A NEXTEXT COURSEBOOK

Consumer Economics

AND PERSONAL FINANCE

Authors

John Burton   Sharon Franklin   Barbara Littman

Robert Mayer   Mary Herd Tull   Diane Wilde

Author Affiliates

Dr. John Burton, Department of Family and Consumer Studies, University of Utah, Salt Lake City.

Sharon Franklin, formerly of Lincoln Elementary School, Eugene, Oregon, writer of educational materials

Barbara Littman, former teacher, toy designer, and Peace Corps volunteer, writer

Dr. Robert Mayer, Department of Family and Consumer Studies, University of Utah, Salt Lake City

Mary Herd Tull, founder of Open Meadow Learning Center Alternative School of Portland, Oregon, writer of educational materials

Dr. Diane Wilde, formerly of Hungarian University, writer of educational and training materials

Cover and interior illustrations: Eric Larsen

Printed in the United States of America

ISBN-13: 978-0-618-22205-6   ISBN-10: 0-618-22205-7

1112131415-DWO-10090807

Table of Contents

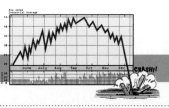

Chapter 9
SMART SHOPPING FOR CLOTHING
156

Chapter 10
SMART SHOPPING FOR ENTERTAINMENT
175

Chapter 11
SMART SHOPPING FOR HEALTH AND FITNESS 190

Chapter 12
SMART SHOPPING ON THE INTERNET 213

Chapter 13
MAKING A HOME
231

Chapter 14
FURNISHING YOUR PLACE
251

Charts and Models

Your Life: Taking Stock

In this chapter, you will learn about:

- knowing yourself
- setting goals
- using your time to meet your goals

For as long as she could remember, Emma wanted to be a nurse. She dressed up as a nurse for Halloween trick or treating. She volunteered at local blood drives starting when she was 10. Of course she did not faint at the sight of blood. It made her feel good to give juice and cookies to people after they had given blood. In high school, she volunteered at the local hospital. There she saw what hard work nursing is but also saw that she could love this kind of work. As she grew to know herself better and better, she realized nursing was the right career path for her.

Most people are not so clear about their life's work. But for everyone, the more you know yourself, the better prepared you are to make important decisions about your life. Let's get started.

Know Yourself

Taking charge of your financial life involves making many decisions: some big, some small, some short-term, others long-term. How does someone decide what kind of work to do in life? Where to live? What kind of transportation to use? Unfortunately, in many situations there isn't a clear "right" or "wrong" answer. No one can make these decisions but you. The more you know about yourself, the more you will be able to make the right decisions for yourself now and in the future.

What Do You Want to Be?

Even when you were very young, people probably asked you, "What do you want to be when you grow up?"

"A cowboy! A dancer! An astronaut!" you might have said without hesitating. Now it may be more difficult. There are so many choices.

You will soon move out into the world as an independent person. Living on your own may seem like a dream, but it's also challenging. The first choice you will probably make is what path you will follow to make money. If you can't earn money, it's hard to live on your own.

A Job or a Career

When you think about making money, naturally you think about getting a job. A job is work you do for a time, like waiting on tables or delivering packages. You may have no special commitment to it. It is simply a way of making money.

At some point, however, many people find themselves settling into an area of work they like. This is called a **career**, a field of work to which you make a commitment over time as you gain more experience, new skills, and often more education.

Another difference between a job and a career has to do with the future. In working at a job, there may be no possibility of advancing through a promotion or the addition of new responsibilities in the future. A career, on the other hand, is something you build over time, hopefully by moving up steps on a career path.

If you choose the right career for you, it can be very rewarding. Today, however, many people change careers several times in their lives, either by choice or necessity. These people often bring a wealth of knowledge and skills with them from one career to the next.

To choose a rewarding career that fits you and the life you want to create for yourself, it's important to know:

* Who are you?
* What do you do well?
* What are you interested in?
* What do you believe in?
* What is your personality?
* What is your learning style?
* What you want to do with your life?

Your answers to these questions will help you chart a course that leads to your life's work.

Your Talents and Skills

What do you do well? What special talents do you have? You will want to look at these questions as you consider what you want to do with your life.

EXAMPLES: Your talents may lie in knowing what to do in an emergency. You may be skilled in teaching young children how to read. Perhaps you're the person your friends seek out to settle disagreements.

Consider these as gifts. If you choose a career in which you use your talents and skills, you won't have to start from scratch in learning them.

Your Interests and Dreams

What are you interested in? Your interests form a large part of what makes you uniquely you. When thinking about career choices, look at what you are interested in now. Interests give important clues about possible directions.

Making it REAL

Discovering Your Interests

Do you find it hard to identify your interests? If so, you aren't alone. Here are some ideas to help you figure out what excites you.

Make a List. If you're not sure what you're interested in, grab a piece of paper and do some brainstorming. Write down activities you like to do, topics you like to read about, subjects you and your friends talk about. Items on your list may range from "drawing" to "planning surprises" to "solving mysteries." Ask friends, family members, or teachers what they think your interests are. Try to come up with as many ideas as you can. Then look back over the list and ask yourself what interests emerge.

Broaden Your Horizons. What is your reaction when you see someone doing something in a way different from the way you and your friends and family do it? What do you think of an idea that goes against the way you usually view things? Do you sometimes criticize people and ideas largely because they're new or different?

Try New Things. Try different foods. Listen to different kinds of music. Read a book or take a class on a subject new to you. Talk to someone with whom you think you have nothing in common. Travel. You'll be surprised at what you'll learn about yourself and about the world. You may find you develop new interests you never dreamed before.

Facing Too Many Choices

Many young people find there are so many choices that it seems impossible to choose which interests them most. In the end, this can be as difficult as having no choices. If you find yourself facing too many possibilities, remember to pace yourself. Try selecting one or two extra-curricular activities this year, and focus on them. If you want to change next year, go ahead! This way, you will take time to experience the things you choose. You will learn more about what really interests you than you can by only dreaming.

Your Values

What do you believe in? Identifying your values helps you stay true to yourself. Your **values** are the things that are important to you, the ideas and principles you live by. Some values many people hold include:

* Honesty.
* Friendliness.
* Compassion.
* Religious beliefs.
* Close family relationships.

Other values relate to how people want to live and can include such approaches to life as:

* Risk-taking.
* Creating or building things.
* Preserving the environment.
* Saving money.
* Helping others.

Some people value having nice things and the means to get them, such as:

* College education.
* High salary.
* Beautiful home.
* Fashionable clothes.
* Expensive cars.
* Latest technology.
* Jewelry.

What are your personal values? Remember, they are *your* values! They may not match those of your friends or even your family. Knowing your values will help you make career choices and life decisions that are compatible with your values.

EXAMPLES: If you value simplicity, you may want to avoid filling your life with things you don't really need, such as expensive jewelry or a car.

If, however, you value expensive possessions, you need to choose a career in which you can make enough money to own such things comfortably.

When you make choices that conflict with your values, you will have trouble, especially in the realm of work. For example, if you are a person who values honesty and have a job in which you are required to lie in order to keep clients happy, you will be unhappy.

Your Style

How would you describe your personality and learning style? They also help you make career and other life decisions.

Your Personality

A big part of your personal style is your **personality**—the combination of unique behaviors, personal characteristics, ideas, and attitudes that make you . . . you! Psychologists define personality as the relatively stable patterns of thinking, feeling, and acting that an individual has.

Your sense of humor, moods, and responses to new situations and ideas are all part of your personality. If you live or work in an environment that goes against your personality in fundamental ways, you are less likely to be comfortable, happy, and successful in that place.

EXAMPLE: If you are outgoing and love being around people, an environment in which you work at a computer day after day may not be stimulating for you.

Get Smart

The Myers-Briggs Type Indicator

Psychologists have created tests to help describe personality types. One very popular one is the Myers-Briggs Type Indicator (MBTI). Schools, career counselors, and even some employers use it to help match personalities to types of work. It describes 16 personality types by looking at how people choose words to describe themselves in four different areas:

* Extrovert (outgoing) *or* Introvert (inner-directed).
* Sensing (practical) *or* Intuitive (imaginative).
* Thinking *or* Feeling.
* Judging (logical, organized) *or* Perceiving (spontaneous and flexible).

Taking the MBTI test can help you recognize how you see and relate to the world. There are no "right" or "wrong" choices in the MBTI test, nor are there "better" or "worse" types. Each of the 16 types has its unique strengths and special gifts.

You can find out more about this and other personality tests by searching the Web using the key words "personality test."

Self-concept

Your **self-concept** is how you see yourself. It is based in part on the mental picture you have of yourself, compared with other people. Do you see yourself as confident? Clumsy? Smart? Sensitive? Artistic? Slow? Funny?

An accurate self-concept is essential to meeting any personal or professional goal. To improve your self-concept, here are **three** hints:

1. **Assess yourself.** Take a fearless inventory of your strengths and weaknesses. Accept yourself honestly, just as you are.

2. **Make changes.** Set realistic goals if there are things you want to change. Build a foundation for yourself made up of small successes. Make changes in small steps, starting with what is most important to you. Suppose you want to start with "being truthful with family and friends." Concentrate on that for awhile, until you can see progress. Then you can add something else, like "starting a regular savings plan." Don't set yourself up for failure by trying to change too many things at once.

3. **Get assistance.** Ask for help when you need it! Choose family members, teachers, and other mentors who can help you make a plan, encourage you, and wholeheartedly celebrate the positive changes you make.

Learning Style

How do you learn best? Your **learning style** is the way you think and learn most easily and naturally. Understanding your style will help you know how to approach learning something new, whether in school or on the job. All of us—including those who have learning disabilities such as dyslexia or Attention-Deficit/Hyperactivity Disorder (ADHD)—can use information about our learning style to develop strategies that maximize our ability to learn.

Psychologists who study how people learn agree that we use our senses to learn. The **three** learning senses are:

1. **Auditory** (hearing).
2. **Visual** (seeing).
3. **Kinesthetic** (muscle motion).

We use all these senses as we learn. However, most people favor one type over the others. The chart on the opposite page will help you discover which kind of learner you are.

Which Kind of Learner Are You?

Auditory	Visual	Kinesthetic
Learns Best by Listening.	**Learns Best by Seeing.**	**Learns Best by Touching, Moving, Doing.**
Description of Learner * Needs to hear text. * Learns well from listening to explanations. * Likes to be read to. * Likes to talk about what he or she is learning.	**Description of Learner** * Likes to read explanations. * Likes to see material presented in charts, graphs, and handouts. * Likes to draw diagrams, maps, and charts and take notes to help learn and remember a subject.	**Description of Learner** * Finds hands-on learning is best. * Finds that manipulating objects, modeling ideas in clay, or making constructions helps to clarify. * Likes to figure things out through doing. * Finds it hard to sit still for long periods of time.
Suggestions * Tape-record class lectures, presentations, and meetings when possible. * When studying, read information out loud. * Participate in class discussions. * Use memory techniques (like the word HOMES to remember the Great Lakes: Huron, Ontario, Michigan, Erie, and Superior) to help remember specific points.	**Suggestions** * Sit near the front in a meeting or classroom so you can see the presenter, board, and other visuals. * Use a highlighter when reading. * Take notes using words and pictures.	**Suggestions** * Volunteer for role-plays and other activities that let you get up and move about. * Choose activities that involve hands-on learning when possible. * If permitted, move around during long presentations. * Decorate study space with bright paintings or posters. * Skim material before reading in detail. * Take short study breaks often. * Chew something when you study.

Multiple Intelligences

Howard Gardner, a psychologist at Harvard University, went further than these three learning senses. He teaches that people have "multiple intelligences." While we have all of them, each of us is stronger in some than in others. Gardner's **eight** intelligences include:

1. **Verbal/Linguistic Intelligence** (ability to understand spoken language and to think, write, and speak with words).

2. **Logical/Mathematical Intelligence** (ability to work with numbers and quantities, to recognize number patterns, and to reason well).

3. **Visual/Spatial Intelligence** (ability to see in visual terms, make mental "maps," and form mental models of physical space).

4. **Musical/Rhythmic Intelligence** (ability to think in rhythms and sounds, to recognize auditory patterns, and to create music).

5. **Interpersonal Intelligence** (ability to work with others, empathize, and see things from other people's viewpoints).

6. **Intrapersonal Intelligence** (ability to understand oneself).

7. **Bodily/Kinesthetic Intelligence** (ability to move purposefully with balance and coordination, and to perform in such activities as acting, dancing, and sports).

8. **Naturalistic Intelligence** (ability to recognize and classify landforms, bodies of water, plants, minerals, and animals).

As you think about these kinds of intelligence, do you see which ones are your strengths?

Setting Goals and Making Decisions

In the movies, people often reach their goals with little effort and few problems. In real life, it's different.

Setting Short-Term and Long-Term Goals

When you start out on a long road trip, it's nice to have a road map. Otherwise, you can get lost and find yourself wandering around, or worse, going in the wrong direction. Goals provide a road map for your life.

Get in the habit of setting both short- and long-term goals. A **short-term goal** is something you desire that can be reached in a short time, from a day to a year. **EXAMPLE:** Power-walking three times a week and saving $10 per month are short-term goals. You can measure your progress toward a short-term goal easily. You can revise the goal when necessary.

Often, short-term goals light the way toward a **long-term goal** that may take a year or five years to reach. Running a marathon and saving up to buy a TV set are long-term goals.

Making Goals Succeed

How do you make a goal work for you? You've probably made New Year's resolutions, or made plans to "do better next year," only to find your bad habits remain unchanged.

There are **six** requirements for goals that help to make them reachable. Be sure your goals are:

1. **Your own.** Your parents or teacher may have worthy goals for you, but those goals are theirs. The goals you set should be your own.

2. **Realistic.** Unrealistic goals are a recipe for failure.

3. **Stated in a positive way.** Describe what you *will* do.

4. **Reachable within a specific period of time.** "I'll save $5,000 for college this summer" is probably not a reasonable goal, but "I'll have $500 in a college savings account by August 31" may be. Your goals should be high enough to be challenging and worth achieving but not so high that you set yourself up to fail.

5. **Concrete.** "Being nice" is not a measurable goal. Neither is "getting better grades" or "trying harder." Mowing your grandmother's lawn once a week, improving your history grade to a B this semester, and making 50 free throws every day are concrete, measurable goals.

6. **Known and shared with someone you trust.** Telling someone your goals keeps you accountable and makes an ally out of the person you told.

Identify the skills and resources needed to help reach your goal. Refer to your goals periodically, assess your progress, and make mid-course corrections if necessary. Success is the ultimate goal. And success breeds success. Each time you reach a goal, you become confident about setting another, perhaps more challenging, goal.

My Notebook

Goal-Setting

Come up with at least two short-term goals and one long-term goal. Describe these goals in detail in your journal. Tell how each one meets the six requirements described. Then imagine what it will feel like when you meet each goal, and describe the feeling in your notebook.

The Process of Decision-Making

So many choices. So little time. How do you decide what choice to make in any given situation? If you have goals for your life, you have a framework for making wise choices. If you are uncertain about what to do, check your short- and long-term goals. Determine which choice will take you closer to your goals.

For example, suppose you have a job, and you are trying to decide whether or not to buy a car to get to the job. Making the decision is a **six**-step process:

1. **Consider the problem.** You need to get to work. A car will get you there, but it will cost money.

2. **Consider the alternatives.** First, will public transportation get you to your job? If so, perhaps it is less expensive than buying a car. On the other hand, with public transportation you cannot get to and from work as quickly, and you do not have a car for other uses.

3. **Consider the outcomes of each alternative.** Public transportation will get you to your job and back, but you will have to wait and work around the bus schedule. A car will cost more, but will give you freedom to come and go as you please, and it will offer other benefits to you.

4. **Consider the outcomes in terms of your goals and values.** Do you want freedom of movement more than you want to save money for college? Do the *benefits* of owning a car outweigh the *disadvantages* of expense in terms of purchase price and insurance? Are you afraid you will not be able to get to work on time, using public transportation?

5. **Choose the best alternative.** Based on how you answer the questions about the

Role Model

Sticking to a Plan

Lynn loved bicycle racing. She set a goal to enter a challenging long-distance race in one year. She began an intensive training program and started saving money for needed equipment. Everything was fine until her friend Monique asked her to go on a trip. Lynn had money saved and figured she could start saving for the equipment when she returned. But then she thought about her goal. Entering the race was something she wanted to do more than anything, so in the end she told Monique she couldn't go—at least, not now.

decision, which solution is best? If you are saving for a long-term goal, then spending money on a car and more money on insurance may not be the best choice.

6. **Reconsider your decision later.** Even if you decided to spend the money on the car, you may conclude you are not saving as much as you need to. You could sell the car if you want to boost your savings. On the other hand, if you decided to save the money the car would have cost, and then you discover that you have a very hard time getting to work on time, you might reconsider buying a car.

It isn't easy, but having the self-discipline to delay something you want now in order to reach a goal shows you are becoming a responsible, mature person.

Using Your Time Wisely

For many people, there's never enough time to finish work assignments, get chores done, and have fun. Having ample time for work and play requires good **time management**, which is the way you organize time you spend on various activities.

Make Time Work for You

Setting priorities is the first step in good time management. Consider this **four**-step process:

1. **Make a two-column list.** In the first column, list the tasks that need to be done this week. In column two, write the date by which you must complete each task.

2. **Decide which tasks are most important.** Label them with one, two, or three stars, or devise another system to rank each task.

3. **Group similar tasks.** If you have six phone calls to make, you can save time by making them all at once. If you have four errands to run, do them all at once and cross four things off your list!

4. **Break up big tasks.** Estimate the amount of time it will take to complete big tasks, and break them down into small steps.

Be realistic.

Tired of secretarial work, Gladys looked for openings as queen.

Choices That Limit Your Future

So far, you've learned ways to find out more about yourself so you can make wise choices regarding your education, career, and finances. You've learned how to set priorities and balance your activities so you can meet your personal goals. Some decisions, however, are guaranteed to *restrict* the choices you will have in the future. These include:

* Getting poor grades.
* Dropping out of school.
* Getting into trouble with the law.
* Abusing drugs and/or alcohol.
* Developing an unhealthy lifestyle or unhealthy relationships.
* Getting pregnant or getting someone else pregnant.

Look around you. Can you identify other things that have limited the choices of some of your friends? If so, learn from their mistakes. Make choices that lead to a future that is full of possibilities.

By the Numbers

Balancing Work and Play

Find out how you use your time now by collecting data over one week's time. In a little notebook that you carry with you, record your time. Every couple of hours, write down everything you did and for how long, in hours and minutes. Don't skip any days or times. At the end of the week, tally up the totals as follows:

* Eating.
* Sleeping.
* Schoolwork.
* Work.
* Home responsibilities.
* Time spent with friends and family.
* Exercise.
* Hobbies.
* Relaxing.

After studying the results, answer these questions:

* What seems out of balance to you?
* In what areas do you feel you spend too much time?
* In what area(s) would you like or need to spend more time?
* How can good time management help you to achieve your goals?

The first step in taking charge of your financial life is to figure out who you are. What are your talents and skills? What are you interested in? What are your values? What type of personality do you have? How do you learn best?

Setting goals for yourself, both short-term and long-term goals, will help you decide what's important in life. You will be more likely to achieve your goals if they are: your own goals, realistic, stated in a positive way, reachable in a specific period of time, and shared with someone you trust.

Learn how to manage your time now while you're young. Time management will go a long way toward helping you achieve your goals.

Consumer Economics

career—field of work to which an individual makes a significant commitment over time; a person's progress in a chosen field, sometimes a life's work. *p. 2*

learning style—way in which you think and learn most naturally. *p. 6*

long-term goal—goal that may take one or more years to reach. *p. 8*

personality—combination of unique behaviors, personal characteristics, ideas, and attitudes of a person. *p. 5*

self-concept—way you see yourself, based in large part on the mental picture you have of yourself, often compared with other people. *p. 6*

short-term goal—goal that can be reached in a short time, from a day to a year. *p. 8*

time management—way you organize time you spend on various activities. *p. 11*

values—things that are important to you; ideas and principles you live by. *p. 4*

CHAPTER 2

Seeking a Career

In this chapter, you will learn about:

- preparing for a career
- creating a resumé
- finding a job

When he was very young, Kevin, like many kids, started thinking about what he wanted to be when he grew up. Early dreams included being a firefighter, a baseball player, and a lobster fisher. But it wasn't until the summer he turned 16 that he found a dream that would stick with him the rest of his life.

That summer, Kevin worked in the kitchen of a pancake house in his hometown. He was hired on as a bus boy, and his main job was to clear and set tables. But he discovered that he loved the atmosphere in the kitchen. The hustle and bustle excited him, and the way the chefs and the rest of the crew joked around with each other made his working day fun. He spent as much time as he could watching the chefs do their work, which looked very creative and satisfying to him.

By the end of the summer, he was hooked. He knew he wanted to be a chef for the rest of his life.

Considering a Career

An important choice you'll be making at some point is what kind of work you want to do. You may be asking yourself, why work? The most important reason people work is to earn money to take care of their basic needs and those of their families. But there are other reasons why people work.

* **It's satisfying.** Work may have a purpose that gives life meaning. People who work with people—as teachers, nurses, or social workers, for example—often choose their profession for this reason.
* **It's challenging.** It can provide interesting problems to solve. Mechanics and engineers, for example, have challenging work. The questions they ask can take a long time to answer, but imagine the excitement when they answer them!
* **It's creative.** Work can give people a chance to express themselves in different ways. Many people choose architecture, graphic design, and other arts-related professions for this reason.
* **It's a way of forming our identity.** Our identity is how we see ourselves and how others see us. When someone asks, "What do you do?" most people answer with a description of the work they do.

Some people don't know what they want to do for a living because they haven't explored what's out there. Don't go through life on automatic pilot, simply being bumped around by circumstances! Steer a course toward something that is interesting and personally fulfilling.

Learning About Careers

Sadly, many people do not like their jobs or careers. It doesn't make sense to spend one-third of every working day of your life in a job you hate. Here is a goal worth striving for: Do work that you love!

Imagine getting paid to do something you would happily do for free. In fact, many people have careers that let them do this. It's up to you to find a career that's just right for you.

Finding Information

Libraries, bookstores, and the Internet contain information on a wide variety of careers. Imagine yourself in many different careers. Which ones fit? Look for signs of energy, curiosity, and excitement within yourself. Think about your skills and play to your strengths.

Research what's out there. Say you'd like to work in the entertainment field, but figure you can't because you're not musical. With some research, you'll discover many other entertainment-related careers, including entertainment lawyer, theater manager, screenwriter, and sound technician. Get more information on careers that interest you from:

* High school, community college, and college career centers.
* Guidance and career counselors.
* Job fairs.
* Library.
* Internet.
* Career Day events.
* Personal interviews.

People Resources

Don't be afraid to interview adult friends and other people in your community who have jobs that sound interesting to you. People are usually happy to answer questions about their work. Take notes and follow up on any leads. Always write a thank-you note the next day to anyone who took the time to talk with you. It's common courtesy.

Carefully put together a team of successful, well respected people to act as mentors for you. Seek out your support team for advice and suggestions. It may include parents or other family members, teachers, coaches, counselors, neighbors, or bosses.

First-Hand Experience

Take advantage of ways to learn first-hand about careers and fields of interest. Apply to volunteer! Offer your services as an intern or apprentice to someone you admire. In volunteer and **apprenticeship** or **internship** relationships, in which you learn a skill from an expert, both parties win.

Role Model

Learning by Doing

When Jackson wanted to learn how to lay down carpeting, he apprenticed himself to the best carpet layer in the city. At the end of his apprenticeship, he had gained excellent skills and experience and, in exchange, his boss had free labor.

On the other hand, Sarah wanted to be a veterinarian until she worked as an intern in a vet's office. Then, she realized what it really took to care for animals that were seriously injured. She decided this wasn't the career for her.

Preparing for Your Career

Careers take careful thought and planning, and for good reason. Although they do not have to, they can influence:

* Where you live.
* Whether you can afford to buy a house or other big-ticket items.
* Your friendships.
* Your overall **standard of living**—the way you live, the quality of what you can afford in goods and services.
* The interests you develop.
* How you feel about yourself.

Even if planning a career seems daunting, do it anyway. You don't want "circumstances" to dictate what happens to you. It's your life. Take charge of it.

In general, more rewarding, better-paying jobs with good benefits require more preparation, specific skills, and relevant experience.

To land such a job, your short-term goals may include at least a two-year college degree, technical training, or participation in an apprenticeship program. In other cases, it may require a four-year college degree followed by graduate work.

Statistics prove the value of a college education in raising earning potential. In 2000, high school graduates earned an average annual income of $27,000, whereas people who held a bachelor's degree earned an average annual income of $44,000.

Search This

Finding Out About Careers

The Internet has a wealth of career-related information. You can find web sites (keywords "jobs," "careers," or "employment") that help you:

* Search for jobs.
* Get career advice.
* Find out salary information.
* Investigate global possibilities.
* Identify the education and working conditions of many jobs.
* Learn more about your own interests and strengths.

Your Life

Volunteer Opportunities

Here are some volunteer organizations that may interest you, now or in the future. Many of these organizations have web sites where you can learn more. You can also find out what organizations in your community need volunteers.

* Peace Corps.
* Earthwatch Institute.
* Americorps.
* VISTA (Volunteers In Service To America).
* Habitat for Humanity.
* Teach for America.
* Sierra Club.
* Local schools, businesses, and nonprofit organizations.

While in High School

You can begin to prepare for life outside of high school now, whether it is college or your first full-time job. Here are **five** suggestions:

1. **Take courses** in fields that interest you or that will prepare you to enter a two- or four-year college.

2. **Do your best** in school and in any job you have.

3. **Investigate on-the-job and employer-sponsored training** possibilities, including the armed forces, if desired.

4. **Take an aptitude test,** such as the General Aptitude Test Battery, to help identify careers in areas of your strengths.

5. **Consider attending a community college** for two years before attending a four-year college. It makes good financial sense. Community colleges often cost a fraction of the cost of four-year colleges and universities. Students may experience smaller class sizes, can live at home, and can work to save money for their last two years—when they transfer to the four-year college of their choice.

What plan can you develop to broaden your knowledge and experience now in an area of interest to you?

Paying for Your Education

Higher education costs are increasing, but don't let the thought of money discourage you from following your dream.

There are many ways to pay for college:

* ***Work/Work Study.*** Many students work in the summer and part-time during the school year to earn money for college. Most colleges offer work-study positions during the school year to qualified students.

* ***Loans.*** Subsidized federal and state low-interest loans are available to qualified students based on need. You begin

Search This

Finding Scholarships

Hundreds of scholarships are available to students. Use the Internet to dig up information on scholarships for which you might qualify. Check the web sites of schools you're interested in for information on scholarships. Take a look at web sites of organizations that provide information on colleges. Hunt for scholarships in your home state. Ask college counselors at your school. Check out organizations that you or your parents belong to. If you simply search the Internet for keywords "scholarships" or "college scholarships," you may be amazed by how many different sources of funds are available.

repaying these loans when you are out of college. Parents may also qualify for loans for their children's education.

* ***Armed Forces.*** Many students enter the armed forces in order to get the type of education and training they desire.
* ***Scholarships.*** Colleges and universities, nonprofit organizations, and many other groups award scholarships to deserving students. College scholarships range from a few thousand dollars to a four-year paid college education. Scholarships do not need to be repaid.
* ***Financial Awards.*** These awards may be given by school or community groups that recognize a student's academic, musical, athletic, or other achievement. It is free money that may be used in any way the student desires.
* ***Relatives***. Sometimes parents, grandparents, or other relatives will make money available as a gift or a loan for college.

Of course, the goal is to acquire as much "free" money, in the form of grants and scholarships, as possible.

Research Pays Off

Benjamin R. Kaplan was an ordinary high school student in Eugene, Oregon, in the late 1990s. Like many high school students, he applied to college and found out how expensive it was. He was determined to find a way to get his college education paid for—in full. So, he started researching. In the end, Benjamin met his goal, acquiring over 24 merit-based scholarships worth $90,000 at any college or university!

Benjamin graduated from Harvard debt-free and has written a guidebook, *How To Go To College Almost For Free* (Gleneden Beach, California: Waggle Dancer Books, 1999), that shows other students how to do the same thing. He has written articles and gives seminars for groups nationwide. Benjamin's personal quest became a marketable skill that made him an expert.

Finding and Keeping a Job

Starting sometime in high school, many students apply for their first job. It's the beginning of a ritual that most people repeat many times throughout their lives.

Finding a Job

When looking for a job, conduct a broad search. Take advantage of:

* School career planning and placement offices.
* Help-wanted ads.
* Employment agencies.
* Job fairs.
* Internet.
* Friends and relatives.
* Your community.

For each place you contact in your job search, make a file that includes the contact person's name, address, and phone number. Add any information about the business that you find on the Internet or through other research. Attach a paper to keep track of your communication with the company.

Finding a job takes time and energy, and at times you'll get discouraged. When this happens, stop for a minute. Relax, exercise, and remind yourself of all the reasons someone should want to hire you. Then, find that positive attitude and go back out there.

Making a Good First Impression

Your resumé, cover letter, application form, and references combine to make up a potential employer's first impression of you. Put your best foot forward!

Resumé

A **resumé** is a record of your job history and education. When creating a resumé:

* Be honest.
* Consider your objective. Make sure your resumé fits the job you're seeking.
* Make every word count. Leave out irrelevant information.
* Keep it to one page.
* Save your resumé in a file on your computer. Title the file "resumé" with the date. That way, you'll always know when it was last revised.
* Create a resumé that is error-free and visually appealing. Make sure you stress the *results* of each job—what you accomplished or learned and how that increases your value.
* Proofread your work carefully.

There are **two** basic types of resumés:

1. A **chronological resumé** lists jobs in order, starting with the most recent. It works best for someone with a short work history or with jobs that are similar. Main headings include:

   * Job Objective.
   * Employment History.
   * Education.
   * Honors/Awards.
   * Special Skills.
   * Interests.

Chronological Resumé

What do you hope to accomplish with this resumé? Spell out your goal. Be specific.

Margaret Jean Cameron
1392 North Caldwell Avenue, Apt. 3R
New York, NY
(212) 555-1234
mjcam@isp.net

List jobs in reverse chronological order, starting with the current or most recent one. Keep your description of responsibilities for each listing brief.

OBJECTIVE
To obtain an entry-level editorial position

EMPLOYMENT HISTORY
Sept. 1999–present **Daily News,** Writer
- Contribute articles weekly and per assignment on freelance basis

1999–present **Copy Man Broadway,** Night Manager
- Responsible for managing Copy Man location three nights each week
- Manage two employees

Feb.–June, 1999 **Tribune,** Journalism Intern
- Assisted investigative team for series on the local housing authority

1997–1999 **Office of the Registrar, Jefferson University,** Administrative Assistant
- Provided office support, phone-service support, and typing

1997–1998 **Jefferson University,** Resident Dorm Assistant
- Responsible for administration and counseling of 36 students in dorm

Where did you go to school? What degree did you get? Consider listing specifics, such as your college major, but save awards and honors for a special section.

EDUCATION
BA, 2001—Jefferson University, New York, NY
Major: Journalism *Minor:* Political Science
- Published articles in student newspaper, edited special features
- Earned 50% of expenses by working 20 hours a week while carrying a full academic load

HONORS AND AWARDS
- 4.0 G.P.A in major
- Named to Dean's List, 4 years
- Named Outstanding Journalism Student, Jefferson University, 2000

Show off your accomplishments. Leave this section out if you have not won any awards or honors.

SPECIAL SKILLS
- Fluent in Spanish
- Proficient in Microsoft Word, Quark Xpress, PageMaker, Microsoft Excel

Describe skills that might interest an employer.

INTERESTS
Creative writing   Concert cellist
Willing to travel and relocate References available upon request

Mention a couple of things that will help a potential employer get a view of how well-rounded you are.

Offer references if they're requested. You may want to add that you're willing to travel or relocate—if you are!

2. A **skills resumé** highlights broad categories of work experience. It presents a diverse work history in a positive and purposeful way. It is useful for someone who has more than one kind of experience. The main headings include:

* Job Objective.
* Career Highlights (arrange your experience under categories, such as retail, medical billing, food services, and so on, followed by the jobs and dates of employment that fall under each).
* Education.
* Honors/Awards.
* Special Skills.
* Interests.

Application Form

Many jobs require an application form. Here are some tips:

* ***Find a sample*** application on the Internet by searching under Careers or Jobs. Read it over to see what kind of information is requested, and practice filling it out. Call on businesses. Make a photocopy of any application forms you take home with you. After completing the copy, transfer the information neatly onto the original copy.
* ***Answer all questions honestly***. It is *never* okay to lie on your application, and it will harm you in the long run. If you don't have a required skill or experience, make a case for why you should be hired anyway.
* ***Keep a copy*** to refer to when you fill out other applications. That way, you'll have all information regarding past jobs, references, and so forth at your fingertips.

Skills Résumé

Margaret Jean Cameron
1392 North Caldwell Avenue, Apt. 3R
New York, NY
(212) 555-1234
mjcam@isp.net

> What do you hope to accomplish with this resumé? Spell out your goal. Be specific.

OBJECTIVE
To obtain an entry-level editorial position

CAREER HIGHLIGHTS ◄

> If your experience is in different fields or uses different sets of skills, divide your jobs into categories, such as "editorial" and "administrative" shown here. List jobs in reverse chronological order, starting with the current or most recent one. Include a brief description of relevant responsibilities for each listing.

Editorial

Daily News, Writer, September 1999–present
- Contribute articles weekly and per assignment on freelance basis

Tribune, Journalism Intern, February–June 1999
- Assisted investigative team for series on the local housing authority

Administrative

Copy Man Broadway, Night Manager, 1999–present
- Responsible for managing Copy Man location three nights each week
- Manage two employees

Office of the Registrar, Jefferson University, 1997–1999, Administrative Assistant
- Provided office support, phone-service support, and typing

Jefferson University, 1997–1998, Resident Dorm Assistant
- Responsible for administration and counseling of 36 students in dorm

EDUCATION ◄

> Where did you go to school? What degree did you get? Consider listing specifics, such as your college major, but save awards and honors for a special section.

BA, 2001—Jefferson University, New York, NY
Major: Journalism   *Minor:* Political Science
- Published articles in student newspaper, edited special features
- Earned 50% of expenses by working 20 hours a week while carrying a full academic load

HONORS AND AWARDS ◄

> Show off your accomplishments. Leave this section out if you have not won any awards or honors.

- 4.0 G.P.A in major
- Named to Dean's List, 4 years
- Named Outstanding Journalism Student, Jefferson University, 2000

SPECIAL SKILLS ◄

> Describe skills that might interest an employer.

- Fluent in Spanish
- Proficient in Microsoft Word, Quark Xpress, PageMaker, Microsoft Excel

INTERESTS ◄

> Mention a couple of things that will help a potential employer get a view of how well-rounded you are.
>
> Offer references if they're requested. You may want to add that you're willing to travel or relocate—if you are!

Creative writing   Concert cellist
Willing to travel and relocate   References available upon request

Cover Letter

May 18, 2003

Margaret Jean Cameron
1392 North Caldwell Avenue, Apt. 3R
New York, NY
(212) 555-1234
mjcam@isp.net

Ms. Lucinda Powell
Editorial Director
Abacus Publications Ltd.
101 First Avenue
Chicago, IL 60611

Dear Ms. Powell:

Professor James Merrill suggested I contact you to apply for the entry-level editor position at Abacus Publications.

Although I have just completed my BA in journalism at Jefferson University, I offer experience and skills that few entry-level candidates can bring to a job. I have contributed to several articles published in the *Daily News* and worked for three months as an intern for an investigative team on the *Tribune*. Both jobs helped prepare me for a career in editorial work.

In addition to my editorial experience, I have gained managerial and technical experience as a night manager for Copy Man Broadway here in New York. I am a very hard worker and am willing to do whatever is necessary to begin my career as an editor and writer.

I hope you will consider me for the job. I am enclosing my resumé and will call you to set up an appointment to discuss the position.

Thank you for your consideration.

Sincerely,

Margaret J. Cameron

Margaret Jean Cameron

References

Three references—people who will vouch for your good work history or personal character—are usually requested on applications. Two references should be job-related and the other should be a personal reference. *Always* ask permission before you list anyone as a reference. For job-related references:

* Select people who have worked with you as supervisors and will be eager to talk about your high-quality work, excellent managerial skills, work habits, and other positive attributes.
* If you haven't held many jobs, use people who know you from volunteer positions, or contact teachers or coaches who know your work in the classroom or in extracurricular activities.
* Let your references know the job you're applying for. That way, they will be expecting a phone call and can tailor their responses to the job you're seeking.
* Tell your references what you would like them to emphasize about you.

For personal references:

* Select family members and friends who have known you for a long time.
* Select people who can speak about your personal attributes, such as honesty, positive attitude, and willingness to learn.

Cover Letter

A cover letter should accompany your resumé. Follow the advice below to develop a professional-sounding cover letter:

* **Address.** Find out to whom you should send the letter and address her by name.
* **Opening.** Tell how you heard about her, the position you're applying for, and why. If someone known to her encouraged you to apply, name the person.
* **Focus.** State why you are the best candidate for the job.
* **Closing.** Repeat your interest in the job and thank her for her consideration. Make sure you include your phone number.
* **Proofread your work carefully!**

The Interview

Face-to-face interviews can be nerve-wracking, but they can also be fun. If you prepare carefully, you can walk out knowing that whatever happens, you did your best. Here are some suggestions on how to prepare for an interview:

* **Research** the company before the interview. That way, you can ask intelligent questions, and the interviewer will see that you cared enough to do your homework.
* **Practice** until you can answer these questions in a clear, succinct, and energetic way: *Why do you want the job? Why should you be hired for this position?*
* **Dress appropriately** for the type of work and make sure you are well

groomed. Make sure your body is clean, hair combed, teeth brushed, and nails clean. Clothes should be clean and pressed. Think about what other people at this office wear to work. Will all the men be wearing ties and jackets, or is it a more casual workplace? Avoid wearing too much jewelry and perfume or after-shave. Also avoid showing off body piercings or tattoos.

* ***Remember*** that first impressions count! Arrive on time. When introduced, make eye contact, shake hands warmly, smile, and say something friendly such as, "It's a pleasure to meet you." If the interviewer asks about your pets or discusses the recent hurricane, talk. It gives the interviewer a chance to know you. Above all, be yourself. Let your own personality shine through.

* ***Be polite*** to everyone you meet at the office.

* ***Speak*** properly and make sure "like" and "um" are absent from your vocabulary. They, like, indicate poor verbal skills and, like, make you, um, appear much younger than you are.

* ***Organize*** your thoughts before answering a question, and don't be afraid to say you don't know. Ask one or two questions that show you've done your homework—for example: "I read that your company did well last year. Do you think this will be a good year for your company?" Never ask about salary,

"It has come to my attention, Picharall, that you have been somewhat less than forthcoming in your resumé."

benefits, or vacation time. These questions can be addressed at the next interview.

* ***Write*** a short thank-you note after the interview. Restate your interest in the position and thank the interviewer for his or her time. Mention your eagerness to learn more. Make sure your note arrives the next day, even if you have to hand-deliver it to the office.

* ***Admit it*** to yourself if the interview went poorly. Think about what you learned for next time, and move on.

Work Habits

Your **work ethic** is your attitude toward the work you do, whether at school, at home, or on the job. Your work habits reflect your work ethic.

Thank-You Letter

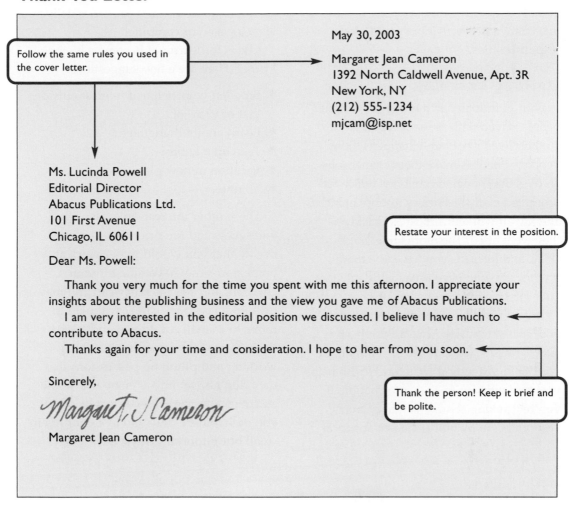

Follow the same rules you used in the cover letter.

May 30, 2003

Margaret Jean Cameron
1392 North Caldwell Avenue, Apt. 3R
New York, NY
(212) 555-1234
mjcam@isp.net

Ms. Lucinda Powell
Editorial Director
Abacus Publications Ltd.
101 First Avenue
Chicago, IL 60611

Restate your interest in the position.

Dear Ms. Powell:

   Thank you very much for the time you spent with me this afternoon. I appreciate your insights about the publishing business and the view you gave me of Abacus Publications.
   I am very interested in the editorial position we discussed. I believe I have much to contribute to Abacus.
   Thanks again for your time and consideration. I hope to hear from you soon.

Sincerely,

Margaret J Cameron

Margaret Jean Cameron

Thank the person! Keep it brief and be polite.

You have good work habits if you:

* Arrive on time and work the required number of hours (or more).
* Dress and behave appropriately.
* Can be counted on to do your part when working as part of a team.
* Complete work on or before the deadline, even if it means working extra hours.
* Have a serious, positive attitude—even under pressure.
* Take pride in your work.
* Accept responsibility.
* Are honest and ethical.
* Take initiative, and do more than is expected.
* Develop good verbal, written, and mathematical skills. They are important in almost any job. Upgrade your skills voluntarily if necessary.

Employers notice employees with a good work ethic. Often, they are rewarded over time with more money and more responsibilities.

Lifelong Learning

In your grandparents' day, many working people stayed with the same company all their lives. That rarely happens today. People's interests make them change jobs. So does the changing economy, which has prompted many businesses to close branches and lay off workers almost as quickly as they were hired. The more knowledge, skills, and interests you have, the more options you will have if you suddenly lose your job or decide to change jobs.

In any field, it's a good idea to update your skills regularly. You can do this by taking classes, workshops, or seminars in your field. Attending conferences also helps you gain new, up-to-date information. If you're thinking about changing careers, you can begin by taking classes at a local community college. Many people also take correspondence courses or classes delivered via television or computer.

Life is for learning! Become a lifelong learner. Here are a few suggestions:

* Broaden your fields of interest outside that of your job.
* Learn another language.
* Take up a hobby.
* Vacation in new places.
* Volunteer.

These other interests may also affect your goals and life priorities. You may decide that you would rather work at home part-time, have time for your children, and sell the fancy car. You may give up a fast-track career willingly to move to a small rural town and start a llama farm. Many people are so busy working and piling up possessions that they don't have time to enjoy life. In the end, happiness is achieved not by what you own, but by how you live your life in small but important ways, day by day.

The career path you choose will play a big role in your financial life. People work to pay bills, including housing costs, food, clothes, and entertainment. But people who choose their careers wisely often find much satisfaction and pleasure in their work.

Take some time to research careers that might interest you. Interview adults you know about their professional lives. Search the Internet for information about positions. Consider an internship or apprenticeship in a field that intrigues you.

Finding and getting a job involves certain steps, such as creating a resumé, honing your interviewing skills, and developing a positive work ethic. It's never too early to start working toward your life's work.

Consumer Economics

apprenticeship—way of learning a job or specific skill by working under the guidance of a skilled expert, often in a trade or through a labor union. *p. 16*

chronological resumé—resumé that lists jobs in order, starting with the most recent and going back in time. *p. 20*

internship—way of learning a job or specific skill by working under the guidance of a skilled expert. *p. 16*

resumé—record of your job history and education. *p. 20*

skills resumé—resumé organized by broad categories of work experience. *p. 22*

standard of living—way you live, the quality of what you can afford in goods and services. *p. 16*

work ethic—your attitude toward the work you do. *p. 26*

CHAPTER 3

Making a Budget

In this chapter, you will learn about:

- developing a budget
- keeping records
- paying taxes

When Jamal first left home to live on his own, he was excited but also nervous. One of the things that worried him was money. At home, his mother had always paid the bills. Now he would have to pay the bills himself. He knew he'd be okay in the beginning because he had some savings and he had just started a new job. But how would he know if he had enough money to make it each month? What would happen if he came up short? Knowing that he needed some help figuring these things out, he asked his mother how she organized the monthly bills. Jamal's mother told him the key was making a budget. One evening, Jamal and his mother sat at the dining room table with all her monthly bills spread out before them, and she showed him how to make a budget. Now, not only does he pay his bills on time every month, but he has even managed to put a little something aside for a rainy day.

Your Financial Well-Being

Living on your own! What does that phrase bring to mind for you? Freedom? Anxiety? Anticipation? Perhaps you feel a mixture of all three.

As you become more independent, many things will affect your happiness and success. Managing your money well is one of those things. It's true that money can't buy happiness. Mismanaging your money, though, can cause unhappiness. It can make it difficult to accomplish important goals, such as going to school or owning a home. It can mean not leading the lifestyle you want. Or, it can mean you're not prepared to handle emergencies.

My Notebook

Where Did It Go?

Does this sound familiar: "What happened to that $10 bill I put in my wallet yesterday?" You know you must have spent it, but on what? This exercise will help you figure that out.

For one week, write down everything you spend money on. Carry a small notebook with you. Try to write the amounts down as soon as you spend them so you don't forget. Look for patterns in your spending. What do you notice about your attitude about buying?

Many people's lives are controlled by poorly managed finances. This doesn't need to happen. Learning to make and follow a budget is the key to managing your money well. Learn how to make a budget and how to stick to it, and your path in life will be easier and more satisfying.

Choosing Financial Goals

Have you ever turned a want into a goal? Maybe you had your heart set on qualifying for the track team. To turn that want into a goal, you had to develop and stick to a training plan. Or, maybe you wanted to travel with your choir to perform in a neighboring state. To turn that want into a goal, you had to come up with a practice plan and stick to it.

Choosing financial goals is no different. You must do **three** things:

1. **Decide on things you want to accomplish** that require money.
2. **Come up with a plan** for earning and saving the money.
3. **Stick to the plan.**

Looking Ahead

What do you want to accomplish as an independent young adult? Do you want to buy a car? Travel? Live on your own? Purchase your own home by the time you're 26? Spend some time thinking about this topic. Discuss it with friends and family. Start a list and add to it as you think of new things. The accomplishments you identify are your goals for young adulthood.

Setting Priorities

If you're like most young people, you probably have more goals than time or resources to accomplish them. If so, you need to set priorities, or select the most important things on your list. What are the five most important things on your list? Rewrite your list with these at the top.

Many of your goals will require money. That's where budgeting comes in. Budgeting will help you manage your money so you can meet daily living expenses *and* plan for longer-term goals.

Developing a Budget

Budgeting is a plan for making the amount of money you earn match the amount of money you spend and save. Understanding how to budget is the first step toward accomplishing your goals.

For many people, *budget* is not a favorite word. When you hear it, you might groan and say something like, "I really should have one, but it's too much trouble." Maybe you have a budget but, like a diet, you can't seem to stick to it. Either way, a budget probably seems like something that restricts your freedom.

Actually, a good budget can do just the opposite. A budget can increase your freedom by giving you control over your finances. Without it, too often your finances control you.

A **budget** is a plan for keeping track of **income** (the money that comes in) and **expenses** (the money that is spent). In a good budget, expenses are less than or equal to income. This allows you to live within your means, or within the amount of money you earn.

Keeping Track of Expenses

To prepare a budget, you have to know **two** things:

1. Your income.
2. Your expenses.

Your income usually comes in chunks in the form of a paycheck, an allowance, presents, or money you receive for providing such services as yard work or baby-sitting. This income is relatively easy to track.

Sometimes you might receive chunks of income from one or more sources each month.

Expenses are harder to track. Most people have daily expenses and also regular monthly expenses. They can lose track of what they are spending.

Regular Expenses

Everyone needs to eat, wear clothes, get around, and have a place to live. The expenses to take care of these needs are made very regularly—daily, weekly, or monthly. When you live on your own, you cannot avoid these expenses:

* Housing (rent or mortgage).
* Insurance (car, health).
* Transportation (gas, bus fare).
* Food.
* Clothing.
* Phone.
* Utilities (electricity, water, gas).
* Taxes.

Some of your regular expenses are the same every month, such as your rent or your car payment. Because these costs don't change, they are **fixed expenses**.

Other regular costs *can* change, depending on your behavior.

EXAMPLES: You ride a bike to save on transportation. You follow energy-saving tips to reduce your utility bill. You change some eating habits to save on groceries.

These kinds of regular expenses are called **flexible expenses**. You have to spend money on them every month, but you can influence the amount you spend.

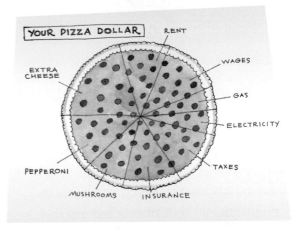

Discretionary Expenses

Discretionary expenses are made for things you can do without. Suppose you want a new CD. What effect will it have on your life if you don't buy it? Not much. However, if you don't pay your phone bill, what will happen? Your phone service will be canceled. Your **credit rating**—reputation with lenders—may go down.

Hobbies, recreational activities, snacks, and movies make life fun and interesting. Your budget should include money for these. However, your plan must take care of regular expenses first. In emergencies, discretionary expenses can be cut back.

Longer-Term Expenses

In addition to weekly and monthly expenses, you will have planned expenses that come less often. Car insurance may be one. Others, like the need to make repairs to a car or other property, may be unexpected. But you should know you will have them. Money to pay these kinds of bills needs to be set aside so it's there when you need it.

Pay Yourself First

Many financial planning books use the phrase: *Pay yourself first.* It doesn't mean give yourself money before meeting your fixed expenses. It means budget for savings as if it were a fixed amount. Plan to save a certain amount each month, and pay that "bill" first. Deposit it in your savings account. If you don't do this, you'll find out what most people learn the hard way. The $50 or $100 you can squeeze out for savings will disappear before it makes it into your savings account.

Savings are important to help you with:

* Longer-term expenses.
* Long- and short-term savings goals.
* Emergencies.

Dividing Up Your Paycheck

Now that you understand the basic categories of expenses, you need to think about how to divide up your paycheck to meet fixed and discretionary expenses.

No one is "average." However, it is helpful to know about how much of their income people spend in these **five** areas:

1. **Housing** takes about 32 percent of an average American's paycheck. If you live in a popular urban area, such as New York, Seattle, or San Francisco, or have a low-paying job, this percentage might be higher.

2. **Food** usually takes about 13 percent of an average paycheck. This includes eating out.

3. **Clothing** usually takes about five percent of an average paycheck. This percentage can vary depending on your clothing needs for work, your personal style, and your willingness to shop for secondhand clothes or make your own.

4. **Health-care** usually takes about five percent of an average paycheck. This percentage will be affected by the type of health-care insurance you have and whether or not your employer provides health-care benefits.

5. **Entertainment.** On average, American households in 2000 spent a little less than five percent of their income on entertainment.

In addition to fixed expenses, there are others that will vary depending on your lifestyle:

* **Transportation.** If you purchase and insure a new car, and drive it frequently, you could spend up to 20 percent of your paycheck on this category. A used car, public transportation, a bike, or walking will reduce the amount you need to spend on transportation.
* **Utilities.** Depending on the energy efficiency of your home, and your use of phone and Internet services, this expense can vary greatly.

* **Savings.** A seven percent savings rate is considered good in this country. However, to meet one of your goals, you might have to save more.

   EXAMPLE: If you're saving for a big purchase, you might find that seven percent will not cover general savings needs and still allow you to put something aside for it.

After meeting your fixed expenses, remaining money can be used for discretionary expenses such as entertainment, vacations, and recreational activities, or it can be used as additional savings.

By the Numbers

Slicing Up the Paycheck Pie

Suzy has just landed her first job after high school. She is still living at home but wants to move out. She has started looking at apartments to rent and is planning to buy a new car.

Her take-home pay is $1,150 a month. The only apartment she has found that she likes rents for $475 a month. The payment and insurance for the car she wants come to $300 a month. These are the only fixed expenses for which she has definite amounts right now.

Do you think Suzy will be able to afford the apartment she wants, a car, and her other fixed and discretionary expenses? To find out, calculate the percentage of her income she will be spending on:

* Housing.
* Transportation.

Do her anticipated expenses fall within the typical American household budget? If not, what advice would you give Suzy so she can afford to live on her own?

Living with a Budget

Most people start by planning a monthly budget. This is because most expenses, such as rent and utilities, are paid monthly. You might need to add or remove categories, depending on your circumstances.

For expenses that are not paid monthly, a monthly amount needs to be calculated. For example, some bills, such as car insurance, can be paid annually (once a year), semi-annually (every six months), or quarterly (every three months). Annual bills should be divided by 12 to come up with a monthly amount. Quarterly bills should be divided by three to get the monthly amount.

A monthly budget will help you understand and control your finances. However, an annual budget is also important. It allows you to compare your annual income with your annual expenses. This can be helpful for many reasons. It allows you to:

* Organize long- and short-term savings plans.
* Adjust your expenses and savings if you have a change in income.
* Adjust flexible and discretionary expenses over a number of months in case of emergencies that require more than your savings plan allows.

Living within a budget is as much psychology as planning. Often, it is the little things that lead us astray. A cup of coffee every day, an extra CD, or a cab ride when you could take the subway may not amount to much by themselves. Add up the expenses, though, and your emergency savings fund can be gone before it's saved. **EXAMPLE:** A $2.50 soda 20 days a month adds up to $50 a month!

Making it REAL

Budget 911 Needed

Barbara just changed jobs. Her new job will pay her $300 more per month, but her transportation costs are going up. Before, she was able to take the train to work, which cost her $84 a month. Now, she must drive to work, and she needs a reliable car to get to her new job.

She traded in her old car for a newer used car. To pay for the car, she will make monthly payments of $390.94 for two years. In addition, because she will be driving more to get to work, her insurance premiums have increased by $210 per year.

Barbara has been told that she can expect her salary to increase after she has been in her new job for a year. Her concern is affording her higher transportation costs for the next 12 months.

Think about ways Barbara could cut back on expenses to handle this increased cost. What would you do if you were Barbara?

Barbara's Monthly Budget			
Income	**Gross Income**	**Net Income**	**Expenses**
	$ 1,700.00	**$1,445.00***	
Expenses			
Housing			$375.00
Utilities			$60.00
Transportation			
* Monthly payment			$390.94
* Insurance ($^1/_{12}$ annual cost)			$86.00
* Gas			$35.00
* Maintenance/repairs			$20.00
Food			$149.00
Phone			$25.00
Clothes			$30.00
Debt (student loan, credit cards)			$50.00
Health care (insurance, copays)			$100.00
Savings			$25.00
Emergency fund			$20.00
Household supplies			$15.00
Charitable donations			$14.00
Entertainment			$30.00
Miscellaneous			$20.00
Total			$1,444.94

* Barbara makes $10.63 an hour and works 160 hours a month. With 15 percent taken out for taxes, her monthly net income is $1,445. She has a roommate, and they split the rent and utilities.

The Electronic Budget

Personal finance software can make budgeting faster and easier than doing everything by hand. Its biggest advantage is that it lets you try out different expense amounts easily.

EXAMPLE: If you are looking at two apartments, you can quickly see how the monthly rental cost affects how much you will have available for other expenses—all without having to redo your calculations by hand.

Imagine being able to do this for every item in your budget, from savings and food expenses to entertainment and transportation costs.

Here are some guidelines to follow when looking for budgeting and personal finance software:

* Look for software that has the features you need. Avoid programs with lots of expensive additional features you probably won't use.
* Make sure the software is compatible with your computer and operating system.
* Pick something that doesn't require that you already know a lot about budgeting.
* If you bank online, select software that will allow you to download your account information.
* Select a program that allows you to easily view the information as charts and graphs. This can be very helpful in getting a picture of how you are spending your money.

Sticking to a Budget

Small behaviors can throw your plan off track quickly. To stick to a budget, try these ideas:

* Continue to keep an expense notebook. It will focus your attention on your spending.
* If you go over one month, reduce discretionary spending the next.
* Post your long- and short-term goals in a prominent spot in your home. It will help you focus on the important things you want from life.
* Don't carry around a lot of cash. That makes it easy to overspend.
* Don't buy on the spur of the moment—often called "impulse buying"—no matter how inexpensive the item. The food, shirt, shoes, or CD will likely still be there tomorrow, after you've had time to think about it.
* Plan major purchases in advance. If you're tempted to buy something you haven't planned for, wait a day. During that day, review your budget to see how it will affect you. If you still want to buy the item, revise your budget to come up with the money.

Revising a Budget

Even the most carefully planned budgets sometimes need to be revised if circumstances change—for example, if you lose a job. Generally, people need to revise a budget because:

* They are overspending and cannot meet all their expenses.
* Their income has gone down.
* Their expenses have gone up.
* Their income has increased.

The easiest way to reduce your expenses is to start with nonessentials, or discretionary expenses. If that doesn't reduce your expenses enough, you will need to reevaluate your fixed expenses.

Here's a **three**-step plan for getting your expenses to match your income:

1. Reduce discretionary expenses.
2. Reduce flexible expenses.
3. Reduce fixed expenses. For example, get a roommate or move to a cheaper home.

At some point, you may find yourself in the lucky position of needing to revise your budget because your expenses have gone down or your income has gone up. **EXAMPLES:** Your expenses might decrease if you're moving and your rent is lower. Your income might go up if you get a raise at work or you take a new job that pays more.

When your financial situation changes, you should complete an annual budget. (Remember: Multiply each monthly income and expense by 12.) This will allow you to compare your new annual income to your changed circumstances.

If you are going to have more income than your current budget is based on, you can enjoy deciding what to do with it.

Get Frugal!

Here's a word you might want to get to know: *frugal*. A person who is frugal is efficient, sparing, or conservative in his or her use of things, not wasteful. It doesn't mean being deprived or being a cheapskate. Being smart about being frugal can mean having a rich, fun life without spending more than you earn. Here are some tips to get you started:

* Walk or bike to work or school instead of taking public transportation or driving.
* Make your lunch instead of buying it.
* Buy snacks in bulk, pack them in plastic bags, and take them with you instead of buying individual snacks.

* Organize a potluck dinner or picnic with friends instead of going out for a meal.
* Buy generic brands instead of brand names at the grocery store.
* Research new services or products before buying.
* Find inexpensive or free forms of recreation and entertainment. Hikes, bike rides, street fairs, and free concerts in the park are just a few of the many fun activities that are often available. Also, don't forget early showings of movies. They are often half-price or less.

Can you think of other areas where you can reduce expenses without reducing your quality of life?

Should you add more to savings, plan a vacation, move to a better apartment, or make other changes in your lifestyle and goals? Is your first inclination to add all the extra income to discretionary expenses or to increase some fixed expenses—like housing or clothes—that are acceptable at their current level? In the long run, you will probably be more satisfied if you put some of the excess toward savings and other long-term financial goals.

Handling Unexpected Expenses

Everyone has emergency expenses from time to time. For example, you might have car repairs. You might have higher-than-expected medical bills, or you might need to travel to help an ill parent or attend an important family event, such as a funeral. If you budget for emergencies, you will be able to handle these unexpected events.

Record-Keeping

Keeping track of expenses and income, planning for emergencies, and being prepared to file your taxes all require keeping track of financial information. These tasks would be very difficult without good paperwork. To control your financial life, get organized right from the start.

Getting and Staying Organized

There are many ways to get organized. Pick a system that fits your style, and then modify it to suit your needs. Here are **three** tried-and-true methods for organizing financial information:

1. **Large envelopes** labeled by category.
2. **File folders** labeled by category in a file drawer or box.
3. **An accordion folder** and labels for identifying each pocket.

Sorting Receipts

To plan a budget that works, you have to know what you're doing with your money. Since you will want—or need—to revise your budget periodically, keeping track of expenses is important.

A set of envelopes or file folders or an accordion file where you store receipts by category will make this task easy. Write your budget categories on the envelopes or file folders. Many office supply stores carry special accordion file folders that come labeled with household expense categories. When you buy something, file the receipt in the appropriate folder.

Add up your receipts regularly. Note the amounts in your budgeting notebook or software. This is an important way to stay on top of how much you're spending on food, transportation, entertainment, and other regular expenses.

By the Numbers

Make Your Own Budget

What are your fixed expenses each month? Which ones are flexible? How about your discretionary expenses? Do you have short-term and long-term goals for which you need to save money?

Think about how you spend and save money now and how you would like to spend and save money in the future. Create a budget for yourself. Start with a monthly one and then calculate your annual budget. Be realistic and create a budget you can stick to!

Personal Records

Keeping and sorting receipts is important, but it's not enough. You also need to organize important documents. Here are some important categories for keeping your personal records in order. Include the ones that match your needs, and add new ones if necessary.

* Automobile (insurance, maintenance, title, registration and license plates, loan information).
* Checking account statements.
* Credit card statements.
* Charitable contributions.
* Contracts.
* Health insurance.

* Investments.
* Medical costs.
* Paycheck stubs.
* Pet records.
* Retirement contributions.
* Savings account statements.
* Social Security statements.
* Tax returns from previous years.
* W-2 forms (forms supplied by your employer in January of each year that show your earnings and deductions for the previous year).
* Warranties (for TV sets and other appliances).

Sort and file these documents in labeled file folders or an accordion file folder as you do your receipts.

Get Smart

Money Management Tips

Brenda W. and Scott T. are both out of high school and living on their own in a small college town in Oregon. Brenda is finished with college and is already thinking about marriage and her future. Scott just finished high school and is going to attend a community college for two years while he saves money to complete his degree.

Here are some practical suggestions they think will help you get off to a good start when you go out on your own:

* Pay the important things first.
* Group bills and pay them once or twice a month instead of when each one is due.
* Over-estimate expenses. It's better to have a little left over than not enough.
* Buy used! Used clothes, cars, and appliances are especially good deals.
* Out of sight, out of mind is the best rule for savings and emergency money. Put your savings in an account every month—or have it deposited into your savings account directly from your paycheck—and then forget about it until you need it.

Students Get Involved

Members of Students in Free Enterprise (SIFE) are out to change the world. With the help of their business professors, students from more than 700 U.S. colleges work to:

* Educate young people about financial issues and responsibility.
* Improve the lives of people in low-income communities by teaching them about business ownership.

In Chico, California, SIFE students set up and ran the Youth Entrepreneurship Camp for children aged 10 to 12 years old. Participants learned about business ownership and got hands-on experience applying math, computer, and writing skills to business-ownership questions.

SIFE students from La Sierra University went to Karandi village in India to help villagers set up The Cow Bank. Instead of lending money, The Cow Bank lends a cow! Families can drink some of the milk themselves and sell the extra milk. Instead of repaying the loan with money, it is repaid with the first female calf produced by the cow.

Understanding Your Paycheck

Getting your first paycheck can be a thrill. It's money you earned yourself! But it can also be a shock. At first, it might seem like the check is too small.

EXAMPLE: Let's see: 40 hours a week at $8 an hour. That comes to $320. Why is the check for only $272? What happened to the missing $48? The answer is: It was deducted to pay your taxes.

Taxes

Taxes are your contribution to running the government. In return for this payment, you receive services and benefits.

EXAMPLE: When you retire you will receive a monthly payment to help with living expenses from **Social Security**.

Your taxes are also used to support public needs, such as schools and roads.

Your Paycheck Stub

Each time you receive a paycheck from your employer, you also receive a **paycheck stub**. This stub shows exactly what taxes were deducted from your paycheck and what the deductions are for.

A typical paycheck stub shows:

* Gross wages.
* Net wages.
* Payroll taxes (including Social Security).

Gross Wages

Gross wages are the total amount you earn in a given time period. But you don't get to take home all of it. Some of it is taken out to cover taxes and other required payments. These amounts are called **deductions** because they are deducted from, or taken out of, your wages before you get your paycheck.

Net Wages

The amount left after deductions are taken out is called **net wages**. This is the amount you will have available to spend for your daily, monthly, and annual living expenses.

Anatomy of a Paycheck Stub

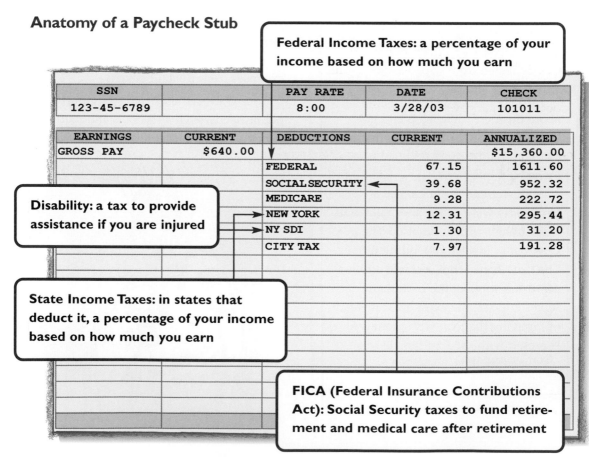

Federal Income Taxes: a percentage of your income based on how much you earn

SSN			PAY RATE	DATE	CHECK
123-45-6789			8:00	3/28/03	101011

EARNINGS	CURRENT	DEDUCTIONS	CURRENT	ANNUALIZED
GROSS PAY	$640.00			$15,360.00
		FEDERAL	67.15	1611.60
		SOCIAL SECURITY	39.68	952.32
		MEDICARE	9.28	222.72
		NEW YORK	12.31	295.44
		NY SDI	1.30	31.20
		CITY TAX	7.97	191.28

Disability: a tax to provide assistance if you are injured

State Income Taxes: in states that deduct it, a percentage of your income based on how much you earn

FICA (Federal Insurance Contributions Act): Social Security taxes to fund retirement and medical care after retirement

Net wages can be quite a bit less than gross wages. Subtract the current deductions from $640 to discover the take-home pay in the Anatomy of a Paycheck Stub example on page 44.

The amount of tax taken out of your paycheck is affected by **two** factors:

1. **Your filing status.** This is the number of dependents you claim. For tax purposes, dependents are people in your household, including yourself, whom you support.
2. **The amount you earn.** Up to a certain high income, the more you earn, the higher the percentage deducted.

Payroll Taxes

Payroll taxes are the different types of taxes deducted from your paycheck. The federal government taxes your income, as does your state government.

Other Deductions

In addition to payroll taxes, there may be additional required or voluntary deductions. For example:

* *Required local taxes.*
* *Contribution toward health insurance.* If your employer provides health insurance benefits, you may be required to pay a portion.
* *Retirement plan contribution.* If your employer provides a retirement benefit, you can have money automatically deposited in your retirement account.
* *Charitable contribution.* Some employers match employee donations and send the total directly to the charity.
* *Union dues.* If you belong to a union, your membership dues will be deducted automatically from your paycheck.
* *Savings.* Some companies will deposit a part of employees' paychecks into a savings account.

Payroll Taxes	
Type of Deduction	**Purpose**
Federal taxes	Deductions used to support the federal government's services and programs.
FICA (Federal Insurance Contribution Act)	Deductions to support retirement programs such as Social Security and Medicare.
Workers' compensation or disability programs	Deductions to provide support if you're injured or unable to work.
State taxes	Deductions used to support state government services and programs.

Paying Taxes

There is an old saying that the only two things in life you can count on are death and taxes. If you earn income in this country, taxes are inevitable. If you're already working, you know taxes can take quite a bite out of your earnings.

What do you receive in return for paying taxes? Every citizen receives both individual and societal benefits—benefits that help society as a whole.

Individual benefits include programs such as Social Security. Societal benefits include programs that use tax dollars to support schools, libraries, road construction, police and fire services, national defense, and many other services.

"Other folks have to pay taxes, too, Mr. Herndon, so would you please spare us the dramatics!"

You have the right to affect how your taxes are used. You can:

* ***Vote for politicians*** who use tax money to support things you believe in.
* ***Vote for or against*** local and state budget measures.
* ***Testify for or against laws*** that are being considered.

Your Life

Beyond Income Taxes

So far, we have talked primarily about taxes that are levied, or collected, against income you earn. There are other kinds of taxes, too. Here are some you should be aware of:

* ***Sales tax:*** percentage added to the price of goods and services by your state or city. Some states have no sales tax, but most do.
* ***Excise taxes:*** percentage added to the price of certain items such as alcohol, tobacco products, and gasoline. Luxury items such as fur coats and yachts also carry excise taxes. The gas-guzzler tax added to the price of certain high-performance cars is another example of an excise tax.
* ***Property taxes:*** amount paid based on the value of property you own, usually a house or condominium. Property taxes are most often collected by your city or county.

April 15th at Midnight

No, it's not a secret party. It's the day and time that must be postmarked on your federal income tax return if you don't want to pay interest and penalties. If the 15th is a Saturday, Sunday, or holiday, the deadline is extended until midnight of the next working day.

Filing Procedures

If you earn more than $4,000 a year, you are required to file taxes in the United States. People whose financial status is complicated often have to complete many tax forms. **EXAMPLE:** For people who own real estate, or receive money from investments, such as mutual funds or stocks, or who are self-employed, completing all the necessary tax forms can be confusing.

Most young people starting out on their own don't have a complicated tax situation. If you've gotten organized and have a good record-keeping system, filing your taxes should be fairly easy.

To file properly, you need to select:

* *An appropriate filing category* (single, head of household, married filing jointly, married filing separately).
* *An appropriate form*. (The 1040EZ and 1040 form are used by most taxpayers whose finances are not complicated.)

Once you've done these two things, you'll be ready to get the forms you need. You can get the forms:

* At most post offices.
* At many public libraries.
* At many banks.
* At your local Internal Revenue Service (IRS) office.
* By calling the IRS.
* By visiting the IRS web site.

Each form, unless it's downloaded from the Web, comes in a booklet that explains how to complete the form. If you download forms from the Web, the explanatory booklets can be downloaded separately.

You have **three** options for filing your completed form. You can:

1. **Mail a paper copy** to the regional IRS office in your area.
2. **Send it electronically** over the Internet.
3. **File by telephone** if you are using a 1040EZ form. To do this, request a Telefile tax package from the IRS.

Deductions

Each year, before the end of January, your employer is required by law to provide you with a W-2 form that shows what you earned and what was deducted for the whole year. The information on your W-2 helps you complete your tax form.

There are some situations in which you have to calculate your own deductions. For example:

* If you earn money working for yourself part-time, or receive enough interest on a savings account.
* If you have expenses that can be deducted from your income, for example, money spent trying to find work.
* If you work more than one job during the year.

1040EZ Form

Most young, single people will be able to use the streamlined 1040EZ form to file their taxes. It's one page with only 12 questions.

Attach a copy of your W-2 to your completed form before sending it in. Employers also send copies of their W-2s to the IRS. This allows the IRS to verify your income and the taxes you owe.

1040EZ Tax Form

Personal information (name and address)

Social Security number

Income information

Payment and tax information

Refund (if you overpaid or have deductions)

Amount you owe

Signature and date

Form **1040EZ**

Department of the Treasury—Internal Revenue Service
Income Tax Return for Single and Joint Filers With No Dependents (L)

OMB No. 1545-0675

Label (See page 12.) **Use the IRS label.** Otherwise, please print or type.

Your first name and initial: MARGARET J.   Last name: CAMERON
Your social security number: 123-45-6789

If a joint return, spouse's first name and initial / Last name
Spouse's social security number

Home address (number and street). If you have a P.O. box, see page 12.   1392 N. CALDWELL AVE.   Apt. no. 3R

▲ **Important!** ▲
You must enter your

City, town or post office, state, and ZIP code. If you have a foreign address, see page 12.   NEW YORK, NY 10020

"Yes" will not change your tax or reduce your refund.
...e if a joint return, want $3 to go to this fund? . . . . ▶ ☐ Yes ☐ No   ☐ Yes ☐ No

Income

Attach Form(s) W-2 here. Enclose, but do not attach, any payment.

1	Total wages, salaries, and tips. This should be shown in box 1 of your W-2 form(s). Attach your W-2 form(s).	1	15360 00
2	Taxable interest. If the total is over $400, you cannot use Form 1040EZ.	2	20 00
3	Unemployment compensation, qualified state tuition program earnings, and Alaska Permanent Fund dividends (see page 14).	3	
4	Add lines 1, 2, and 3. This is your **adjusted gross income.**	4	15380. 00

Note. You **must** check Yes or No.

5	Can your parents (or someone else) claim you on their return? **Yes.** Enter amount from ☐ worksheet on back. **No.** If **single**, enter 7,450.00. ☒ If **married**, enter 13,400.00. See back for explanation.	5	7450 00
6	...ine 5 is larger than line 4, enter 0. ▶	6	7930 00

Credits, payments, and tax

7	Rate reduction credit. See the worksheet on page 14.	7	
8	Enter your Federal income tax withheld from box 2 of your W-2 form(s).	8	1611. 60
9a	**Earned income credit (EIC).** See page 15.	9a	
b	Nontaxable earned income. 9b		
10	Add lines 7, 8, and 9a. These are your **total credits and payments.** ▶	10	1611. 60
11	**Tax.** If you checked "Yes" on line 5, see page 20. Otherwise, use the amount on **line 6 above** to find your tax in the tax table on pages 24–28 of the booklet.	11	1189. 00

Refund
Have it directly deposited! See page 20 and fill in 12b, 12c, and 12d.

		12a ▶	422. 00
	...outing number		☐ Savings
d	Account number		

Amount you owe

	...ubtract line 10 from line 11. This is ...l for details on how to pay. ▶	13 ▶	0

...Do you want to allow another person to discuss this return with the IRS (see page 22)? ☐ **Yes.** Complete the following. ☐ **No**

Third party designee
Designee's name ▶   Phone no. ▶ ( )   Personal identification number (PIN)

Sign here
Joint return? See page 11. Keep a copy for your records.

Under penalties of perjury, I declare that I have examined this return, and to the best of my knowledge and belief, it is true, correct, and accurately lists all amounts and sources of income I received during the tax year. Declaration of preparer (other than the taxpayer) is based on all information of which the preparer has any knowledge.

Your signature: Margaret J. Cameron   Date: 4/15/0   Your occupation: CLERK   Daytime phone number: (212) 234567

Spouse's signature. If a joint return, **both** must sign.   Date   Spouse's occupation

Paid preparer's use only
Preparer's signature   Date   Check if self-employed ☐   Preparer's SSN or PTIN
Firm's name   EIN
Phone no. ( )

For Disclosure, Privacy Act, and Paperwork Reduction Act Notice, see page 23.   Cat. No. 12617R   Form **1040EZ** (2001)

A good budget can pave the way to financial well-being. Tracking your income and expenses puts you in control of your money and helps you achieve your short and long-term financial goals. Getting and staying organized, keeping records, and sorting receipts are important habits to develop. They will help you stick to your budget.

You will need to revise your budget, if you lose a job or get a raise. If you move into a more or less expensive home, your expenses will change. Revising monthly and annual budgets will help you cope with changes in your circumstances.

One set of expenses you cannot avoid is taxes. When calculating your income, keep your net wages in mind. That's what you get to take home.

Consumer Economics

budget—spending plan designed to balance income and expenses. *p. 32*

credit rating—evaluation made by lenders based on ability to pay and bill-paying history. *p. 33*

deductions—required and voluntary amounts removed from your paycheck to cover taxes and optional benefits. *p. 44*

discretionary expenses—costs for items or services that are not essential. *p. 33*

expenses—money spent to purchase goods and services. *p. 32*

fixed expenses—costs of living that are the same amount every month. *p. 33*

flexible expenses—costs of living that vary. *p. 33*

gross wages—amount you earn before deductions *p. 44*

income—money received for labor or services (your work), for the sale of goods or property, or from financial investments. *p. 32*

net wages—amount you earn after deductions; your take-home pay. *p. 44*

paycheck stub—slip that shows your pay and gives you an accounting of all amounts deducted from your paycheck. *p. 44*

Social Security—federally funded government program designed to provide partial retirement benefits for older Americans; program is funded with worker payroll taxes. *p. 43*

taxes—required contribution all workers must make to support government services. *p. 43*

Handling Your Money

In this chapter, you will learn about:

- banks and other financial institutions
- checking and savings accounts
- shopping for interest rates

Picture this: It's a beautiful sunny day. You're relaxing on a park bench, soaking up the rays. After a few moments, you're joined by a man with a small metal box. You greet each other warmly, and then you hand him all the money you made for the last week. He writes you a receipt for the money, puts it in the metal box, and promises to safeguard it until you need it. On another day, you might meet on the bench again, but not to give him more money. On this day, you might request a loan and then linger on the bench to work out the details of how you'll pay him back.

Sound improbable? Well, if you had lived in Italy in the 15th century, that is probably how you would have handled your money. Most people did, which is why our word "bank" comes from the Italian banca, *which means bench—the location where many banking activities took place.*

How Banks Work

Banks and other financial institutions provide an important service to society. When most people say the word *bank*, they are referring to several different financial institutions, including commercial banks—what most of us call a *bank*—savings and loans, savings banks, and others. There are differences between the institutions, but for most ordinary purposes, these differences are slight. Whatever you call them, banks allow people to:

* Protect their money from theft.
* Borrow money.
* Smoothly carry out **transactions**—deposits, withdrawals, and payments in checks you write to pay your bills.
* Earn money by receiving **interest**, or a percentage of the amount in the account that is paid to you in return for keeping your money with the bank.

Banks are businesses. To stay in business, they need to make money, or a **profit**, just like any other business does. The **two** main ways they make money are by:

1. **Providing loans** (lending money to their customers).
2. **Charging for financial services,** such as loans and checking accounts.

Banks and the Government

In the United States, banking is a regulated industry. This means financial institutions that take your money have to follow certain laws. For example, to protect customers' money, banks are allowed to lend only a percentage of the amount they take from depositors. **Depositors** are people, like you, who deposit money in a bank. The amount of money they put in each time is called a **deposit**.

With the billions of dollars circulating in the United States, you might wonder how all that money is regulated. It's done by a national agency called the Federal Reserve. Often called "The Fed" for short, the Federal Reserve:

* Manages the federal government's money.
* Controls the flow of money in this country.

To handle both these activities, the Federal Reserve functions as a regulatory agency and as a bank. (It has one main bank in Washington, D.C., and 12 regional banks around the country.)

Banks and the Community

Banks keep money moving through a community, which helps the economy. For example, banks loan money so consumers can buy houses and cars. Since most people do not have enough cash on hand to purchase such expensive items, a bank loan makes it possible. These kinds of purchases stimulate, or spur, the economy. In the same way, bank loans to businesses also benefit the local economy.

Understanding Fees and Interest Rates

Banks are businesses that make money by charging for services and by lending money. The costs for their services are called fees.

Banks don't only charge fees. They also pay depositors interest. You might wonder how they can afford to do that. The answer is simple. They lend money at a higher **interest rate** (percentage paid on a loan or deposit) than they pay out. This difference between the interest they pay depositors and the interest they receive from loan payments is an important source of income for banks.

Other Financial Institutions

Each type of institution offers advantages and disadvantages, primarily involving differences in fees and services. In some cases, the main advantage is that a particular institution offers all the services you need. For example, commercial banks and **credit unions**, whose members are affiliated in some way (work for the same organization or graduated from the same college), offer the widest range of services and products. This includes checking and savings accounts, loans, and investment tools. While fees can be higher at commercial banks than some other institutions, the convenience of one-stop banking can make them a practical choice. Credit union services and products compare well with those

What Banking Institutions Do	
Type of Institution	**Services Offered**
Savings and loans	First set up to promote home ownership, they offer home mortgages, and car loans, savings, and checking accounts.
Credit unions	Nonprofit cooperatives whose members are affiliated in some way. They offer full banking services at lower costs.
Commercial banks	Referred to as full-service banks because they offer complete lending, checking, and saving services.
Savings banks	Services limited to savings accounts, loans, and safe-deposit boxes.
Virtual banks	Full-service banks without branches; all transactions are conducted electronically.
Loan companies	Primary function is consumer loans.

offered by commercial banks. In addition, fees can be lower because credit unions are **cooperatives** (groups owned and managed by members). If you are eligible for membership in a credit union, this can be a good choice.

Other institutions offer specialized products. As a result, they can offer more choices in their area of specialization. For example, a loan company may be able to find a loan for you that better meets your needs than one from a commercial bank. Even if you use a commercial bank or credit union for your banking needs, it can pay to research fees and choices with more specialized institutions, such as loan companies, savings banks, and savings and loans.

Checking Accounts

Writing someone a check is like giving them cash. It's just a more convenient and safer substitute. It's hard to function in our society without a checking account. Since you'll probably stick with the bank you choose for a number of years, spend some time researching account options. Compare:

* Fees.
* Interest rates.
* Check costs.
* Check-writing restrictions, if any.
* Overdraft policies.
* Minimum requirements for your balance (the amount of money you have in the account).

Anatomy of a Check

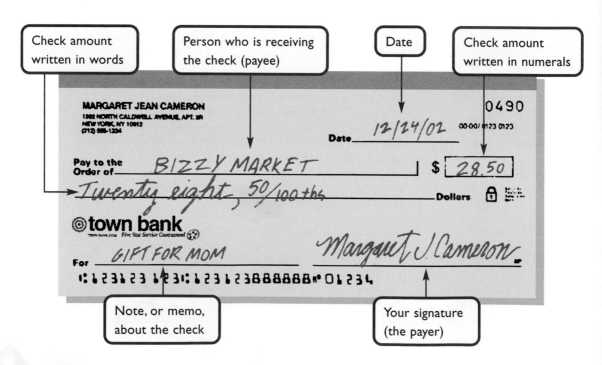

Check amount written in words

Person who is receiving the check (payee)

Date

Check amount written in numerals

Note, or memo, about the check

Your signature (the payer)

Opening an Account

To open an account:

* Select the bank and type of account that meet your needs.
* Gather personal information to complete an application.
* Take your personal information to the bank to meet with a customer service representative (or, complete your online application for a virtual bank).
* Complete a signature card so the bank knows what your signature looks like.
* Make a deposit.

Don't forget to bring the following when opening a checking account:

* Photo identification.
* Money for an initial deposit.
* Address and phone number.
* Name and address of a relative or reference.

Using Checks

When you write checks, you should always follow these **three** steps:

1. **Fill in all the information.** This will include the name of the **payee** (the person or company to whom you wrote the check), date, amount of the check in numerals, amount spelled out in words, and your signature. Otherwise, the check may not be accepted. Then you'll have to spend time straightening out the mess that results.

   "Memo" is optional. You can use it to write a note reminding yourself what the check is for, such as "electricity bill," or to provide information for the payee, such as the account number of your cell phone if you're paying your cell phone bill.

2. **Complete the check register.** Write the amount of the check, the date, the check number, and the payee in the **check register** (the booklet where you record checks and track your bank balance).

Anatomy of a Check Register

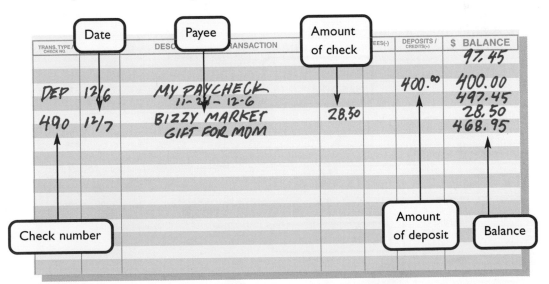

3. **Figure your balance.** Subtract the amount of your check from the balance, which is the amount you had in your account before you wrote the check. This will give you a new balance.

When you make a deposit or put money in the account, record that in your check register, too. Each time you deposit money, you need to fill out a slip telling the bank the amount of the deposit. Your checkbook will have deposit slips in the back. Make sure you also record ATM or debit withdrawals.

How to Read a Bank Statement

Every month, you will receive a bank statement. This monthly statement shows all the checks you wrote during the month. It also shows all your deposits, withdrawals, and other important information.

Anatomy of a Bank Statement

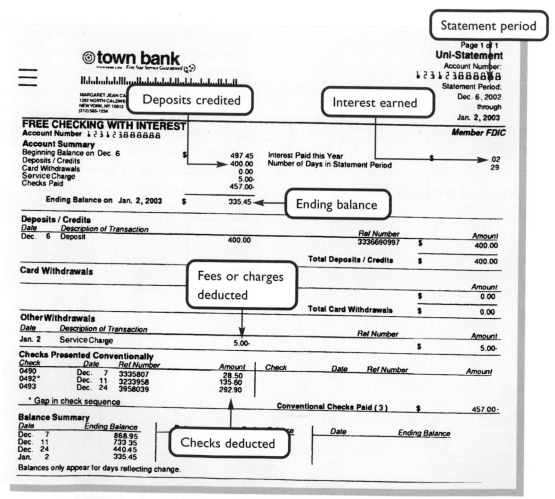

A bank statement includes the following information with which you need to be familiar. At a minimum, a bank statement includes these **six** pieces of information:

1. **Statement Period** The period of time covered by that statement and the transactions that occurred during that period. The statement period is usually one month, most often from the first day of the month to the last.

2. **Ending Balance** The amount of money in the account on the last day of the statement period.

3. **Checks Deducted** A list of each check and debit card transaction for which money was taken out of the account.

4. **Deposits Credited** A list of all money put into the account during the statement period.

5. **Fees or Charges Deducted** A list of deductions made against your account during the statement period. These deductions can include a charge for checks, or a fee for dropping below the minimum balance or writing a bad check (a check that bounced).

6. **Interest Earned** The amount of money the bank paid you on the amount of money in your account during the statement period.

What Banks Charge	
Fee	**Description**
Monthly service charge	A fixed amount deducted from your account each month.
Check costs	Charges for printing new checks.
Minimum balance charge	A charge if the balance falls below a certain dollar amount.
Returned check or overdraft charge	A charge for checks that were written when there wasn't enough money in the account to pay for them.
Overdraft protection	A service in which banks will move money from a savings account to a checking account when you don't have enough money in the account to cover the check.
Teller usage fees	A charge for speaking with a teller if you select an account in which you carry out all your transactions online or with an Automated Teller Machine.

Balancing Your Checkbook

Balancing a checkbook involves making sure:

* The amount you have in your checkbook balance matches the amount the bank says you have.
* You have enough money in the account to cover checks you write.

When you receive your statement, it will come with an account-balance reconciliation form, which you use to make sure your records match the bank's records. *Reconciling* your account means balancing your account based on the information in the bank statement. If your account is balanced, it means you and the bank agree on the amount of money in your account.

Balancing your checking account involves these **five** steps:

1. **Check the current balance.** Determine what your account balance was on the last day of the statement period by looking on the monthly statement (ending balance).
2. **Check deposits and checks written.** Compare the deductions and deposits in your check register to those on the bank statement.
3. **Include new deposits.** Add up all the deposits made after the ending date on your monthly statement, and add them to the ending balance.

4. **Include new deductions.** Add up all your deductions—checks you've written, ATM fees, and the like—after the end of the statement period, and deduct them from the balance you got when you added your deposits to the ending balance.
5. **Balance the totals.** The amount in step 4 is the amount you have now in your checking account because it includes transactions you've made since the statement was prepared.

Here are some tips to help you keep track of items when you're balancing your checkbook so you don't add or subtract the same item more than once. As you compare the statement to your check register:

* Put a check mark next to each withdrawal (check, ATM, or debit card) that is in your check register and on the statement.
* Put a check mark next to each deposit that is in your check register and on the statement.
* If some checks or deposits don't have checks next to them, determine why. **EXAMPLES:** was a deposit you made not recorded by the bank? Are there checks, debit card transactions, or deposits on the statement that you forgot to add to your register?

Can you think of other items that might not match? Why?

Endorsing Checks

Sometimes you will not be the one to write a check. You will be the one to receive a check from someone. When this happens, you can do one of two things with it:

* Cash it.
* Deposit it into an account.

No matter which option you choose, you have to **endorse** the check. When you endorse a check, you write your name on the back. This signature indicates that you accept the transfer of someone else's money to you.

In addition to a signature, you might want to include other information on the back, depending on whether you plan to cash or deposit the check. If you plan to

cash the check, write only your signature on the back. However, wait until you are at the bank. If someone finds or steals an endorsed check, it is as good as money. It can be cashed at a bank.

If you plan to deposit the check, add the following information above or below your signature:

* "For deposit only."
* The account number to which you want the check deposited.

This information will tell the bank that the check is meant to be deposited only to the account with the number written on the back. If someone tries to cash the check or deposit it to another account, the bank will not accept it.

Anatomy of an Endorsed Check

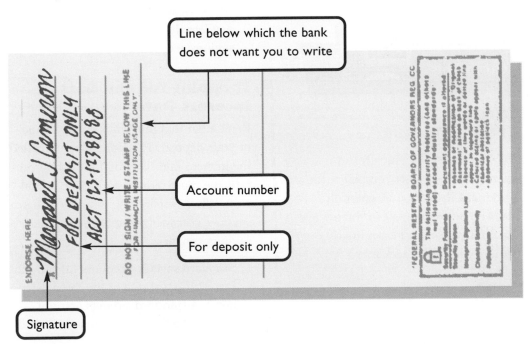

Line below which the bank does not want you to write

Account number

For deposit only

Signature

Handling Mistakes

Even if you keep track of every check you write and balance your checkbook every month, the day will probably come when there will be a mistake with your account. Here are some common mistakes that everyone experiences now and then:

* Your balance doesn't match the bank's. (If this occurs, balance your account again. If it still doesn't balance, contact the bank. If a mistake is due to bank error, check your next statement carefully. You should not be charged bank fees for any problems that might result.)
* A check written quite some time ago has not cleared. (Contact the payee to see if the check was cashed.)
* Your checkbook is lost or stolen. (Report it to your bank immediately.)

Search This

Safeguard Your Checking Account

Don't get taken by check fraud. Learn how to protect yourself at the National Check Fraud Center on the Web or by phone. List three ways the information you learn might protect you from check fraud.

* You believe someone has forged one of your checks. (Contact the bank immediately. You should not be responsible for the amount of the check. If the bank cashed the check without verifying the signature, it will have to reimburse, or pay back, your account.)

Savings Accounts

What should you do with the money you have earmarked for savings and an emergency fund? Avoid keeping this money in your checking account for **two** main reasons:

1. **The money is too easy to reach.** It should take extra effort to get to money saved so you don't use it for the wrong purpose.
2. **Savings accounts earn more.** Generally, checking accounts don't pay interest or pay less than what you'll receive on a savings account.

Shopping for the Best Interest Rate

Remember that interest is a percentage of your deposit. This percentage is called the interest rate. The higher the interest rate, the more money your deposit will earn. When researching where to put your savings, consider these **three** types of savings vehicles:

1. **Standard savings accounts** (usually the lowest interest rate of the three listed here). A standard savings account is the place to keep enough money to handle

an emergency, but it is not a good place for the largest share of your savings. The advantage is, you can get your money whenever you want it.

2. **Money market accounts** (usually a higher interest rate than a standard account). A **money market account** allows you to write checks, but only up to a certain number each month. Usually, you must keep a minimum balance in a money market account, whereas a regular savings account has no minimum balance requirements (or a much lower minimum).

3. **Certificates of deposit,** called CDs (higher interest rate than other options). The money placed in a **certificate of deposit** cannot be touched for a certain amount of time,

usually at least six months, without paying penalties. It's a good way to increase your earnings on savings, as long as you know you will not need the money for any other purpose.

Getting the Right Kind of Account

Your reasons for saving influence the kinds of accounts you use. For example, emergency funds need to be "liquid," or easy to reach. For these funds, standard savings accounts and money market accounts are appropriate. Look for accounts with:

* The highest interest rate.
* The lowest fees.
* The minimum penalty if your balance falls below a certain amount.

Your Highest Returns

Vincelle L. is a high school junior. He has a job and a savings account that he has had since he was a small child. He needs to pay for car insurance, but he doesn't have other monthly bills.

Because he will not need his savings for at least another year, he put three-quarters of his savings in a 12-month certificate of deposit. The CD earns 4.9 percent interest.

To pay his car insurance premiums, he put most of his remaining savings in a money market account, so he can write checks while he earns 3.2 percent. In his savings account, he keeps monthly amounts that are being saved toward less regular payments (like his car insurance) and for planned repairs. It pays only 2.9 percent, but he can get the money out whenever he needs it.

While you need easy access to emergency funds, that is not necessarily true for non-emergency savings. The account you select depends on the purpose for which you are saving. For example, short-term savings needed in less than six months can be placed in a regular savings or money market account.

If you use a money market account, find out how many checks you can write on the account in a given time period. Most money market accounts restrict the number of checks you can write. This has advantages and disadvantages:

* *It can help you stick to a savings plan* because you can't make unlimited withdrawals.
* *It can be difficult to withdraw money* if you've already reached the allowed number of withdrawals.

For savings that won't be touched for at least six months, consider CDs. You'll get a higher interest rate than in a savings or money market account. You'll also get the benefit of forced savings, since you can't get the money out easily.

My Notebook

Tracking Savings

Write down the amount you save each time you spend less on something than you used to. There are many reasons you might spend less. Perhaps you've waited to buy until a needed item came on sale. Maybe you've decided to start buying generic items instead of brand-name products, or skip the expensive popcorn and soda at movies, or take your lunch to school or work everyday. Whatever the reason, make a note of the amount saved and the reason you were able to save.

Also, keep a record of times you decide not to spend money at all when you might have in the past. At the end of the month, add up your savings. How did you do for the month?

By the Numbers

Compare the Savings

Let's say you've been following your savings plan every month. Some of your savings are still sitting in your checking account. You've saved up enough money now that you can begin to divide it into funds for emergencies, short-term savings, and long-term savings.

Research interest rates for a savings account, a money market account, and a certificate of deposit.

Now, imagine you are going to put $100 in each account for six months. You will not withdraw money from or deposit money into the account during that time. Calculate how much you'll have in each account in six months:

* First, multiply $100 by the interest rate of each account. (For example, if the interest rate is 2.5%, multiply $100 by .025 to get $2.50 in interest.)
* Next, determine your earnings. Since the interest just calculated is for one year, divide it in half to get the interest for six months (2 into $2.50 = $1.25).

Where will you go in your area to get the best interest rate?

Protecting Your Savings—From Yourself

No matter how well you stick to a savings plan, you always run the risk of undoing all your hard work. All it takes is one withdrawal for the wrong reason. That's why it's a good idea to have a plan for protecting your savings from yourself.

Here are **four** guidelines to help you avoid jeopardizing your savings:

1. **Don't mix savings** funds with funds for paying daily and monthly expenses.
2. **Transfer money regularly** from your checking to savings accounts.
3. **Make it hard to get to your savings.** For example, put money in CDs. You can't remove it early without paying a penalty.
4. **Save automatically.** Ask your bank to set up automatic monthly deposits into savings vehicles through the automatic deposit of your paycheck or through banks and other financial institutions.

Debit Cards and ATMs

Debit cards, ATM cards , and **ATMs (Automated Teller Machines)** work together to provide bank customers with convenient access to their money. ATMs are computer terminals that read your ATM or debit card and follow the instructions you punch in on the ATM's keypad. An ATM or debit card is a small plastic card that looks very much like a credit card.

Saving Lessons

As a college senior in the Southwest, Lindsey A. will soon be graduating from college debt free. It all started 20 years ago when her parents opened two certificate of deposit accounts for Lindsey when she was still a baby. As a child, she contributed part of her allowance to the accounts. Later, when she started working as a bank teller her senior year of high school, she contributed larger amounts.

Here are Lindsey's tips for saving:

* Keep savings for different purposes separate. Set up different accounts and make regular deposits.

* Don't dip into your savings for things they're not earmarked for. (But if you do, treat it as a loan and pay yourself back as soon as possible. Consider paying yourself "interest" on the loan.)

* Stay on top of debit card withdrawals. If you overdraw your account, you will be charged a hefty fee. "It's not worth a $30 bank charge to buy a $5 lunch when you're not sure what your account balance is," she says.

* Be active in your banking. Don't wait for the monthly statement. If you're not sure what your balance is, ask your bank—by phone, online, or in person.

An ATM card allows you to:

* Deposit money.
* Transfer money between linked accounts.
* Withdraw cash at ATMs.

A debit card allows you to:

* Deposit and withdraw cash at ATMs.
* Purchase goods.
* Receive cash from some stores when you make a purchase. This is called cash back.

Even though a debit card looks like a credit card, it is very different. Use of a credit card is like getting a loan. You don't have to have the cash on hand to make a purchase. A debit card, though, takes money out of your checking account to cover your purchases or withdrawals. You must have the cash in the account to cover the purchase or withdrawal. If you don't, your checking account will be overdrawn.

If properly managed, the use of ATM and debit cards offers a great deal of convenience.

Benefits

Debit and ATM cards allow you to do one or more of the following:

* Withdraw cash when banks are closed.
* Make purchases without writing checks or carrying a lot of cash around.
* Deposit funds when banks are closed.

ATMs allow you to:

* Bank in many locations, in your home city and while traveling to other locations.

* Handle transactions when the bank is closed.
* Keep a record of your most recent transaction by requesting a printed receipt.
* Make payments on bank loans.

Disadvantages

Debit and ATM cards can create the following problems if you aren't careful:

* Easy access to cash can make it hard to stick to a budget.
* The balance in your checking account can fall too low or be hard to reconcile if you forget to record each transaction in your check register.
* Other people can access your account if they learn your personal identification number (PIN).

"Hold on—I was putting my card in upside down."

Banking Carefully

When Robbie Robertson and Sheryl Manning offer tips on how to bank wisely and handle money, it pays to listen. Literally. Robertson works for a credit union, and Manning works for a bank. Both have helped young adults organize their banking and saving practices.

Manning suggests starting out with a savings account that has a debit card, instead of jumping right into managing a checking account. This allows you to get used to tracking deposits and withdrawals and using ATMs. In six months, if you've handled the debit card well, add a basic checking account. Once you add a checking account, don't let a month go by without balancing it against your monthly statement. Robertson cautions you to look carefully at anything that claims to be a "free" account. There are often hidden costs.

EXAMPLE: Many accounts require that you use the ATM for all your transactions. If you use teller services by phone or in person, you're charged a service fee! In some cases, there might also be a limit on the number of ATM transactions allowed each month. If you make more transactions, you pay again!

Robertson also encourages young people to get the savings bug. "As you make more money, you don't have to spend it," he says. "Don't get caught in the spending trap. Learn to save excess money."

Track Your Withdrawals

The most reliable way to keep track of ATM and debit card withdrawals is to write them in your check register as if you had written a check. Try to develop the habit of writing the withdrawal in your check register at the time of the purchase or cash withdrawal, just as you would when you write a check. This means getting in the habit of pulling out your checkbook every time you pull out your debit card. As a safeguard, always get a receipt or transaction slip so you can check to see if your check register is up to date.

Electronic Banking

Electronic banking allows you to bank online. It also allows you to arrange for automatic transactions to be carried out by the bank so you can pay bills without writing a check each time.

Checking Account Balances

By using electronic banking services, you can check your account balance any time of day or night. You can also check to see if a particular check has cleared. (When a check has cleared, it means the money has come out of your account and gone to the payee, or recipient, of the check.) This can be more convenient than calling the bank, going to an ATM, or waiting for a monthly statement.

Automatic Transactions

By using electronic banking, you can also arrange to have:

* **Automatic deductions** from your account. For example, regular monthly loan payments can be automatically deducted and sent to the payee.
* **Transfers** from one account into another. **EXAMPLE:** A certain amount can go automatically from your checking account into a savings account or other savings tool.
* **Automatic Deposits** in your account. **EXAMPLE:** Your paycheck can be deposited by your employer.

Institutions to Avoid

Of course, banking isn't completely free. There are costs such as minimum-balance fees, for using banking services. In general, though, the benefits of using banking services outweigh the disadvantages. This is especially true if you handle your money well and avoid unnecessary service charges. This is not true, however, for some institutions. If you use services from the ones described in this section, it can be very hard to handle your money wisely.

Pawnshops

Imagine it's been a difficult month financially. Your phone bill was much higher than usual. You also had an unexpected car repair bill. Now, it's the end of the month, and your rent is due. For the first time since you've been on your own, you don't have enough money in your checking account to cover the rent check.

Last month, though, you bought the big-screen television for which you'd been saving for months. Your friend suggests taking the TV to the local **pawnshop** to get the money to pay your rent. You've never heard of this idea before, and you're wondering what a pawnshop is and if it's wise to use one.

A pawnshop is a store that loans money with interest and keeps a valuable item you own as security. The interest rate you pay is higher than a bank loan. You have a certain amount of time to pay off the loan, and then the shop has the right to sell your item. Many people lose their property this way, because once they get behind, they can't catch up enough to pay off the pawnshop loan.

Do you think it would be wise to try to make ends meet by using a pawnshop?

Loan Sharks

Imagine that you have been hoping to buy a car. You've even picked out the make and model you want. Unfortunately, in the past you used your credit card too much and got behind on your payments. When you went to the bank to get a car loan, they looked up your credit history. They were not willing to give you a loan because you didn't have a good record of making your credit card payments on time. The loan officer was concerned that you might not make your car loan payments on time either.

You've seen car loan ads for people who have bad credit. You're wondering if you should contact one of these lenders. You know how credit works, though: If you're a bad risk, people don't want to lend to you.

Why would someone be willing to lend to people who have a bad payment history? The answer: they charge very high interest rates for the loan. These kinds of lenders are known as **loan sharks**. When you borrow from a loan shark at high interest rates, it takes a very long time to pay off even a small loan. Most of what you pay goes toward interest, not toward paying down the amount of the loan.

On TV and in movies, loan sharks often appear as unsavory characters with a reputation for breaking a leg or two when a loan isn't repaid. In real life, loan sharks may look like reputable loan companies. Think carefully before borrowing money from anyone.

The High Cost of Loan Sharks

Jonathan wants to buy a car. Unfortunately, he has a bad credit history and cannot get a loan from a bank. He's thinking about buying the car from a company that many would call a loan shark because the interest rate is so high. The loan is for $12,000, to be paid off in three years.

Look at the difference in the interest rates and monthly payments in the chart at the left. How much more will Jonathan pay for the car if he buys it from a loan shark instead of from a conventional bank? Do you think he should get a loan now from a loan shark or wait until he can get one from a regular bank? What would you do?

From the Loan Shark	From a Conventional Bank
$12,000 loan	$12,000 loan
Pay it off in 3 years	Pay it off in 3 years
Interest rate: 21%	Interest rate: 8%
Monthly payment: $452.10	Monthly payment: $376.04
Total you pay: $16,275.60	Total you pay: $13,537.44
Your cost to borrow $12,000: $4,275.60	Your cost to borrow $12,000: $1,537.44

Check-Cashing Centers

Your best friend can never seem to get ahead. You've helped her set up a reasonable budget. Every month, she resolves to stick to it, but every month there is some new gadget she just has to buy. As a result, she has a lot of credit card debt and she is often short on cash.

Yesterday, she told you she was going to get a paycheck loan at a **check-cashing center** that just opened in your neighborhood. You don't know very much about check-cashing centers, but you remember hearing something bad about them. You don't want your friend to get into more financial trouble, so you get on the Web to do some research. You learn that the centers give people an advance, or cash, against their next paycheck. The interest rates are very high, though. This makes it hard for people to pay off the loan. In fact, it's often so hard that they have to get another paycheck loan to pay off their first loan. Soon, people are trapped in a vicious cycle of borrowing money they can never pay back.

What can you tell your friend to convince her that she should avoid check-cashing centers?

Debt Consolidators

Do you know someone who owes money to a lot of different companies and has trouble making the payments? Many people in this situation often think it would be easier to write one check for everything. In one way, they're right. They wouldn't have to keep track of many different payment dates.

In another way, though, they're wrong. That's because the usual way to combine all your payments is to go to a **debt consolidator** . A debt consolidator combines your payments on a number of debts, then loans you the total so you can

pay off all your debts. Then, you have only one monthly loan payment to the consolidator. There are **two** reasons working with a debt consolidator can create problems:

1. **Rates are high.** Interest rates on the loan can be high because borrowers are usually a bad risk.

2. **Your property is at risk.** The loan is guaranteed, or secured, with something valuable the borrower owns, like a house or car. If the loan is not paid, people lose the item used to guarantee the loan.

If you have a number of debts, it is often better to work out a payment plan with the companies you owe rather than to go to a debt consolidator. The interest rates will usually be lower. In addition, you will pay less in interest overall and pay off the debt sooner.

Chapter 4 Wrap-up
HANDLING YOUR MONEY

Handling your money effectively will help you achieve your goals. It will also improve the quality of your daily life by allowing you to avoid unnecessary worry about money and your financial status. Understanding what different financial institutions offer and selecting the best ones for your needs will support your efforts to handle your money well. Once you've selected particular institutions, knowing how to track and manage your accounts is another way to be in charge of your money. As important as it is to select good institutions, it is just as important to avoid others, like check-cashing centers, that prey on people who are barely getting by financially.

ATM (Automated Teller Machine)—computer in a public place, such as a bank or grocery store, that accepts a debit or ATM card and allows customers to withdraw or deposit money without interacting with a person. *p. 64*

bank—business that receives, safeguards, and lends money, and offers related financial and monetary services. *p. 52*

certificate of deposit—savings tool in which you loan money to the bank for a fixed term (a specific amount of time). In return, you receive a higher interest rate than a traditional savings account, but you must wait to make withdrawals. *p. 61*

check-cashing center—office that provides high-interest loans guaranteed by the amount of your next paycheck. *p. 69*

check register—small booklet used to keep track of each check written and your bank balance. *p. 55*

cooperative—group in which members band together to form a business or association that's owned and operated by the members themselves. Members share the profits. *p. 54*

credit union—cooperative savings and lending institution in which members are affiliated in some way, such as working for the same organization or attending the same college. *p. 53*

debit card—small plastic card that can be used at an ATM to allow you to withdraw money from (or deposit money into) your checking account. Debit cards can also be used to make purchases. *p. 64*

debt consolidator—lender who makes loans to customers to pay off multiple creditors. Customers then make a single

monthly payment to the consolidator. Interest rates are often high, and loans are secured with property, such as a house or a car. *p. 70*

deposit—amount of money placed in an account, such as a checking or savings account. *p. 52*

depositor—person who puts money in an account. *p. 52*

endorse—to sign one's name on the back of a check, indicating approval of the transfer of money from one party to another. *p. 59*

interest—amount of money received as a benefit of keeping funds in a bank or other financial institution, or the amount paid to borrow money from a financial institution. *p. 52*

interest rate—percentage paid on a loan or deposit. *p. 53*

loan shark—informal term for a provider of high-interest loans to people who can't get conventional loans. *p. 68*

money market account—specialized savings account that has limited check-writing options and offers a higher interest rate than a regular savings account. *p. 61*

pawnshop—company that loans cash at interest and keeps personal items as security until the loan is paid off. *p. 67*

payee—person or company being paid. *p. 55*

profit—amount of money returned after all of a business's operating expenses have been paid. *p. 52*

transactions—bank activities, such as deposits and withdrawals, conducted as part of doing business with the bank. *p. 52*

CHAPTER 5

Using Credit Wisely

In this chapter, you will learn about:

- understanding credit
- keeping a good credit rating
- avoiding getting into debt

Alex and Shauna each got a credit card. Both were tempted to get the things they wanted by charging the purchases. Alex caved in to his temptations. He wanted a new stereo system for his apartment, so he put it on his credit card. He also used credit to buy a car, and he opened charge accounts at several stores so he could buy the latest trendy clothes. Soon, Alex was deeply in debt. Most of his income went to making his credit card and loan payments, leaving him with no money to have fun.

Shauna, on the other hand, used credit only when it was really necessary and when she knew that she would be able to pay it off right away. Her clothing and her car were not always the coolest among her friends, but, after a year or two, Shauna had money left from her paycheck to buy new clothing and even to take a trip. She also had no debt.

Understanding Credit

Omnika wanted a cool set of speakers that cost $500, and she had only a few dollars in her checking account. The salesperson suggested she buy the speakers on **credit**. "Buy now, pay later!" he encouraged Omnika.

Getting what you want on credit seems easy, but what the ads fail to tell you is that credit often causes many financial problems and heartaches. If Omnika gets several cash loans and if she charges many purchases, she may find herself so heavily in debt that she cannot enjoy life because she is always worried about paying her bills. However, Omnika can avoid sleepless nights, having her car taken away, and being harassed by people to whom she owes money. She can make credit work for her rather than against her. So can you. The way to make credit work for you is to understand how it works and when to use it.

What Is Credit?

Credit goes by many different names, such as borrowing, charging, and getting a loan. Credit is really using someone else's money. Credit may be borrowing cash, or it may be buying something now and paying for it in the future. In either case, not only must the amount borrowed or charged be paid back, but also a fee will be charged that is some percentage of the amount borrowed. The amount charged or borrowed is called the **principal**, and the fee that is paid for the use of the money is called the interest.

Immediate Versus Delayed Gratification

Let's say you really want a new CD. If you go out and buy it right away, you're getting something called **immediate gratification**. Using credit is a way of getting immediate gratification. However, if you wait a few weeks to save up the money to buy the CD, you have **delayed gratification**.

Buying on credit helps you get immediate gratification, but there are disadvantages. You may not have money you need at some later date because you have committed your future income to pay for things you get now. Some of your earnings also must go to pay credit fees rather than to purchasing things you might need or want.

"Someday, son, all this will be mine."

Commercial and Personal Credit

Like individuals, businesses and even governments often borrow money. When a business wants to expand or increase its inventory, it gets a loan, called **commercial credit**, to cover the costs. There are times when a government spends more than it raises in taxes. When this happens, it also has to borrow money.

Credit used by individuals is called **personal credit**. Personal credit also affects the economy. Having credit available makes it easy to purchase more goods. When people buy more, jobs are created for those who make and sell those products. What happens to the economy if consumers use too much credit? If people buy on credit and save little, a time may come when they have to pay off their debts and cannot buy anymore. When this happens, there are fewer people to purchase goods and fewer jobs for people who make and sell the products.

Uses of Credit

Credit is neither good nor bad in itself. It is *what* you use it for and *how* you use it that make it good or bad. When is it to your advantage to use credit? When should you pay cash or give up the purchase? These are often not easy questions to answer. Here are some guidelines to help you make these decisions.

Advantages of Using Credit

Credit is necessary for almost everyone. For example, very few people could buy a house without credit. Here are **three** examples of the advantages of using credit:

1. **If you don't have ready cash,** buying something on credit makes it possible to use the product while you are paying for it, rather than waiting until you save enough to buy it. If you buy a DVD player on a one-year credit plan, you can use it immediately. If you saved for it first, the satisfaction of having it will be delayed for a year. Buying now and using the product while you pay for it is most appropriate for major purchases, such as homes and automobiles, since it's difficult to save in advance for the full purchase price.

2. **Using credit may help you save money.** Suppose you see inline skates that you've been wanting. They are on sale for a limited time for $20 off. If you don't have the money but have a credit card, you can take advantage of this sale.

3. **Credit comes in handy** for short-term needs and emergencies. Suppose your car breaks down and you have no ready cash for repairs. If you had no other way to get to work, you might lose your job without using credit to make the needed repairs.

Disadvantages of Using Credit

Along with the advantages that credit offers, though, there are risks when you use credit to make your purchases. Here are **three** examples:

1. **Credit makes it easier to overspend** and to make impulse purchases. It's so easy to buy things today thinking you'll pay for them "in the future." But the future is uncertain. Suppose you use too much credit? What if you're laid off from your job or have unexpected medical expenses?

2. **Very little in this world comes free.** Not only do you have to pay back the money you borrow, but credit requires you to pay for the use of the money in interest.

3. **When you buy many things on credit, payments sometimes pile up** so much that you may have little money left to do anything beyond the essentials. Even taking care of basic needs may be at risk. You may have your property taken away, have part of your wages taken by creditors, or even be forced into bankruptcy.

My Notebook

Buying Now or Later?

Describe a time when you waited to save up the money to buy something you wanted. What happened? Did you still want the item by the time you saved up the money for it? What can you learn from this experience?

Now describe a time when you purchased something big without waiting. What, if anything, did you give up to buy the item? If you had to do it again, would you purchase the item in the same way, or at all? Why or why not? What did you learn to help you in the future?

Rates and Fees

Have you ever heard the saying, "Knowledge is power"? If you know how credit works and the meaning of terms used in credit advertising and contracts, you will have the power to get the best rates on loans and protect yourself from being cheated. Remember, the better the interest rate on the loan (the lower it is), the more money you will have to spend on other things.

When comparing different kinds of credit, the most important piece of information is the **annual percentage rate** (or APR). The APR is a number stated as a percentage, such as 20 percent, which means that each year you have the loan, you will be paying the lender a fee that equals 20 percent of the amount you owe.

In most cases, the calculation of the interest charges is quite complicated and too difficult for the average consumer to calculate. However, because there are laws that tell lenders exactly how they must do the interest calculations, you don't have to do the calculations on your own. (If you want to calculate the APR and other elements of a loan, there are web sites that will help you.)

What you really want to know is the APR number the lender quotes for the loan, because the lower the APR, the less costly the loan is to you. Because all lenders are required to state an APR, it is the best comparison point to use when shopping for the cheapest loan.

Another important credit term is the **finance charge**. This term tells you in dollar amounts what the total cost of the loan will be to you. By knowing this dollar amount, you can understand your immediate cost of borrowing and be able to budget for the repayment of the loan. Although it is important to know the finance charge, the APR is a better way to compare loans when other terms of loans are different.

The Three Cs of Credit

Most people qualify for some type of credit. There are many forms of credit to choose from. Some cost much more than others. The challenge is to do everything possible to qualify for credit with the most favorable terms (the lowest APR).

Lenders look at three indicators of a borrower's ability to repay a loan: character, capacity, and capital. These are called the "**three** Cs of credit:"

1. Your **character** is measured by your past record of paying bills on time. Creditors don't like to lend money to people who make late payments or fail to make payments altogether.

2. Your **capacity** is determined by whether you have steady employment with enough income to make payments on the loan.

3. Your **capital** includes money you may have saved, any investments, and any property you own, such as a car or house. Lenders know that if the loan isn't repaid, they can get what is owed by taking your capital.

Loans

Loans come in many forms and amounts. Although many purchases may be made with credit cards, some of your largest credit transactions will be installment purchases for big-ticket items, such as televisions, washing machines, cars, and homes. Before financing a major purchase, do some research in order to get a loan with the best rates.

* **Banks:** These privately owned businesses have been lending large and small amounts of money in the form of secured and unsecured loans for decades.
* **Credit Unions and Savings and Loan Companies:** These offer similar credit services as do the banks, except they are owned by the people they serve. This means they may give better service and offer lower loan rates.
* **Retailers:** Many retailers offer their own credit on the products they sell. The goods you buy often serve as collateral (security) for the loans.
* **Sales Finance Companies:** Many retailers may offer you credit for products that you buy, but *they* are not giving you the credit. Rather, they arrange for you to get credit from some other lender, called a sales finance company. A sales finance company usually does not lend money directly to the borrower, but only makes consumer loans through the retailer selling the product.

Types of Loans

Many different kinds of loans are offered to businesses and consumers by financial institutions. For individuals, the most common loans are used for very expensive purchases: cars, an education, and a home.

Car Loans

Max is considering buying that hot red convertible he always wanted. He wants to get the best deal he can so he will have money left over to buy accessories, insurance, gasoline, and all the other things that go with automobile ownership.

As part of his shopping, he looks at ads that say, "best credit term in town;" "we finance anyone;" "a few dollars down and drive the car home;" and "0.0% financing."

What do these ads really promise? In most cases, the messages in advertising for automobile financing are meaningless at best and fraudulent at worst.

Max could finance his car purchase in several different ways. The first option he should try is to apply for a car loan at his bank or credit union. The loan officer will not only check his **credit history**—his record of borrowing and repaying debts—with a **credit bureau** (a company that gathers credit information), but also look up the loan value of the car. Based on this information, the loan officer will decide if Max qualifies for a loan and how much the lender is willing to lend him to buy that particular car.

Many dealers advertise that they will finance the cars they sell. If Max has not already gotten a loan in advance, the dealer will try to convince him to finance it with the dealer. When the dealer says it will finance, this usually means the dealer will make the financial arrangements along with doing all the other paperwork involved in the purchase. In most cases, the dealer is not giving the loan but is arranging the loan through a sales finance company.

Although dealer-arranged financing is usually quicker and more convenient, it is often a more expensive way to finance than if Max had applied for a bank or credit union loan on his own, because the dealer makes a profit on loans it arranges. Here are some of the tricks a less-than-honest auto dealer may pull on Max:

* Quote a low APR in conversation and then sneak a higher APR into the written contract.
* Say he must buy a service contract or extended warranty in order to get financing.
* Say he must buy all kinds of insurance from the dealer.

Student Loans

Are you planning on going to college? Because of rapidly rising tuition and other college-related costs, many students can't afford to go. Fortunately, there are relatively low-cost loans to help with college expenses. Depending on which school you attend, you may borrow from the federal government, from your state government, or from a private lender.

If you can prove financial need based upon your and your parents' finances, you may qualify for a subsidized loan. With a subsidized loan, the government pays off part of the amount borrowed, so you won't have to pay back the full amount of the loan.

Student loans can add up fast, and the amount can be staggering. Make sure that you understand the amount you will be required to pay back, when you will need to start making payments, and that you are able to assume this debt.

Student Loan

Mary F. knew she wanted to go to a private college, and that it would be expensive. To save up money for school, she started working at a toy store when she was 15 years old. While she was in high school, she worked at the store every day after school and all day on Saturdays. She also baby-sat for neighbors' kids a couple of evenings per week.

During college, she worked at a financial-aid job serving food. During winter and summer vacations, she worked at the toy store or as a waitress in restaurants.

Even though she worked part-time, her parents paid half her tuition, and she got a small scholarship from her college, it still wasn't enough. So she took out a loan from the state of Illinois, her home state. Over the course of four years, she borrowed $10,000 at an interest rate of nine percent, which she was originally supposed to pay back within 10 years.

When she graduated from college, she had a year grace period before she had to start paying back the loan. Once she started making the payments, it was very difficult to come up with the $125 loan payment every month. Twice, she couldn't make the payments and had to renegotiate the loan. Once, she lost her job, and another time, she got behind on her bills.

Finally, when she was 35 years old, she paid off the loan! It took her 20 years to pay for her education. Was it worth it? "Absolutely," says Mary.

Mortgages

The loan you obtain to buy a home is called a **mortgage**. It's much like other installment loans, in which your monthly payment includes both part of the principal (the amount of money borrowed) and interest. Since homes are expensive, mortgage loan terms are generally from 15 to 30 years. The home is collateral. If you don't make your mortgage payments, the lending institution can take your house.

When you buy a home, in most cases you will need to invest savings in addition to the money you borrow. This is called a **down payment**. As you make your mortgage payments, part of the payment is for principal, and part is for interest. The combination of your down payment, the principal you have paid, and any increase in the home's value in the years since you took out the mortgage loan is the **equity** you have in the home. Your equity is the difference between what your home would sell for and what you owe on the mortgage.

If you already have a mortgage and need to borrow a large amount for another purchase, such as home improvements or college, you can apply for an additional mortgage called a **home equity loan**. This type of loan usually has a lower APR and a longer repayment period than other types of loans. But, if you can't make the payments, you could lose your home.

Troublesome Loans

Have you seen billboards or heard radio ads for "Instant Cash!" "Easy Loans!" "No Credit Checks!" "Friendly Credit!" and other such claims?

Think of a situation where you might need cash quickly and don't have an established credit history or have a bad credit record. Under such circumstances, you may be lured into getting one of these loans. Lenders who do this type of advertising usually give you cash on the spot with no credit check and few questions asked.

Remember, if it's that easy, there must be a catch. There is one *big* one—you will pay interest charges many times greater than for other types of loans.

Search This

Comparing Credit Costs

Use the Internet and other sources to research different types of loans. Investigate the ones listed here in terms of typical length and APR. What is the cost of each type of loan per $100 for one year?

* Mortgage loans.
* Automobile loans.
* Credit card loans.
* Pawnshop loans.
* Payday loans.

On the basis of your research, which types of loans would you recommend, and why? Which loans cost consumers the most? Are there any you would definitely avoid? Why?

Credit Cards

Do you already have a credit card, or are you thinking about getting one? Do you seem to be on every credit card company's "most wanted" list? More than a half billion cards have been issued, and the average American credit card debt is around $8,000. Credit card issuers know that teenagers are big spenders. They want to profit from them. Many people just out of high school find themselves with huge credit card problems—and debt—fast. You don't want to be one of them.

Surviving in our economy without a credit card is very difficult, although some people challenge themselves to do just that. Still, it is almost impossible to buy something over the phone or on the Internet, or to rent a car or buy a plane ticket, without a credit card. Knowing how credit cards work will help you make good choices about how and when to use them.

How Credit Cards Work

Having a credit card is like having a pre-approved line of credit—that is, you can borrow or charge up to a certain amount agreed to by you and the lender. For credit cards, the pre-approved line of credit is called your **credit limit**. You may make charges at any time during the payment period as long as you don't exceed your limit.

There are ways to use a credit card without paying interest charges. In most cases, if you pay the full balance on time, you don't pay any interest or other fees. However, if you pay less than the full balance owed, you will be charged interest. When you pay less than the minimum due or if you pay late or go over your credit limit, you may be required to pay additional fees.

Advantages of Credit Cards

Carrying a credit card is usually safer than carrying cash. If your credit card is lost or stolen, and you report it immediately, you lose nothing. If cash is lost or stolen from you, it is usually gone for good.

Reviewing the charges on your credit card statement is a good way to keep track of spending and may even help you with budgeting.

One of the biggest advantages of credit cards is the **charge back** feature. Suppose you purchase a DVD player on your credit card and find it defective. When you return it, the seller refuses to credit your account. If the product cost more than $50 and was purchased within your home state or within 100 miles from home, you can withhold payment for the purchase until the problem is resolved.

Disadvantages of Credit Cards

Because you are buying something and won't pay for it for a month or more, it's easy to overspend. Many people in financial trouble are there because of credit card spending sprees. They end up able only to pay the minimum balance each month. The amount they owe continues to rise, along with the interest they must pay. It is very difficult to pay down a credit card once you get to this stage.

One of the biggest disadvantages of credit cards is their cost. In recent years, most credit card companies have added many new fees, increased existing fees, and raised the APR.

Choosing the Right Card

Choosing the right card is not easy, because interest rates, terms, and fees vary greatly from one card to the next, even though they may look alike. Although your credit card may say "Visa" or "MasterCard," the actual credit comes from a bank, credit union, or other lender. Some may be good choices, while others should be avoided.

Most credit cards are **revolving credit** accounts. Visa and MasterCard accounts use revolving credit. These types of cards permit you to make charges to your account at any time without paying the full balance each month. A **charge card** is similar to a credit card, but you must pay your balance in full each month. However, there may be high annual fees. American Express and Diner's Club are examples of charge cards.

Retailers offer credit and charge cards. They are similar to most other types of cards, except they may be used only at the store or chain that offers them.

Get Smart

My Wallet Is Missing!

You reach for your wallet and suddenly, anxiety runs though your body. It's not there! What do you do now? Follow these **three** steps:

1. **Notify authorities or law enforcement.** If you are in a store, restaurant, or other public place, notify the management. If you are in a foreign country, contact the American Embassy.

2. **Notify your bank and credit card companies *immediately*.** Only by promptly notifying the bank and credit card companies of your loss can you limit your responsibility for charges that may

be made on your card and checks written on your account. Then you will be billed only for charges made on your account *before* the notification, with a maximum charge of $50 to you.

3. **Keep a copy of all relevant credit card information in a safe place.** Your list should include each credit or debit card number and the toll-free number of each institution. For an annual fee, some banks and credit unions will register all your credit cards with one company. This lets you make just one call to cancel all your cards. Update your list every year to keep it current.

Cost of Credit Cards

The biggest factor in choosing a credit card is the cost. For all the convenience credit cards provide, there are costs to you that are not obvious at first glance.

* **Annual fees.** Some credit card companies charge annual membership fees that can be as high as $60. The amount is automatically added to your account balance. If you don't read your statement carefully, you won't even notice it.
* **Interest charges.** Almost all credit cards charge interest, but you may not have to pay it. In most cases, if you pay the full balance on time at the end of each payment period, you are not charged interest.

* **Grace period.** The number of days between the billing date and the payment due date is called the **grace period**. You are charged a stiff fee if the credit card issuer does not receive payment before the end of the grace period.
* **Fees, fees, and more fees.** You might think you are a savvy consumer because you shopped around and found the lowest APR available. However, you may have missed the most important part of the contract—the fine-print information about fees charged. Charging fees is a very lucrative way for credit card companies to increase profits. New fees are often added to the contract and old fees are frequently increased.

Making it **REAL**

Evaluating Credit Card Offers

How do you know which credit card is best for you? Gather several credit card offers that either you or your parents receive in the mail. Evaluate each card to see which one has the:

* Lowest APR. Be careful of introductory teaser rates that go much higher after a short time.
* Longest grace period.

* Highest credit limit.
* Lowest (or no) fees for: annual membership, going over credit limit, late payments, paying with bad check.
* Lowest penalty APR for: exceeding the credit limit, paying late.

What language or terms in the credit contract don't you understand? How can you find out the answers to your questions?

ATM Costs

Jack plans to borrow $100 for his weekend date using a credit card cash advance from an ATM machine.

How much will this cash advance cost him?

* Fee for the use of the ATM machine: $4.
* Fee from Jack's bank for not using its machine: $2.
* Fee for getting a cash advance from a credit card account: $5.
* Interest paid on the cash advance: $2.
* Total cost for getting the $100: $13.

What if Jack gets a cash advance every week for a whole year? How much will that cost him?

Credit Card Fees

Often the most costly part of having a credit card are the fees and penalty interest rates that go along with it. These include:

* *Late fee:* fee charged when the payment is received after the due date.
* *Over-the-limit fee*: fee charged when your balance goes over the specified credit limit.
* *Penalty or punitive interest rates:* big increase in your APR if you have paid late or exceeded your credit limit.

Cash Advances

If you need cash quickly, your credit card company makes it easy for you to get a **cash advance**, which is really a loan from your credit card company. You simply insert your credit card in an ATM machine, key in your personal identification number, and out comes the money. You may get a momentary rush seeing those bills come out of the machine, but is this really a good way to get cash? Only if you don't mind paying ATM fees, cash-advance fees, and an APR for the advance that is a few percentage points higher than for a credit purchase.

Credit Card or Debit Card?

When you purchase that computer game, should you use a debit or a credit card? Because debit cards are heavily advertised as a convenient alternative to credit cards, they have become very popular. Although they may look like credit cards, they are very different.

With a credit card, you are increasing your debt each time you use it, but when you use your debit card, you are immediately withdrawing money from your checking account without having the inconvenience of writing a check. Not only are debit cards more convenient, but for some people, it helps them control their spending. A person can only use the debit card when there is money in his or her checking account.

A smarter strategy is to use a credit card *and pay the full balance each month to avoid credit charges*. Why use a credit card instead of a debit card? You have greater responsibility for loss with a debit card. If you lose your debit card, you may have to cover unauthorized charges up to $500, while your liability limit for a credit card is only $50.

Another advantage is that it is much easier to correct improper charges to a credit card account than to a debit card account.

"You see that dark, spooky image on the screen? That's your credit history coming back to haunt you."

Avoiding Trouble

More trouble comes from using credit cards than with most other types of credit, yet with careful planning, it's possible to handle credit cards responsibly.

Living Within Your Means

Unless you keep track of each charge purchase, the balance owed can quickly become much higher than you plan. Reality sets in when you get your statement, and you find you can only make the minimum payment. If you only make minimum payments, the balance owed decreases only slightly. If you continue to make purchases, the balance will rise. You may reach your credit limit, apply for more cards, and head toward your credit limit on these cards by making only minimum payments. Soon, you are trapped! You can do little to enjoy life because most of your income goes to pay credit card bills.

Live within your means! Here are some guidelines to help you:

* Look carefully at your monthly budget. Decide whether it can handle a new expense. If not, create some options for yourself.
* Make sure your paycheck isn't all going to paying off credit card debt.
* Save some emergency money for car repairs or other unexpected expenses.
* If you decide to charge a new item, set a schedule for paying off the new debt. Each month, pay on time and keep to your schedule.

Making Minimum Payments

Why do credit card companies require you to pay only a small part of the balance due each month and sometimes even give you the opportunity to skip a payment? They prefer that you don't pay your balance in full or even a large part of it. Why? Because the larger your credit balance, the more profit they can make from you.

For example, if you made only the minimum payment of $40 on a $2,000 balance with an APR of 21 percent, how would you answer the questions given below:

1. How many years would it take to pay off the balance without making additional charges?

2. What is the total amount of interest that you would pay (not including payment to principle)?

3. What is the total amount, including principle and interest, that you would pay?

You won't be able to do the math yourself, but there are web sites that will let you plug in the figures and give you the results. Use the keywords "credit card calculators" to find a number of sites that will help you. Is it really to your advantage to make only the minimum payment when you can afford more? Look at the numbers. You might be shocked.

Credit Card Fraud

Not only can excessive use of credit cause you to exceed your budget, credit card fraud can create additional problems for you. There are **three** types of credit card fraud, all of which can cost you money and damage your reputation:

1. **Fraud by credit card companies.**

2. **Fraud by sellers.**

3. **Fraud by other people.**

Fraud by Credit Card Companies

Do you think that all credit card companies are ethical and operate within the law? Not so. Some companies send you credit cards without your asking. Some charge high rates and fees. Others advertise competitive interest rates and low fees and then quickly raise them soon after you get the card—a form of bait and switch. Many say you will have a credit limit "up to" some amount, but after you request the card, you're given a credit limit of only a few hundred dollars.

Fraud by Sellers

Do you check all charges on your credit card statements? Because of a practice called **cramming**, you should check to see if all the listed charges are made by you. Cramming is where businesses involved in fraudulent practices obtain your credit card number and then charge you for purchases you didn't make or bill you more than once for purchases you did make.

Check your statement as soon as you receive it and immediately notify the credit card company of any suspicious charges. Usually, they will help you eliminate any fraudulent charges.

Get Smart

Watch Your Card!

* Don't leave the restaurant copy of a credit card receipt on the table. Hand it to the waiter.
* Tear up carbons of credit card slips.
* Make sure you were given back your own card.

Fraud by Other People

Many dishonest individuals are ready to fraudulently use your credit card. This happens in a variety of ways:

* A person may snoop in your wallet to get your credit card number.
* A restaurant server or store clerk may discreetly copy your credit card information.
* Someone may steal your wallet.

Once people have the information on your card, they can start making purchases and other transactions for which you will be charged.

Sometimes friends may ask for your account number to make a purchase, saying they'll "pay you back" when you get your statement. This is like giving them free access to cash. You have no control over when and where they use your account. If you have freely given your account number to someone, the credit card company may not be sympathetic to your request to have charges removed.

Identity theft is the worst thing that can happen. In identity theft, a person not only gets your credit card numbers, but your Social Security number and other personal data. The thief becomes you on paper. She can make all kinds of transactions, including using your credit card and opening new credit card accounts in your name. To prevent identity theft, always check your credit card statements, and periodically check your credit bureau files.

Rating Your Credit

Have you ever wondered how a lender decides whether to give you credit and what rates to charge? To apply for credit, you must typically complete a lengthy application form that asks questions that establish your three Cs of credit worthiness. Credit bureaus collect credit-related information on consumers and sell this information to businesses.

Your Credit Score

The information credit bureaus sell to lenders is in the form of a **credit report**, which may contain a **credit score**. This score is a number based on many pieces of information found in your credit record. The higher the score, the more likely you are to get a better loan rate.

Your credit score comes from information related to **four** areas:

1. **Employment and income.** Consumers get a higher score when they have a history of having a steady job and enough income to pay the bills.
2. **Housing.** Do you rent or own your home? Creditors believe that people who own homes are more financially stable.
3. **Assets.** What do you own of value, such as investments and savings accounts? The higher the value of your assets, the higher your score.
4. **Credit history.** How many loans and credit cards do you have? What balances do you maintain? How prompt have you been in paying your debts? This tells how well you will likely meet future credit obligations.

Getting Your Credit Report

By law, consumers have access to their files. If there are mistakes, the consumer can demand they be corrected. If there is a dispute between the consumer and the creditor, the consumer has the right to have his or her side of the story in the file.

Most consumer credit experts suggest checking your credit file with at least one bureau once a year or six months before making a large credit purchase, such as taking out a mortgage to buy a home. Here are some tips:

* Although you can request a copy of your file by telephone or U.S. mail, the simplest way is through the Internet. Search for national credit bureaus and follow the instructions. Each will charge about $10, but if you were denied credit because of a negative report, there is no charge.
* Be careful of Internet sites that offer "free" credit reports. They typically require personal information and credit card numbers, and there is always risk when you divulge this information on the Internet. What's more, you only get the "free" report when you subscribe to a credit service that costs much more than simply paying for the report in the first place.
* Always avoid firms that promise to repair your credit rating or remove all bad credit information from your file. They can't do it, and if they try, not only are they violating the law, but you are, also.

Keeping a Good Credit Rating

A good credit rating is important. How do you keep it that way? First, continually track how much you are borrowing or charging. Before applying for any more credit, ask yourself the following:

* Am I able to pay my current bills without any trouble?
* Do I have enough income to make an extra credit payment?
* Will I be able to make my payments if there is an unexpected emergency?
* Will I be able to make my payments if I lose my job or my income decreases?

If You Become Overextended

What do you do if you find you're **overextended**, meaning you have more bills than you can pay? This can occur if you're careless in using credit, incur an expensive emergency, or lose your job. When this happens, not only will your credit rating be damaged, but you may create other serious financial problems as well.

* *Your property may be repossessed.* To get out of financial trouble, it may be tempting to just let the creditor take back your car or some other property, especially if the amount owed is not much more or even less than the value of the item.
* *Your wages may be garnished.* One way creditors collect money owed is to put a claim, called a garnishment, on your wages. This means that a creditor will take money out of your paycheck before you even see it.
* *You may be forced into bankruptcy.* If you are heavily in debt with little or no prospect of ever paying off your bills, you may be forced to file for bankruptcy.

Paying Off Debt From Several Credit Cards

What would you do if you found you had large balances from several credit cards? You might consider getting a consolidation loan. Study the chart below and then answer the questions that follow.

1. How much money could you save each month by taking out a loan to pay off the balance owed on all four cards?

2. What might be the danger in doing that?

3. If a consolidation loan weren't possible, what would be your second-choice strategy, and why?

Card Company	Monthly Balance	APR	Monthly Interest
Card #1	$1,000	15%	$12.50
Card #2	$2,000	24%	$40.00
Card #3	$500	18%	$7.50
Card #4	$4,000	21%	$70.00
Consolidation loan:	$7,500	12%	$76.30

Bankruptcy

There are two types of **bankruptcy**. In one type, if you can pay at least a part of your debts, the bankruptcy court will create a plan for you to pay a portion of what you owe over a set period of time. If the court doesn't believe you have enough money to pay any part of your debts, it will cancel all your debts except for taxes and child support. If this happens, you must give up much of the property that you own.

Having a bankruptcy in your credit file may prevent you from getting the job you want, make it hard to insure your automobile, and make it difficult to get credit for a long time. If and when you do, you will pay much higher rates.

Help for Credit Problems

Once you find that you have serious problems with credit, is there a way out other than bankruptcy? In most cases, there is. Some people are able to solve the credit problems on their own, while some may need professional help.

Self-help

To solve your own credit problems will take a lot of discipline. Here are some steps to take:

* You must cut up your credit cards (but do not cancel them until they are paid off, as companies often raise rates if you cancel the card). Do not apply for any new credit.
* You may have to go without things you want in order to pay for what you bought in the past.
* Most important of all, you will have to budget your finances not only to get out of your current debt problems, but to avoid getting back into them in the future.

There is one immediate step you can take to help resolve your problems. Sometimes you can get your creditors to help you. Because creditors frown on people who just stop making payments without any explanation, you should contact your creditors and explain your situation. They may work with you by lowering the monthly payments, letting you skip a payment, or lowering the interest rate. Seldom will they forgive the loan, but they may be more patient with you in making the payments.

Professional Help

Sometimes it is beyond your own resources to get out of financial trouble. When this happens, you should seek outside help. Nonprofit credit counseling agencies are a major source of help. Counselors at these agencies may help you in two ways. They may contact your creditors and, because of their experience, may be more successful than you are in reducing the payments and possibly even reducing the interest charges. In most cases, the agencies force discipline on you by handling your bills. You pay them a specific amount of money each month, and they will pay your bills out of that. These counselors will also advise you in how to budget your finances to put you back on the road to financial health. A small fee is usually charged for such services.

Signs of Financial Difficulty

Financial problems don't just happen all at once. Usually, they creep up on you. Here are indications that you might be overextended:

* More than a quarter of your take-home pay, other than car and mortgage payments, goes to pay off debt.
* You are able to make only the minimum payments on your credit card balances.
* You make payments after the due date because you don't have the cash.
* You open new credit card accounts because the old ones are maxed out.
* You are harassed by creditors to pay your bills.
* You worry about paying bills and avoid answering the phone.
* You experience strains in your family and close relationships because of increasing stress and credit anxiety.

If you are overextended, seek professional help—from a consumer credit counselor and perhaps also from a therapist.

Staying Free of Credit Problems

If you have credit problems, not only will resolving them require a lot of effort, but staying out of trouble in the future will take discipline. Here are some strategies you can practice now to avoid credit problems later:

* Pay off the full balance each month to avoid any interest charges.
* Maintain only one credit card and use it sparingly. Once you pay off a card, cut it up and notify the company to close the account.
* Charge purchases only if you can afford to pay for them now.
* Don't apply for other loans unless absolutely necessary.
* Realize you don't have to buy everything that you want. In other words, don't buy on impulse.
* Realistically budget your finances.
* If you have saved money, take money from that account rather than using credit, and start putting money back in savings as soon as possible.

Another way to avoid credit problems is to continually make yourself aware of the disadvantages of credit. Before you get a loan or buy something with the credit card, ask yourself: *What will I be giving up by buying this item on credit*? Not making the purchase at all may be the best way to avoid the costs and problems that often come with credit.

You are very likely to use credit in some form sometime in the future, whether it is in the form of a credit card, mortgage, car loan, or some other type of loan. Most of the time, using credit can be a help if you use it only when necessary and then use it wisely.

Far too many people have abused credit either because they wanted everything right away or they did not have the skills to get the best credit terms available. They often suffer from anxiety, strains in family relations, unwelcome calls and mail from creditors, repossessions, and even bankruptcy. However, those who limit their use of credit and employ their skills to get the best credit deals will have a more carefree life.

Consumer Economics

annual percentage rate (APR)— interest rate stated as the percentage charged on the unpaid balance of the debt for the period of one year. *p. 76*

bankruptcy—legal arrangement to deal with the affairs of individuals unable to pay their debts. *p.90*

capacity—borrower's ability to earn enough to make debt payments. *p. 76*

capital—wealth in the form of money or property. *p. 76*

cash advance—cash that may be borrowed against a credit card account. *p. 84*

character—borrower's history of making debt payments on time. *p. 76*

charge back—option of withholding payment on a credit card for a disputed purchase. *p. 81*

charge card—type of credit card where the entire balance must be paid each month. *p. 82*

commercial credit—loan extended to a business. *p. 74*

cramming—fraudulent practice in which charges are billed when no purchases were made. *p. 87*

credit—system of buying goods and services with payment at a later time. *p. 73*

credit bureau—company that gathers credit information on consumers and sells it to other businesses. *p. 77*

credit history—record of borrowing and repaying debts, either loans or credit card purchases. *p. 77*

credit limit—highest balance permitted on your credit account. *p. 81*

credit report—statement by a credit bureau that gives the credit history of a consumer. *p. 88*

credit score—number calculated by a credit bureau that indicates the credit-worthiness of a consumer. Also known as a credit rating. *p. 88*

delayed gratification—satisfaction postponed, usually because the person is willing to wait for something wanted. *p. 73*

down payment—amount of money you must pay up front in order to obtain a loan. Home mortgages and car loans usually require a down payment. *p. 79*

equity—value of a business or property after debts and mortgages are subtracted. *p. 79*

finance charge—total cost of a loan expressed in dollars. *p. 76*

grace period—number of days between a billing date and the due date. *p. 83*

home equity loan—loan secured by the owner's equity in the home. It is in addition to the mortgage and is usually at a higher rate of interest than the mortgage, but lower than most other forms of loans. *p. 80*

identity theft—unauthorized use of another person's Social Security number, birth date, driver's license number, or other identifying information to obtain credit cards, car loans, phone plans, or other services in the victim's name. *p. 87*

immediate gratification—satisfaction of getting something as soon as you want it. *p. 73*

mortgage—consumer loan for the purchase of a home or other building where the building is collateral. *p. 79*

overextended—state in which a borrower has more debt than can be paid. *p. 89*

personal credit—loan extended to an individual. *p. 74*

principal—amount of money borrowed from a lender. *p. 73*

revolving credit—type of account in which the consumer is not required to pay off the balance before making new purchases. *p. 82*

sales finance companies—lenders that finance purchases for the consumer through retailers. *p. 77*

CHAPTER 6

Understanding the Economy

In this chapter you will learn about:

- ups and downs in the U.S. economy
- how the economy affects your life
- what factors indicate the economy's overall health

Gold was first discovered in the United States in the foothills of the Sierra Nevada Mountains in California in 1848. Gold fever swept the nation, and people from all over the country ventured west in search of gold and wealth. Louisa Clappe, the wife of a Gold-Rush doctor, wrote about the experiences of those who tried to become rich. She reported that in July 1850, two men turned over a huge stone near Feather River and found a large piece of gold beneath it. They washed a small panful of the dirt and sold it for $256. Within two weeks, each man had dug up $6,000 worth of gold. They were rich! But within a year, they had lost it all, and both men were penniless. They were not alone. Many people made their fortunes, only to lose them again. Some people struck it rich, while others did not. Still others prospered, invested their money, and managed to hold their own, even in down times. People who understand the economy and how it works are able to have more control of their lives than those who expect that luck will help them strike it rich.

The Economy

A powerful saying in the 1992 race for president was, "It's the **economy**, stupid!" It suggested that voters cared about the economy more than any other single issue. When the president, George Bush, lost that election to Bill Clinton, many observers blamed Bush for being out of touch with the country's economic concerns.

Don't you make the same mistake. The earlier you understand the importance of the economy and how it affects your life, the sooner you'll be able to handle economic ups and downs.

The word "economics" comes from the Greek term meaning "home management." **Economics** is the science that deals with the ways in which goods and services are produced, transported, sold, and used. It also studies the effects of taxes and the distribution of money within an economy. But its roots lie in the careful management of the resources of a home. If you understand the principles of economics, you can manage the resources you have. Economics can help you make big decisions:

* Is it a good time to quit your job and look for a new one?
* Should you put your money in a savings account or spend it on a summer vacation?
* Should you get a loan to start your own business now or wait for a better time?

Understanding economic cycles gives you information to help you to make well reasoned economic decisions in your own life.

Defining the Economy

The range of economic activity of a country is called its economy. A healthy economy needs both **producers**, the people who make goods and provide services, and **consumers**, people to buy the goods and services that are produced.

Throughout human history, groups of people have had to figure out:

* What to produce.
* How to produce.
* How much to produce.
* Who needs and will consume what is produced.

Picture a society in which all land, natural resources, and labor are focused on the production of ice cream and everyone gets as many scoops as they want. (People live short but happy lives!) If there are enough land, resources, and labor related to ice cream production to go around—that is, not too much and not too little—everything is in balance. However, what happens if things change?

Expansion and Inflation

We'd like all good things to "stay the same," but the truth is, everything is in a constant state of change. During a time of **expansion**, the economy grows. More ice cream is produced, and there are more people who buy it. But, what if the economy grows too fast? What if people have so much money they are able to buy ice cream at a faster rate than ice cream makers can supply it? If this happens, the price of ice cream will go up. When the amount of ready money people have grows faster than the amount of goods and services, **inflation** occurs. This results in continuing increases in price levels. Inflation can have many causes.

In this case, inflation occurs because there is too much **demand** (the amount of a particular item, like ice cream, that people are willing and able to buy) and too little **supply** (the amount of ice cream that producers are willing and able to provide at a given price). In such cases, prices increase.

Other times, inflation is due to big increases in the cost of producing goods. To make up for the rising costs, producers pass their costs onto consumers by increasing prices.

However, increased prices reduce demand for the product. Layoffs and unemployment figures may rise as companies try to save money by "downsizing," which means reducing their workforce.

Someone in your family or circle of friends may have been laid off work for a period of time. Sometimes companies lay off workers for just a few months. Other times, workers are laid off for so long that they must find a new job. It is often a time of great frustration and hardship for families.

During a time of inflation, people who don't have the ability to earn more are hurt the most. The government usually tries to

Get Smart

What Is a Dollar Worth?

For most of recent history, we have had some inflation in the economy. Inflation eats away at the value of money over time. This means that one dollar today will be worth less than a dollar a year from now. Here's another way of looking at it: What you can buy for one dollar today will cost you more than a dollar a year from now.

Even when the inflation rate is very low—say, two percent—the value of the money in your pocket is declining. What you can buy for $100 today will cost you $102 a year from now. That may not sound like much, but it adds up over time. If you wanted to buy the same things that would have cost you $100 in 1950, you would have had to spend $739 in 2001!

Because of inflation, it is unwise to save your money under a mattress or in a locked box somewhere. You need to earn interest on the money you save in order for it to grow and keep up with inflation.

You also need to work somewhere where you can get regular raises. Inflation increases the **cost of living**—the average cost of basic necessities, such as food, clothing, and housing. So your income at the least needs to keep up with inflation.

help by decreasing its own spending and increasing taxes and interest rates. These actions result in less money in circulation, which slows down economic activity.

Recession

A **recession** is a slowdown in economic activity and growth for an extended period of time. People usually spend less during a recession. This slows the economy even more, resulting in:

* Decreased spending by individuals and businesses.
* Rising unemployment.
* Difficulty in finding and keeping jobs.

The government may try to help the economy by decreasing taxes, lowering interest rates, and increasing its own spending in order to put more money into circulation. The hope is that, with more money to spend, demand will increase, which in turn will lead to increased production and more jobs.

Depression

A **depression** is like a recession, only worse. It signals a deep decline in the nation's economy. It means financial hardship for businesses and individuals, as there is less demand for goods.

In a depression, many people are out of work. They aren't making *or* buying much. This, in turn, leads to the loss of more jobs. It's easy to see how the economy can spiral out of control in a downward cycle.

EXAMPLE: The Great Depression began in 1929 with the stock market crash. People's property lost value, many banks went out of business, and many people lost their jobs. For many people in the United States, it was a time of misery that lasted several years.

A depression continues until the need for goods increases again. At that point, businesses can begin to increase production and more jobs are created.

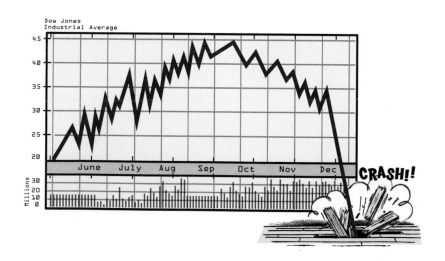

The Economic Challenge

You can see how consumers affect the state of the economy by their actions (or inaction), just as the state of the economy has an effect on consumer decisions. Economic cycles are marked by periods of up and down movement between prosperity and growth and degrees of slowdown that signal a recession. The challenge is to sustain growth in a slow, steady way with minimal price increases.

When you look at your own life in the long term, you may be able to identify cycles. **EXAMPLE:** Perhaps you tend to start each year slowly in basketball practice, but over several months' time your free throw percentage increases as you get in shape.

The economy also has recurring ups and downs called the **business cycle**—the pattern of alternating periods of economic growth and decline; the ups and downs of economic activty as a whole.

Identifying and understanding cycles in the economy and in your own life can help you:

* Predict what will happen next.
* Be more patient with the way things are in the present.
* Give you clues as to how to respond intelligently at a given time.

The challenge of a healthy economy is how to balance:

* Limited resources with unlimited needs and wants.

* Business profits with adequate wages for workers.
* Consumer spending and consumer debt.
* Supply of and demand for goods and services.

To understand the cycles that mark our economic system, it's important to consider **five** concepts that have an impact on the ups and downs of the economy:

① Scarcity

Imagine living in a world where everyone has more money than they could ever spend, businesses produce an infinite supply of goods we want to buy, and, to top it off, you live indefinitely. It would be a world without **scarcity**. There would be no shortage of money, goods, or time.

Unfortunately, we live in a world of scarcity. Resources such as time and money are limited, while our needs and desires for goods and services are unlimited. Economists call this the basic economic problem.

② Factors of Production

Resources available to a business or a nation are called **factors of production**, the things needed to produce goods and services. Factors of production are limited. They include:

* Natural resources (raw materials, such as land, oil, coal, or trees).
* Capital (factories and the equipment in them).

* Labor (work done by employees).
* Entrepreneurship (skill in acquiring and managing the other three factors of production).

Because factors of production are limited, we must make careful choices about how to use these factors efficiently. This involves using available resources so you get the most out of them.

EXAMPLE: If you want to buy a car, it would be short-sighted to spend all your money on the car itself. That would leave you with no resources for the license plates, insurance, and gas.

❸ Opportunity Cost

Due to scarcity, using available resources in one way means that they're not available to be used for something else. Economists—

Factors of Production

Capital

Natural Resources

More Capital

Labor

BLDG. 4

Capital

Entrepreneurship

More Natural Resources

people who study the economy—use the term **opportunity cost** to describe what has been given up when a decision to use resources is made. It is usually described in terms of the next best use of those resources. We gain the benefits of what we produce, but we lose the potential benefits of the next best item that could have been produced from those same factors of production.

EXAMPLES: If a firm uses all its machines, workers, and managers to make cars, those same factors of production can't be used to produce bicycles or energy-efficient trolleys. The opportunity cost of saving money by eating a sack lunch is how much value you put on eating lunch at a cafe with your coworkers.

Whether an individual or a country is faced with the choice, it's important to carefully weigh the pros and cons before making a decision.

④ Supply and Demand

The law of supply and demand says that the demand for a good or service influences the price and supply. In the beginning of the computer revolution when everyone wanted a personal computer, demand quickly went up. Prices were high. But in response to the demand, many new workers were hired, facilities were enlarged, and prices came down. If an item maintains a rather steady demand over time, the price and production remain steady.

When the demand for an item goes down, manufacturers lower prices in order to entice consumers to buy the item. If the demand does not pick up in response to the lower prices, production slows. Factories may close and workers may be laid off.

Making it **REAL**

Community College or Work?

To save money, you have to choose between going to a community college for your freshman year or waiting a year to start college while you save money to attend the four-year college of your choice.

You choose to wait a year and work. What is the opportunity cost of your decision?

Now imagine making the opposite decision. What is the opportunity cost of attending community college? Considering the opportunity costs of each choice, which choice would you make, and why?

Goods and Services

Issues of scarcity, factors of production, and opportunity costs apply to both goods and services. **Goods** are tangible items that we buy, use, store, and eventually discard. Goods can be durable, lasting many years, or nondurable, intended for use in the near future. **Services** are the less tangible things we buy. Hats, paintings, and houses are goods. Haircuts, art lessons, and home insurance are services.

Prices and Price Controls

Taken together, the laws of supply and demand drive a marketplace where buyers and sellers meet. If producers are willing to supply a good or service at a price consumers are willing to pay, a transaction will likely occur. If producers charge a higher price than most consumers will spend, sales may be sluggish, and producers may realize they must lower their prices. If producers charge a price substantially *below* the price consumers are willing to pay, consumers will buy eagerly and cut

Create Your Own Money!

You might think that it's against the law to print your own money, but many cities and communities have done just that! This special money, called *scrip*, can be used at certain agreed-upon places.

* During the Great Depression, newspaper publisher Samuel Bowles paid his employees in scrip that could be used at stores in the community. The stores used the scrip to pay for advertising in the paper.
* In 1989, one Massachusetts deli owner who needed cash was turned down for a bank loan. Undaunted, he started issuing "Deli Dollars" to his customers. The deli dollars cost $8 but could be used to buy $10 worth of products at his deli. Customers flocked to his deli, and the increased sales helped him finance the store's move to a new location.

Scrip encourages people to keep their money in local communities. It bands consumers and business owners together with a common goal. It feels good to be in charge of your own destiny and not dependent upon a bank loan, the stock market, or the state of the economy to reach a goal.

How might scrip be used to meet a need in your community or school?

deeply into supplies. The buying spree will send a message to producers that they can probably charge a little more. Eventually, a stable price emerges at which producers are willing to sell and consumers are willing to buy.

Sometimes the market for a particular good or service creates prices buyers may consider too high.

EXAMPLE: Imagine it's the beginning of the school year and you're buying required school supplies. Suddenly, the prices of school supplies sky rocket. "Unfair!" would be the cry of many students and their parents! When this happens to essential goods in the national economy, government price controls may be imposed. We believe in letting the marketplace determine prices. So price controls, or limits, are only likely to be imposed on goods and services that are viewed as necessities, such as food, electricity, and housing.

EXAMPLE: During wartime, food and heating may be in short supply, so price controls may be implemented.

Making it REAL

Take It or Leave It

Demand doesn't operate exactly the same way for all goods and services. Sometimes the amount of a good we will buy is very sensitive to price. For example, if someone offered to sell you your favorite candy bar for 25 cents rather than the regular 50-cent price, you'd probably buy it immediately and maybe ask if you could buy a few more at that price. In the same way, if the price doubled from 50 cents to a dollar, you'd probably stop buying it and try another candy bar. Can you think of other goods or services where a change in price up or down greatly changes your desire for the item? Do they tend to be luxuries or necessities?

Now imagine you have a baby and are feeding her milk formula. You go to the store to buy more and notice the price has doubled. Will you buy it anyway? Probably, because it is essential to your baby's health and well-being, and you don't have a good alternative. If money is scarce, you will find something else to do without.

List some other products where the amount you buy won't change much, regardless of price.

Wages

The concepts of supply and demand are most frequently applied to tangible items, such as donuts or diamonds. However, supply and demand can be applied equally well to work or human labor. The price of labor to employers is the hourly wage or a salary they pay workers. Employers can attract more workers by paying higher wages. When there are many people looking for work, there is a high supply of labor, and the price for it—wages—goes down.

Think about it, if you were out of work for a long time, wouldn't you take a job that paid less than you thought it ought to because you needed work? On the other hand, if you were an employer who needed a skill in your employees that many people didn't have, wouldn't you pay more for that work in order to get the best people to come to work for you rather than for your competitor?

By the Numbers

Minimum and Living Wages

The requirement that workers be paid an hourly minimum wage began in the United States in 1938 when the Fair Labor Standards Act was passed. The minimum wage then was 25 cents per hour. The minimum wage has been raised several times over the years, but it has not kept up with inflation.

There is much debate about raising the minimum wage. Some people argue that the minimum wage should be high enough for an adult to support himself or herself or even a family. Others say that if the wage is raised, employers will hire fewer people, and students and others who work for minimum wages will find it harder to get jobs.

Some U.S. cities have replaced the minimum wage with something higher, called a "living wage." This higher wage applies to city employees or companies doing business with the city. In 2001, Santa Monica, California, became the first U.S. city to require private employers in its jurisdiction to pay a living wage of $12.25 an hour.

Calculate the difference between the annual salary of someone earning $5.15 for 40 hours a week, 50 weeks a year, and someone earning $12.25 for that same period. If you were a small business owner with 15 employees, how much more would you have to pay in wages if you sold your services to the city of Santa Monica?

5 Competition and Profit

Competition and profit are at the center of what is called the **free market**, the free enterprise system, or capitalism. Common to all of these terms is the idea of individual buyers and sellers making their own economic decisions. Consumers enjoy a particularly favorable position in the free market because businesses have to compete with each other to earn the consumer's purchase. In a free market, business competition means that many companies will use price or nonprice incentives, such as product quality, to try to sell their products or services to individual buyers.

The Competitive Marketplace

The free market operates a bit like the political system, with each dollar spent by consumers representing a kind of vote for one company versus another. Just as politicians with the most votes stay in office, companies with the most "votes" stay in business. Ideally, companies get consumers' votes because they offer a product or service that is better or less expensive than that of their competitors. In this way, the free market rewards the best companies and weeds out the worst.

EXAMPLE: When you need to buy pants, you have many choices available. There are many different brands sold in many different stores. The brands and stores are competing for your purchase. You may want the lowest-priced pair of blue jeans, or you may prefer a particular brand. The choice is yours.

Making it **REAL**

Making a Profit

Think back to the lemonade stand you may have had when you were young. If the day was hot and your stand was well located, you might have made a lot of money. You probably thought of the money you made as "profit," but was it really?

* Did you pay for the lemonade and cups, or did your parents pay for these items?
* Who paid for the sign you made to publicize your lemonade stand?

* Did you pay rent for the table, the chair you sat in all day, and the ground on which you placed your stand?

In a larger-scale business, all these expenses would have been paid to someone, and those expenses are subtracted from the revenue to reveal any profit. Now that you think about it, did your lemonade stand make a true profit?

The Role of Profit

In a free market, profits are a good measure of how well a company serves consumers' needs and wants. A firm's **profit** is simply the amount by which its **revenue**, or what it takes in, exceeds costs or expenses. The possibility of making a profit is what motivates most people who run or invest in a business. These **entrepreneurs** and investors believe they will be rewarded in the form of profit if they are able to offer consumers a better product or service than that available from other businesses. The possibility of making a profit keeps our economy dynamic, growing, and oriented to what consumers want.

Some people think companies make huge profits. They don't. A few are able to take advantage of periods of shortage, when sellers can charge prices that are very high relative to their expenses. Typically, though, profits amount to less than ten percent of a firm's total revenues.

Monopolies

Profits are good for our society. The *profit incentive*, or desire for profits, encourages businesses to develop new products and better services. But what happens when little competition exists?

Without competition, prices to consumers increase, and the services consumers buy get worse and worse.

U.S. laws protect competition. If companies that should be competing make agreements with each other to charge a certain price, for instance, or only to pay so much for the materials they need, they are breaking the law. If a company becomes so big and strong it buys up all its competitors, the government will step in.

When a company has complete control of a market, it has a **monopoly**. There is no check on what that company can charge for its services. No other firm is developing better products or offering better service. So the company has little incentive to satisfy customers. Customers can buy the monopolist's product or nothing at all.

EXAMPLE: Software maker Microsoft had a near monopoly on the market for personal computer operating systems. When it bundled its internet browser with its operating system, other internet service providers claimed they were being excluded from competing in the marketplace. To remedy the situation, a federal judge required Microsoft to let computer makers separate the browser from the operating system.

Some businesses require such a huge investment, and are so necessary, the government has permitted monopolies.

EXAMPLE: Electric power companies.

To address the problems of poor service and high prices, the government regulates such monopolies.

EXAMPLE: State governments limit how much local utility companies can charge their customers. They may also require them to meet certain service standards. When a series of electric power failures during one hot summer sent many people to hospitals and the morgue, the state of Illinois required the electric company that did business in that state to make repairs and guarantee better service.

Measuring the Economy

Just as your body's temperature is used to indicate whether or not you are sick—or how sick you are—there are indicators, or measures, of overall health in the nation's economy. Economists study these indicators and pass the information on to the general public. These **economic indicators** include statistics related to the:

* Gross Domestic Product (GDP).
* Rate of inflation.
* Consumer Price Index (CPI).
* Unemployment rate.
* Personal income level.
* Consumer confidence.
* Interest rates.

Gross Domestic Product (GDP)

The **Gross Domestic Product (GDP)** represents the current value in dollars of all goods and services produced in the U.S. for one year. This figure includes everything you buy, from CDs, music lessons, and movie tickets, to government spending. It considers only finished products and not the items produced to make the final product. This means it would focus on the dollar value of a car but not on the fabric used to make the rugs and seats. It also does not include items made by U.S. businesses but produced in other countries.

If you study the GDP over several years, you can usually see a trend. If the GDP decreases, the economy is in a recession or

depression. In general, a steady increase in the GDP signals a healthy economy that has:

* Jobs for workers.
* Increased productivity.
* A higher standard of living.
* More money for consumers to spend.

Rate of Inflation

Inflation represents an ongoing increase in prices. As inflation rises, consumer purchasing power decreases. To understand whether the GDP is a true figure, the rate of inflation must be factored in. For example, if the GDP increased four percent over the previous year, but prices (the rate of inflation) increased two percent, the real change in the GDP would be just two percent after adjusting for inflation.

Search This

Investigate the GDP

Use the Internet to investigate the GDP over the past five or ten years. Draw a graph to represent your findings. How would you summarize the movement of the GDP from five years ago to the present? What events do you think could affect this figure in the future?

Consumer Price Index (CPI)

The **Consumer Price Index (CPI)** is one basic way economists measure the rate of inflation. The CPI identifies the monthly change in prices of about 400 selected goods and services. These items are a part of most people's general budget categories in:

* Housing.
* Food.
* Transportation.
* Clothing.
* Medical expenses.
* Personal expenses.
* Entertainment.

The average prices of the goods and services included in the CPI are combined to come up with overall prices for the month. They are compared with a percentage change from a base figure (for example, the years 1982–1984) to come up with how much money you would need to purchase something today *as compared with* prices in the base period.

In general, since the late 1930s, prices have continued to rise. You may have heard your grandparents talk about when it cost 25 cents to go to the movies, hamburgers and candy bars were 10 cents, bubble gum cost a penny, and it took just 3 cents to mail a letter. Remember, wages were lower back then as well!

Unemployment Rate

The **unemployment rate** is the percent of all employable people who don't currently have jobs and are looking for work. An unemployment rate of four to six percent is considered to be a sign of a healthy economy.

The level of employment in the U.S. is a good indicator of the nation's economic health. If the unemployment rate is high, it means the economy's growth has slowed. Fewer goods and services are being produced. When people are laid off from work or cannot find jobs, they don't have money to buy things that help the economy recover from a recession or a depression. Even more, a high rate of unemployment means that our society is wasting its most precious resource—the energy of its people. **EXAMPLE:** During the Great Depression in the 1930s, unemployment was nearly 25 percent! If the United States had experienced the same level of unemployment in 2001, it would have meant that more than *40 million* people were out of work!

Unemployment rates do not include:

* People who are retired.
* People who aren't trying to find work.
* People who work in a family business for no pay .
* Children who are not old enough to work.

Personal Income

Personal income data shows how much money people in the country have in their pockets to save and to spend. This figure is used to compare the health of the economy from one year to the next and reflects the overall standard of living in the United States. Personal income is figured on gross income (income before taxes) and not disposable/net income (money available after taxes). Personal income includes money from:

* Wages and salaries.
* Self-employment income.
* Interest income.
* Investment income.
* Rental profits.

If personal income is high, people generally have more money to put into the economy.

Consumer Confidence

Consumer confidence means the degree of confidence, or trust, that people feel in a business, product, or the economy in general. When you feel confident, you think the conditions are right for success. You are more likely to act, whether that means applying for a new job, asking for a raise, or making a big purchase.

When people feel their jobs are secure and they will have enough money in the near future, this consumer confidence often means increased spending, which helps the economy.

If consumer confidence is low, people spend less money. That reduction in spending can, in turn, have a negative impact on the economy, pushing the country into—or further into—recession.

Interest Rates

When you borrow money from a friend or perhaps your parents, you typically don't pay them interest. When individuals, businesses, and the federal government need to borrow money, they do not get the money for free. The money they must pay in order to borrow money is called *interest*. This cost is expressed as a percentage of the amount borrowed. The percentage is the *interest rate.* Interest rates are important to businesses and individuals because in order for a business to expand, or for an individual to buy a house or car, borrowed money is usually needed.

The Role of Government

Besides setting rules for the behavior of certain types of businesses and consumers of specific products, there are other ways that the U.S. government influences the overall condition of the economy.

The federal government can indirectly control the spending of businesses and consumers by increasing or decreasing the supply of money. This, in turn, affects the interest rates offered for loans, savings accounts, and investments. The government's plan for controlling the amount of money in the overall economy is known as its **monetary policy**. Monetary policy tries to address problems such as unemployment or inflation.

Government as Consumer

The government is, itself, a huge consumer. Its budget for 2001 was about $2 trillion. Much of this huge amount of money goes to taking care of people who are retired or sick. Another big chunk of the budget is used for national defense.

Government economic policy involves not only spending, but also taxing. The U.S. government may increase or decrease taxes in order to help stabilize the economy or encourage economic growth.

Some of the U.S. federal budget is specifically designed to assist certain industries and groups of consumers. For instance, the federal government spends billions of dollars on scientific research. Sometimes spending in one area, like the development of new materials and fuels for use in the space program, ends up providing new options for consumers. **EXAMPLE:** The materials developed to protect the space shuttle from extreme temperatures are now used on NASCAR racing cars to protect drivers from the extreme heat generated by their engines.

Federal Reserve

The Federal Reserve is the main bank of the United States. Its business is to implement monetary policy.

The Federal Reserve tries to maintain the stability of the financial system. One way it does this is by determining how much money is in circulation at any given time. Think of it this way. You may set aside a certain portion of the money you make "in reserve"—for savings for emergencies or for college. When it's "in reserve," you don't have it available to spend. In the same way, the Federal Reserve determines the amount of money to be held in reserve in the country—that is, held back from circulation. When more money is held back, there is less money available for loans and interest rate rise. If less money is held back, there is more money available to borrow and interest rates fall.

The Federal Reserve influences the interest rate of banks and other lending institutions in the U.S.

The Federal Reserve does not set all interest rates. It sets the "federal funds rate," which is the amount of interest banks must pay the Federal Reserve, for example, to borrow money overnight.

Making it REAL

The Fed Responds to a Crisis

Just six days after the September 11, 2001, attack on the World Trade Center, the Federal Reserve cut the federal funds rates one-half percent, the eighth such drop in interest rates in 2001, in an effort to reassure nervous consumers. Banks quickly matched the one-half percentage point to lower prime lending rates to six percent, the lowest prime rate in nine years. The Federal Reserve also put billions of dollars into the banking system by bolstering bank reserves and providing emergency loans to banks.

* How do you think such an event could effect people's economic decisions?
* Why do you think the government would increase spending? Why did the Federal Reserve step in?

This percentage rate is what drives the **prime rate** (the amount of interest banks charge their most credit-worthy customers) and all other lending rates. When banks and other financial institutions are paying less to borrow money themselves, they are able to pass the savings on to their customers.

Many people eagerly watch for news that interest rates have been raised or lowered. Businesses try to wait until interest rates are low to purchase new equipment. Likewise, individuals are enticed by low interest rates to start a new business, buy or refinance a house, or purchase the car they've been wanting. If interest rates are too high, potential borrowers tend to hold on to their money and wait for interest rates to drop. When that happens, how do you think it affects the overall economy?

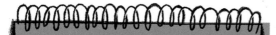

The interest rate for different types of loans varies. You usually pay a higher rate of interest for a personal or car loan, for example, than on a loan to purchase, remodel, or refinance a house.

You might think that everyone likes low interest rates, but that is not true. Retired people in particular, who live off their bank savings, lose money in times of declining interest rates. This is because the interest they make on their savings is lower.

Throughout your life, the economy will have a huge impact on your financial well-being. In times of expansion, jobs, for example, are more plentiful. In times of recession, jobs are harder to come by. In times of depression, many people are out of work.

It's important to watch signs of the economy's overall health. These signs include: Gross Domestic Product (GDP), rate of inflation, Consumer Price Index (CPI), unemployment rate, personal income level, consumer confidence, and interest rates.

As a consumer, you are part of the U.S. and world economies. The more you know about the state of the economy at any given time, the more you'll be able to predict changes in progress, have patience in the midst of negative economic changes, and make wise economic decisions for yourself and your family.

Consumer Economics

business cycle—pattern of alternating periods of economic growth and decline; the ups and downs of economic activity as a whole. *p. 99*

consumer confidence—degree of confidence, or trust, that people feel in the economy in general. *p. 109*

Consumer Price Index—number that identifies the monthly price change in about 400 selected goods and services. *p. 108*

consumers—people who buy and use goods and services. *p. 96*

cost of living—average price of basic necessities—such as housing and food—in an area. *p. 97*

demand—desire and ability to purchase a product or service. *p. 97*

depression—deep decline in the nation's economy. *p. 98*

economic indicator—measure of the U.S. economy's general health. *p. 107*

economics—science that deals with the ways in which goods and services are produced, transported, sold, and used. *p. 96*

economy—range of economic activity in a country; also, its system for producing and distributing goods and services. *p. 96*

entrepreneurs—people who organize and run a business and take on the risks involved. *p. 106*

expansion—general period of sustained growth. *p. 96*

factors of production—things needed to produce goods and services, including natural resources, capital/machinery, labor, and entrepreneurship. *p. 99*

more Words to Know

free market system—type of economy in which buyers and sellers determine prices with limited government interference. *p. 105*

goods—tangible items that people buy and use, such as cars, pencils, shoes, and food. *p. 102*

Gross Domestic Product (GDP)— current value in dollars of all goods and services produces in a country for one year. *p. 107*

inflation—rise in the general level of prices. *p. 97*

monetary policy—government plan for controlling the amount of money in the overall economy. *p. 110*

monopoly—complete control by one company of the means of producing or selling a product or service. *p. 106*

opportunity cost—value of the next best use of resources when a choice is made. *p. 101*

prime rate—interest rate banks charge their most credit-worthy customers. *p. 111*

producers—people who make goods and provide services. *p. 96*

profit—money from a business activity, sale, or investments that remains after expenses have been paid. *p. 106*

recession—slowdown in economic activity and growth. *p. 98*

revenue—income. *p. 106*

scarcity—basic economic problem: resources for the production of goods and services are limited while human wants and needs are unlimited. *p. 99*

services—work products people buy, such as haircuts, insurance, medical care, education, and so on. *p. 102*

supply—amount of a particular good or service that producers are willing (and able) to provide at a given price. *p. 97*

unemployment rate—percentage figure representing the number of people who don't currently have jobs and are looking for work. *p. 109*

CHAPTER 7

Becoming a Wise Consumer

In this chapter, you will learn about:

- **what influences your buying decisions**
- **how to be a smart shopper**
- **how to use your power as a consumer**

For Maria's 16th birthday, her Aunt Rita gave her a generous present: a check for $100. Maria decided to spend it on a new jacket. The seasons were changing, and her old jacket didn't fit anymore. She went to the mall with some of her friends.

On her way to the coat department of her favorite department store, one of her friends stopped to look at all the pretty blouses hanging on the racks. A sign said, "Bargain Blouses: 2 for $99." Maria thought the blouses were beautiful, and they came in her favorite colors: blue and purple. Her friend grabbed a bunch of blouses and whisked her into a dressing room. Maria tried on a couple of blouses, and they looked great on her. "Maria, you should get two of these," her friend said. "After all, you've got that check from your aunt to spend!" Maria was very tempted.

However, then she remembered that she really did need a new jacket. She took another look in the mirror, and thought, "The blouses do look very pretty, but I've got a lot of blouses in my closet already. I can do without these." She went to the jacket department and found a jacket she liked very much. Walking home wearing her new jacket, she felt good. She knew she had made the right decision.

nderstanding Your Buying Behavior

Think of all the things you'll buy this week. Maybe you'll buy your lunches or other meals. Maybe you'll buy transportation to and from school or work. You might spend money on some entertainment, such as a movie. Maybe you'll buy newspapers or books. Perhaps you'll buy someone a present. We buy things all the time for many different kinds of reasons.

You might be asking, "What's the big deal? We buy stuff because we need it or want it. It's not rocket science!" It's true that buying isn't rocket science, but it can be complicated.

Why we buy what we buy is the result of a mixture of influences:

* Psychological (our emotions, personal values, beliefs, and self-image).
* Sociological (how our culture and society influence us).
* Economic (how much money we have, our attitudes toward money, how we choose to spend it).

Needs and Wants

Our shopping behavior is affected by what we want and need. What is the difference, though, between a need and a want? A **need** is something necessary to survival, such as food and shelter. A **want** is something you desire, but is not necessary for survival. It can be difficult to separate needs and wants.

EXAMPLE: Both food and clothes are necessary—they both fulfill needs. But when do they become wants? When are they luxury items?

Evaluating Our Needs

We are bombarded every day with advertising that tells us we "need" the latest, greatest gadget. This can make it hard to differentiate, or tell the difference between, needs and wants.

Needs and Wants		
Item	**Definition**	**Examples**
Need	Something required for survival.	Basic food, shelter, clothes, safety.
Want	Something desired but not required for survival.	Special clothes, candy, CDs, jewelry.

Psychologist Abraham Maslow developed a theory about human needs. He called it the **hierarchy** of needs. (A hierarchy organizes things according to importance. The most basic is at the bottom. The most advanced is at the top.) Understanding Maslow's hierarchy will help you differentiate needs from wants.

Maslow's hierarchy has five levels. Before the needs of one level can be fulfilled, the needs of the level below it must be met. For example, it is difficult to be a creative artist or scientist when you are hungry.

Maslow's Hierarchy of Needs

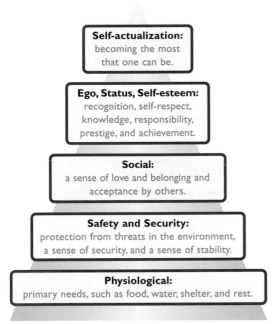

Self-actualization:
becoming the most
that one can be.

Ego, Status, Self-esteem:
recognition, self-respect,
knowledge, responsibility,
prestige, and achievement.

Social:
a sense of love and belonging and
acceptance by others.

Safety and Security:
protection from threats in the environment,
a sense of security, and a sense of stability.

Physiological:
primary needs, such as food, water, shelter, and rest.

Maslow's hierarchy shows that physical or physiological needs are our most primary or basic human needs.

In general, it is hard to meet higher needs when basic needs have not been met. Keep this in mind as you become an independent adult. Develop spending habits that allow you to meet basic needs responsibly. This will ensure opportunities to fulfill higher-level needs that provide satisfaction in life.

Higher-Level Needs

As self-aware, social beings, we have a drive to fulfill more than primary survival needs. The top three levels in Maslow's hierarchy describe these higher-level needs. Higher-level needs affect our spending habits.

EXAMPLE: With increased self-understanding, you might realize you want to go into an unusual line of work. This could require specialized training or experience. Saving for that education will become an important goal that will affect how you choose to spend your money.

Evaluating Our Wants

It is not always easy to tell when a need is really a want. One clue is cost. Fulfilling wants often costs more than fulfilling needs.
EXAMPLE: A luxury condominium is more expensive than a modest home or apartment.

There's nothing wrong with fulfilling a need with a want, in most cases. A luxury condominium is fine if you can afford it. But when basic needs are sacrificed, that is a problem.

Psychological Aspects

Our psychological make-up affects our wants. Owning certain items—and even the process of buying—can provide psychological satisfaction.

EXAMPLE: Wearing certain clothing might make some people feel attractive and accepted. A fancy car might serve the same purpose for someone else. A cozy couch might provide a sense of comfort or security. Tools or recreational gear might help some people feel competent, effective, and alive.

There is nothing wrong with getting psychological satisfaction from purchases. It is important, though, to make sure the satisfaction doesn't encourage overspending. When this happens, your financial goals can be jeopardized. Also, it is important to find satisfaction in other areas of life.

Your Life

Shop-aholic Syndrome

Do you shop to lift your spirits? Do you spend more than you can afford? Do you buy things you never use? Are you in debt from excessive shopping? If you answered yes to these questions, you might suffer from a compulsive shopping disorder. This disorder can lead to difficult financial and emotional problems. Nip it in the bud by getting help from a mental health professional.

My Notebook

Needs or Wants?

Make a chart with four headings: "Item," "Need," "Want," and "Need or Want?" Under "Item," write the names of three things you are considering buying. In the "Need" column, write down all the reasons you need the item. In the "Want" column, write down all the reasons you want the item.

Review your reasons carefully. Consider Maslow's hierarchy and how advertising works. After thinking through all the issues, indicate in the last column if the item is a need or a want.

Advertising

Basic human needs influence many of your purchases. Your individual psychology and values play a role. In addition, your environment exerts a strong influence.

Advertising, your peers, special offers, and affordability are some of the most common things in the environment that affect your buying decisions.

Market Research

American companies spend more than $200 billion annually on **advertising**. The purpose of every one of these ad dollars is to try to get you to buy goods or services. In addition to money spent on ads, companies also spend over $5 billion on market research. **Market research** is the study of people in order to understand their buying behavior.

Let's say a company wants to sell more jeans to young people. It will conduct market research to discover the characteristics of the group being studied—teens your age. Such a company might create a survey with the following questions:

* How old are you?
* Are you a boy or a girl?
* What is your family income?
* How do you spend your own money?
* What are your favorite colors?
* Name two of your most important values.
* Name two public figures you admire.

Answers to these kinds of questions will help the company create ads that appeal to the needs and wants of people like you.

How Ads Influence People

It's no surprise that ads are carefully designed to influence you. To be successful, an ad has to:

* Get your attention.
* Make you want the product.
* Persuade you to buy the product.
* Tell you where you can get it.

Advertising accomplishes this by creating psychological, intellectual, or social desires.

Making it **REAL**

Checking out Ads

Your family is considering the purchase of a computer. For one week, gather computer advertisements from magazines and newspapers. Watch television ads. At the end of the week, compare the ads. Which computer do you most want to buy? Write down five reasons.

FASTEST COMPUTER EVER! Version 8.0.5.3

Types of Advertisements

Type of Ad	Description	Example	Appeal
Informational	Describes features to convince you to buy the product.	*Get your new WOW computer now. Its 900-megahertz processor is the fastest on the market. The 50-gigabyte hard drive can't be beat, and the price is lower than any other new model.*	Appeals primarily to the intellect: It looks like a great deal for the amount of money.
Persuasive	Tries to create desire by giving you the impression you will feel fulfilled, satisfied, or happy if only you have this product.	*Tummy Tucker slacks make every woman look great. With our new special design, you'll look and feel like a new woman. On sale now in stores across the country.*	Appeals primarily to our emotions, since little factual information is provided.
Image-Enhancing	Tries to make you feel like you will belong to a special group if you buy the service or product.	*It's no accident that superstars Josie Jose and Tanya Tonya love their new Phoenix sports cars. The Phoenix is the best and made for the best. That's why you'll love yours, too.*	Appeals to emotions and social needs.
Brand	Reassures you that you can count on the quality because the product is coming from a well known, reputable manufacturer.	*Now, from the people who brought you the wildly popular ChocoCrunch snack bar, comes the PeesaPizza meal in a pocket for busy teens who want taste and nutrition.*	Appeals to emotions. Relies solely on success by association.

It should be clear by now that ads:

* Are designed to get you to buy.
* Use a variety of techniques to accomplish that goal.

Knowing that, can you make wise buying decisions with the help of advertising? Ads can be useful for letting you know:

* Where you can purchase products.
* When products are on sale.

However, ads should not be the only source of information you use when considering an important purchase. While some ads do include factual information, none will tell you about problems with the product. You need to find that information on your own.

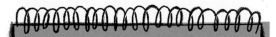

My Notebook

Which Ads Work?

Learn what pushes your buttons. Make notes for a week about at least five ads that catch your attention and make you want to buy. Analyze how they make their point with you. Do they appeal to your image of how you would like to be? Do they connect with someone or something you admire? Do they offer to solve a problem for you?

How could understanding the appeal of those ads help you make smart purchasing decisions?

Deceptive Techniques		
Technique	**Description**	**Problem**
Exaggeration	Claims are puffed up with words like *fabulous, the best,* and *super-strength.*	Something starts to sound awfully good, even though there is no information to back up the claim.
Testimonials	A celebrity or someone who has used the product is quoted as saying the product is great.	What authority or experience does the person have? Has he or she ever used a similar product? If not, how would he or she know which is best?
Offer a Gift	When you make a purchase, you get something along with the purchase for which you don't pay any more money.	Gifts are free. If you have to buy something before you get the "gift," it isn't free.

Truth in Advertising

Advertisers cannot say anything they want to about their products or services in an ad. They cannot lie. In fact, if they make false claims, it is considered to be **fraud**. Fraud, which deceives or tricks people with lies to get them to spend their money, is illegal. However, advertising can be misleading without being illegal. Misleading ads are deceptive but do not lie.

Avoid being taken in. Analyze ads carefully. Do your own research before you buy.

Peer Influences

Most people want to feel they belong to a group. For this reason, people are influenced by their **peers**, the people most like them with whom they spend time. This desire to belong is a natural and healthy human desire. Much of the time, this desire is constructive.

EXAMPLE: Belonging to a service or church group encourages people to help those who are less fortunate.

In some cases, though, the desire to belong influences you inappropriately. Sometimes this can affect your spending habits.

EXAMPLE: Imagine you are working to save for an important goal. Should you buy the brand-name shoes your friends have? Would it be better to buy less expensive shoes and

Get Smart

But the Survey Said . . .

You've seen the ads that use numbers to persuade you to buy. They usually go something like this: "Four out of five doctors recommend . . ." or "100 percent of teens chose . . ." If advertisers can't lie, it must be true. Right?

Well, yes and no. For example, a clothing manufacturer hired a market research company to identify the top clothes items high school students would pick from a pre-selected group of clothes. However, there was only one pair of jeans included—the manufacturer's.

When the company reported the survey results in an ad, it said 90 percent of high school students preferred their jeans. What the ad didn't tell you was that the company's jeans were the only ones the survey participants could choose.

Did the ad lie? No. Did the numbers really mean anything? No. Be skeptical. It's your best defense.

put some money in your savings account? If you want to meet your goal, the answer is probably "buy less expensive shoes."

Resisting peer influence can be a challenge. It is made harder by advertisements that appeal to your desire to belong. Here are some tips to help you resist peer influences and advertising:

* Stay focused on *your* goals.
* Learn to tell the difference between your needs and wants.
* Analyze ads.
* Remember that ads tell only one side of the story.
* Base your purchases on independent research.

Special Offers

A special offer tries to induce, or encourage, you to buy a product or service offered by the advertiser. Common special offers include:

* Two-for-one sales.
* Coupons.
* Contests.
* Rebates (you get money back later from the manufacturer).

Special offers can be valuable if:

* You buy something you had intended to buy anyway.
* You get something you were going to buy anyway, but at a better price.

The problem with special offers is that they often encourage you to buy something you don't need or want, or that you wouldn't have purchased at the time.

Affordability

Sometimes, you will find that the forces conspiring to get you to buy something will assure you that it is **affordable**. That means that you can pay for it. How would they know? How do you know when something is truly affordable? Answer these **four** questions:

1. Did you plan to buy it?
2. Does it cost the amount that you had budgeted?
3. Is there another planned purchase you can give up or postpone?
4. Did you earn extra money or receive a gift that your budget didn't plan on? Is this the thing you would most want to spend that extra money on?

You need to be especially honest and careful with yourself in answering question 3. Can you really get along without the item you would give up?

Also, beware of spending money before you have it. Many people think they can afford something because they are expecting to earn extra money or are sure they are going to get a raise. Then, guess what happens? It's only affordable if you can pay for it now.

Becoming a Smart Shopper

By now, you understand many of the factors that influence your buying decisions. The next step is to understand how to make buying decisions that:

* Will meet your requirements.
* You won't regret later.

Deciding What to Buy

The information about differentiating needs and wants, peer influence, and values can help you decide whether to make a purchase or not. But once you've decided to make a purchase, how can you be sure you'll be pleased with your final choice?

The best way to accomplish this is to use a rational, or logical and reasonable, approach. This requires:

* *Gathering information* (product research).
* *Evaluating alternatives* (price-value comparison, comparison shopping, brand loyalty).
* *Evaluating your satisfaction* after the purchase.

Researching Products

Advertising and peer influence do give you information about products or services, but they have their pitfalls. To buy with confidence, it's important to:

* Follow a systematic approach to gathering and organizing information.
* Use several different sources of information.

This process may not be necessary for small purchases, such as a CD—if it's in your budget—but it's important for more expensive items, such as a CD player, that you expect to use and own for a long time.

Gathering and Organizing Information

Creating a grid that compares products can be a useful way to help you gather and organize information. A grid will help you:

* Compare the same features, or characteristics, of different models.
* Keep track of the information you gather.
* Compare choices once you've gathered all the information you need.

To set up your own grid, do a little preliminary research to determine how many features you want to compare.

EXAMPLE: If you're buying a CD player, you might compare these **five** features:

1. **The number of CDs it will play.**
2. **Recording capability.**
3. **Cord and battery operation.**
4. **Sound quality.**
5. **Repair and durability record.**

In your grid, set up a column for each of the five features. You'll always want a price column. A column to indicate where different models are available is also helpful. Keep in mind that you will often have more than one price and availability location for one model. For this reason, you should make the spaces large enough for all your notes. Try to compare at least four to six models, but no fewer than three.

Sources of Information

Since the purpose of advertising is to sell you something, the information in an ad is likely influenced by the advertiser's motive to sell. When you make important purchases, you want objective, or unbiased, information.

Where can you get unbiased information? There are a number of sources:

* **Consumers Union.** Consumers Union is an independent product-testing laboratory. Its magazine, *Consumer Reports*, publishes the results of the lab's tests. Almost all public libraries subscribe to this magazine. Look up the product you want to purchase in the index. From shoes and ice cream to cars, CD players, and nearly everything in between, you'll find test results.

* **Specialized magazine reviews.** For example, if you want to buy a computer, research product reviews in computer magazines.

* **Certifications or seals of approval.** To obtain these, a manufacturer has to meet certain standards.

* **Salespeople and manufacturers** can provide some information about features, but do not rely on them alone.

* **Friends, family, and coworkers** can provide useful information about their purchases and degree of satisfaction after the purchase.

Price-Value Comparison

A price-value comparison analyzes the cost as compared with what you get, or the value. **EXAMPLE:** In researching CD players, you might find you definitely want to be able to play five CDs. A CD player that only plays three might cost less, but it won't meet your needs. In this case, the results of the price-value comparison indicate you will have to pay a little more to get the value you want.

By the Numbers

Evaluating Price and Value

Does the least expensive model always give you the best value? Here's one way to find out:

1. Select a product you want to buy.
2. Research it in magazines.
3. Select at least one model that has a high repair rate.
4. Call repair shops and ask the price of each repair.
5. Add up the cost of the possible repairs. Add them to the price of the less reliable models.
6. Compare that cost with the cost of more expensive but more reliable models.

Which product really costs less? Which product gives you the best value for the price?

Comparison Shopping

Now you're ready to find out who has the best deal on exactly what you want. In this case, you want a five-disc CD player, model 123 or XYZ. Both models got the highest ratings in your independent research. Now you need to get online or use the phone to do some **comparison shopping**, which means looking for the best product at the lowest price you can find.

Price is the most common reason people comparison shop, but there may be other reasons as well.

EXAMPLE: You might want to buy from a company that is environmentally or socially responsible. If so, you'll compare manufacturers' records in these areas.

Brand Loyalty

Sometimes you already own a certain brand of product. You like it, and it has held up well. You are inclined to buy that brand again, even if it costs a little more. You feel you can't go wrong. Sometimes brand loyalty makes good sense.

Deciding Where to Buy

Once you have decided on the product you want to buy, you'll need to figure out where to buy it.

Search This

Comparison Shopping

Shop for an item valued at approximately $100 in a department store and online. Create a comparison grid to decide what features to research and how to organize your information. When your grid is complete, compare costs and availability between the two shopping methods. Don't forget to include shipping and handling charges. Which gives you a better deal on this item, stores or web sites?

Shopping Choices

From shopping malls to neighborhood stores, to flea markets, you have many choices about where to spend your dollars.

Different Kinds of Stores		
Retailer	**Description**	**Advantage/Disadvantage**
Department Stores	Offer items in clearly defined departments, such as shoes, apparel, kitchenware, and others.	* They offer a wide variety of merchandise. * They offer some specialty merchandise. * Prices can be higher than other retail outlets.
Specialty Stores	Offer items in a specific category, such as shoes, books, office supplies, and others.	* Many choices are offered in that specialty category. * Salespeople tend to be more knowledgeable about what they're selling. * Prices may be higher than in other stores.
Discount Stores	Offer lots of merchandise in many categories at lower prices.	* The physical setting may be plain, like a warehouse. * It may be hard to find a salesperson or get your questions answered. * Salespeople may be less knowledgeable than in specialty or department stores.
Online Stores and Catalogs	Offer ordering and product selection from an Internet site or by phone or mail.	* They offer convenient shopping from home. * Merchandise that is not available locally can be found. * You cannot try on or look at the product before buying. * They can pose security issues. * You need to verify return policies and contact information before ordering in case there is a problem with the order. * You often must pay shipping fees.

Warranties and Contracts

Warranties and service contracts are agreements about how problems with products will be handled. A **warranty** covers problems that occur because the product was not made properly, including defective materials or workmanship. It comes at no extra cost when you buy a product and guarantees that a defective product will be repaired or replaced for free.

Service and repair contracts are designed to cover the costs of some kinds of repairs that might be needed after you have used the product for a while. However, most service and repair contracts are not worth the additional cost.

Most products do not require special servicing or repairs during their useful lives. Besides, by setting aside a small amount each month, you can save up enough to cover repairs yourself if it becomes necessary. If you never need to make the repair, you can use the money for something else. If you've paid the money out on a service contract, though, the money is gone even if repairs are never needed.

After the Purchase

Once you've made a significant purchase, it's important to keep track of how the product:

* Holds up.
* Meets your needs.

This information will tell you if your purchasing process was effective.

Take Care of Your Things

Treating your purchases properly is the best protection against the cost of repairs. Remember, warranties won't pay for repair costs if *you've* damaged or misused the product. If you cause the damage, you'll be stuck with the cost even if the product is still under warranty.

Here are some tips to help you take care of your things:

* Follow the manufacturer's instructions for care and maintenance.
* Use the product only for the purpose intended.
* Treat the product in a reasonable manner.

Avoid Problems

They say the best defense is a good offense. Translated to the realm of consumer economics, this means:

* Don't get taken.
* But if you do, fight back.

Your best protection against fraud is to recognize and avoid it.

Recognizing Problems

Type	Description	How It Works and What to Watch For
Bait and Switch	You're encouraged to come to the store (the "bait") because of a good sale price. The sale item is no longer available and you're shown other, higher-priced models (the switch).	✳ The sale item is "out of stock" or "sold out." ✳ The salesperson suggests you look at other models that are more expensive.
Phone Fraud	Products or services are sold with high-pressure phone calls trying to convince you to act now.	✳ You feel pressured or as if you might be losing an opportunity if you don't act quickly. ✳ Someone asks for your credit card or Social Security number. ✳ The caller won't give you a phone number or address.
Pyramid Schemes	You must pay to participate in a business that supposedly sells products. People who signed up before you "are higher in the pyramid," and get a percentage of your payment.	✳ You are more encouraged to bring in new members than to sell products. ✳ Most of the revenue comes from signing up new participants, not from selling products.
Contests and Sweepstakes	You cannot participate for free.	✳ You're required to pay a fee or buy something to be eligible for the prize.
Loss Leaders	You're attracted to the store by an unusually low price on a high ticket item. (Loss leaders are not technically fraud, but they are illegal in some states because they are so deceptive.)	✳ The store is selling at a loss to get you into the store. ✳ No other items are comparably priced. ✳ You were lured into the store where you end up buying other things because you're there.

Don't Get Taken

The Federal Trade Commission (FTC) helps consumers avoid fraud. Visit the FTC web site to learn how to avoid everything from identity theft, diet, health, and fitness scams to abusive lending practices, and much more.

Resolving Problems

No matter how wise a consumer you become, you still may encounter problems. When you try to resolve a problem with a company, be sure to:

* Document every contact you have with the company.
* Keep a log of all visits or phone calls to the company, including date, person you spoke with, and a summary of the conversation.
* Keep copies of all correspondence (regular mail and e-mail).

Dealing with Defective Products

The first step in trying to deal with a defective product should be a visit in person or on the Web or a phone call to the company where you bought it. If you go in person:

* Take the product and your receipt and log book.
* Explain in detail the problem you are having and show your receipt.
* If the salesperson says he or she cannot do anything, ask to speak to the manager.

* If the manager will not help, explain that you are going to contact the manufacturer directly, and also consumer advocacy groups.

If phone calls or visits don't get any results, write a letter. The letter needs to include these **seven** pieces of information:

1. **The make and model** of the item purchased.
2. **The date and location** of the purchase.
3. **The problems** you are experiencing with the item.
4. **The date of your visit(s)** and/or phone call(s).
5. **The name(s) of the person(s)** you spoke with.
6. **A summary** of your conversation(s).
7. **A statement** of what you want (a replacement product or your money back).

Stick to the facts. Do not threaten or accuse.

After a week from the date you sent the letter, contact the company if it has not contacted you. If you are not going to get a refund or replacement product, seek assistance. If you have made phone calls and written letters and have gotten nowhere, it's time to contact a professional organization or consumer advocacy group. See page 134.

Consumer Rights and Responsibilities

Even if you research thoroughly before making a major purchase and you avoid deceptive and fraudulent selling practices, the time may still come when you will have a problem that needs to be resolved. That's when it becomes important to know your rights, responsibilities, and power as a consumer. You have more power as a consumer than you probably know.

Make Your Spending Dollars Speak for You

As a consumer, you may not realize how much influence you have, or *could* have, on businesses.

You can "vote" with your dollars. Take the time to be a smart consumer and give your business—and your hard-earned money—to those whose products and service you like. Business owners know that stories of experiences, especially bad ones, spread like wildfire within a community. If enough people hear about the over-priced—and over-cooked—food at a new restaurant and choose not to eat there, the business will notice. Either it will try hard to create a new, less damaging reputation or it will likely go out of business.

Consumers also pass along news of:

* Fair prices.
* Great products.
* "Good deals."
* Excellent customer service.

However it comes, feedback from consumers is critical for all businesses and service industries. It helps them with their short-term and long-term planning. Information and feedback from consumers helps businesses to know how to improve their product development, service, and, ultimately, their sales.

The Rights of Consumers

In his 1962 address to Congress, President John F. Kennedy outlined **four** basic rights of consumers. This "Consumers' Bill of Rights" included the right to:

1. **Buy products that are safe.**
2. **Be informed.**
3. **Have a choice.**
4. **Be heard.**

Other rights were added as Congress passed laws to further protect consumers. They include the right to:

* Redress (to seek and receive money or other compensation for a wrong done).
* Satisfaction of basic needs.
* A healthy environment.
* Consumer education.

Consumers also have responsibilities when it comes to using products. **EXAMPLES:** We must buckle car seatbelts. We must wear helmets when riding our bikes. When the air quality falls below a certain standard, we may not use our outdoor barbecue grill in some places. When water levels drop below a certain level in some places, people may not wash their cars or water their gardens.

Consumer Help and Protection

Federal, state, local, and private consumer-protection agencies assist consumers with consumer-related problems. The responsibilities and authority of agencies vary. The agencies may:

* Enforce laws and regulations.
* Set product standards (for example, exhaust emission standards for cars).
* Protect consumers from unsafe and unscrupulous practices.
* Give consumers a place to complain and make their voices heard.
* Provide general information on consumer-related issues and information on local, state, and federal laws.

The Role of Government

Federal agencies and departments work on a national level to protect consumers. They each specialize in certain areas to:

* Watch over a specific area of consumer concerns.
* Set up and enforce rules and regulations to guard consumers.
* Penalize those who break the law.

We need government to help protect consumers. But government regulations can add greatly to the costs of businesses. Furthermore, some requirements, such as various warnings manufacturers are required to give consumers, are downright silly. A smart consumer does not expect government to solve all our problems.

How the Government Protects Consumers

Federal Agencies and Departments	Some Responsibilities
Department of Agriculture (USDA)	* Inspects, grades, and sets safety and production standards for meat, poultry, and canned fruits and vegetables. * Oversees farming and international trade. * Manages food programs for people in need. * Publishes consumer information booklets.
Department of Labor	* Supports wage-earners through improved working conditions and increased work opportunities. * Fights child labor, job discrimination, and unsafe and unhealthy practices and working conditions.
Department of Health and Human Services (HHS)	* Helps to protect people's health and well-being through financial assistance programs, public health programs, and drug and alcohol abuse programs. * Supervises and coordinates work of other agencies, including the FDA and the Centers for Disease Control and Prevention.
Food and Drug Administration (FDA)	* Enforces food labeling laws. * Oversees safety of food, drugs, and cosmetics. * Certifies new drugs. * Runs national centers for drug research.
Consumer Product Safety Commission (CPSC)	* Works with businesses to protect workers and the public from unreasonable risk of injury and death. * Promotes voluntary safety standards by manufacturers. * Sets and enforces safety standards for many consumer products. * Orders recall or replacement of defective or hazardous products.
Federal Trade Commission (FTC)	* Promotes free, fair business competition. * Investigates unfair and deceptive trade practices. * Enforces consumer protection legislation. * Protects businesses from unfair competition.
Environmental Protection Agency (EPA)	* Enforces environmental laws. * Determines air and water quality standards. * Monitors businesses for compliance with environmental laws. * Oversees safe disposal of hazardous waste.

Consumer Agencies and Groups

There are many hundreds of national, state, local, and private, nonprofit consumer protection agencies and groups. The memberships of some national organizations are made up of consumer groups rather than individuals. National groups are often made up of people in the same profession.

Some of the many consumer groups include:

* **The U.S. Office of Consumer Affairs:** federal agency that helps consumers by providing advice and information but has no power to uphold laws or reach legal decisions.
* **The National Consumer League (NCL):** private nonprofit organization that focuses on marketplace and workplace issues including child labor, privacy, food safety, and medication.
* **Consumer Federation of America (CFA):** a private nonprofit organization that advances pro-consumer legislation and views to Congress, state and federal regulatory agencies, and the courts.
* **Better Business Bureau:** nonprofit organization that helps resolve disputes but has no legal authority to settle them.
* **State consumer agencies** centralize responsibility and give consumers a clear place to turn for advice and redress. Many times they are under the control of the state attorney general who can bring legal action against businesses that violate consumer protection laws.
* **Local agencies and groups** act as clearing houses of information. They can also make referrals to appropriate state or federal agencies.

Media Attention

Newspapers, magazines, the Internet, radio, and television shows provide consumer product information and support in resolving consumer product complaints. They research consumer questions and follow up on complaints that may go unanswered. News reports often highlight and then find a remedy for specific problems, such as money not refunded for a defective product or services where the contracted promises are not honored.

The Power of the Consumer

On a grassroots level, consumers affect the free market system in **two** substantial ways:

1. **Consumers can withdraw their support** in the form of money from the market, either by refusing to do business with a specific store or manufacturer or by pulling their money out of a conventional store or institution and instead investing it into a member-owned and operated group.

2. **Consumers can influence and lead the debate** on important issues. They can push for new consumer legislation.

Boycotts and consumer cooperatives are two effective ways to make an impact on the financial bottom line for a business.

Boycotts

To **boycott** means to deny or withhold economic or other support from an individual, group, manufacturer, store, or even a country because of disagreement with its policies or conduct. A boycott is a group action. It is an effective way to make a business take notice.

Boycotts have been around for a long while. In 1773, the Boston Tea Party climaxed a series of colonial boycotts of English goods to protest various taxes.

In the 1960s and 1970s, many people boycotted table grapes to show support for farm workers in their struggles with grape growers for better wages and working conditions.

The tenants of an east coast apartment building all refused to pay their rent until the landlord made the necessary repairs they had requested for so long. It took a boycott to cause him to listen.

You, as an individual or as part of a group, might boycott a product or business to protest:

* Poor working conditions.
* Unsafe living conditions.
* Low wages.
* High prices.
* The company's environmental policy.
* The company's political stance.

Consumer Cooperatives

Consumers have another powerful way to affect their own economic well-being. In a cooperative (or co-op), members band together to form a business or association. The members own the business and share any profits. (They may also take no profits in order to keep consumer costs down.) They run the business to meet their own goals.

EXAMPLE: People have set up food co-ops in order to get farm-fresh food and to buy at lower prices than their neighborhood grocery stores offer.

Often, members of a cooperative donate time and energy to do some of the work they would otherwise have to pay someone to do. This also helps them keep their costs—and therefore the prices of their goods—down.

Being a wise consumer takes work and practice. Once you've decided what you need and what you want, you can decide what, where, and from whom to purchase an item at the best price.

Businesses rely on different kinds of advertising to get customers. Learn how to spot deceptive techniques before you buy. Check into the product's warranty, and know where to go for help if you have problems in dealing with a store or manufacturer.

The choices you make as a consumer are very important to businesses, which rely on your "voting" dollars to keep them in business. Sometimes, you may decide to vote by boycotting a particular product or business, or you may choose to be part of a consumer cooperative.

As a consumer, the more you know the better decisions you'll make.

Consumer Economics

advertising—business act of attracting attention to products or services with information designed to stimulate consumer buying. *p. 119*

affordable—able to be paid for. *Affordable* doesn't mean "cheap;" it means the item is at a price you can pay. *p. 123*

boycott—group action of refusing to buy a product or use a service or deal with a business, especially as an act of protest. *p. 135*

comparison shopping—process of gathering pieces of information about products (price, features, ratings) and sources and comparing them to make a wise purchasing decision. *p. 126*

fraud—deliberate deception by one party to get an unfair or unlawful gain from another party. *p. 122*

hierarchy—list of things in order of importance. *p. 117*

market research—collection and interpretation of data about a specific group (or groups) of consumers. *p. 119*

need—something required for survival. *p. 116*

peers—people who have similar characteristics, such as age, gender, income, or hobbies. *p. 122*

want—something desired but not required for survival. *p. 116*

warranty—guarantee by a manufacturer or service provider. *p. 128*

CHAPTER 8

Smart Shopping for Food

In this chapter, you will learn about:

- **why we eat what we eat**
- **how to shop for food**
- **how to make sure your food is safe**

Win Jing wanted to have a special dinner party for her friend Lee on his birthday. Her first idea was to take him to dinner at his favorite Italian restaurant. Then she worried it would cost more money than she could afford. She wondered if there was a less expensive way to give Lee a special Italian dinner. Perhaps she could cook it!

She knew Lee liked linguini with clam sauce. Win Jing went to Lee's favorite Italian restaurant, Luigi's, and looked at the menu. At Luigi's, linguini with clam sauce cost $14. Dinner for 6 would cost $84, plus tax and tip.

Win Jing went to the grocery store and priced the ingredients needed to make linguini with clam sauce at home. She discovered that for only $13, she could make the pasta dish for six people and also buy ingredients for a tossed salad and garlic bread to go with it! Lee loved the dinner, and he was very impressed that Win Jing went to the extra effort to cook it herself.

Why We Eat What We Eat

Food is fundamental. All of us must eat or we will die. From the day we are born, we must eat at more or less regular intervals to get the energy we need to survive and grow. However, food represents much more to us than fuel for our bodies. Food connects us to our family, friends, community, and even our country. It also affects our health. What we eat and how we produce or acquire what we eat affect the economy and the environment.

We use food not just to nourish our bodies, but to soothe our feelings, celebrate with friends, and gather with family. Holidays throughout the world are celebrated with feasts. Food can be symbolic. Think about the parts different foods play in your life. What foods do you want when you're feeling down? Which foods do you choose when you're having a party? What traditional foods does your family eat at holiday gatherings?

Four factors influence why we eat what we eat:

1 Family and Culture

What comes to mind when you think about cookies and milk? Do you sometimes crave popcorn or potato chips? Just as your family's habits influence many of your choices in life, the eating habits you develop at home influence which foods are likely to make you feel safe and comforted. If your dad, who loves you, feeds you meatloaf and mashed potatoes, you'll tend to crave meat and potatoes when you feel the need for "**comfort food**."

A major factor that influences what we like to eat is the **cuisine** of our country or culture. Different parts of the world have different cuisines. *Cuisine* is a French word that literally means "kitchen," but it is used to refer to different styles of cooking and the food prepared in those styles. In America today, we are exposed to many different cuisines. Most cities now have Italian, Greek, Chinese, Mexican, Vietnamese, German, and many other restaurants that serve regional cuisines. We are exposed to a greater variety of food now than at any time in the past.

2 Advertising and Media

Start paying close attention to how many food ads you see in the next few days. Look for ads in magazines and newspapers. Notice how many food ads you see when you're watching television or listening to the radio.

Advertisers spend millions of dollars every year to influence what you eat. They generally use images that show youthful, healthy people, but they are frequently trying to sell you food that contains a lot of fat, sugar, and salt. These ingredients certainly don't make you healthy and good looking, but advertisers know that the images you see will create this impression anyway and make you want to buy their products.

Today, lots of food advertising relies on terms such as "natural," "organic," and "homemade." These words conjure up values and images that advertisers know people find attractive, but they are often misleading. Obviously, something that you buy in a package wasn't homemade, no matter what it says.

There are also hidden ways that marketers influence what you buy. Supermarkets take your shopping experience very seriously. They spend a lot of time and money designing their stores in ways that manipulate what you buy. There are good reasons why they place magazines and candy next to the check-out counter. They know that while you're waiting in line, you'll get bored and be more likely to buy these items to kill time. In fact, the entire store is laid out to influence your shopping habits.

❸ Nutritional Education

We have learned more about how nutrition influences our health in the past 50 years than we ever knew before. We've discovered how vitamins and minerals can help to protect our bodies from damaging exposure to smog, X-rays, and other environmental pollutants. We've learned how different kinds of fats affect our bodies. We also know that eating plenty of fiber-rich food is good for our health.

More than at any time in the past, well-researched information is available to help us choose foods that promote good health and longevity. In fact, keeping up with all the latest data on nutrition can easily be a full-time job! As with many aspects of life in the 21st century, one of the challenges is sorting out all the information that is available. In some cases, nutritional information can be contradictory. So, unless you're interested in becoming a professional nutritionist, you have to depend on experts, and even they sometimes disagree.

You owe it to yourself to become as knowledgeable as you can about the nutritional content of food and how it affects your health and well-being. This means keeping up with the latest research. Try to find reliable sources and look at more than one source of information. There is a lot of conflicting information, because most researchers approach the facts with some bias. When you get information from a variety of sources, you will begin to see areas of clear agreement. Then you can feel confident that the information is pretty accurate.

Making it REAL

Reacting to Food

There's one thing you can do without any outside research—learn to pay attention to messages from your own body. Start to notice how you feel after you eat different foods. Do you feel clear and energized or do you feel stuffed, heavy, and drowsy? Food should give you energy, not drain you and slow you down.

The next time you buy some groceries or order a meal, think about making choices that will make your body feel better. What will you pick?

④ Personal Preferences

We each have our own preferences for foods. You might find it hard to believe, but you probably eat things that other people—even your friends—consider strange. Kara loves peanut butter and banana sandwiches, which Mark finds disgusting. He, however, puts ketchup on his grilled cheese sandwiches and adds apple to tuna salad. What unusual tastes in food do you have?

Planning

When you're eating at home, you need to plan what you're going to stock on your shelves and in your refrigerator. In this section we'll look at:

* Food budgeting.
* Food preferences.
* Nutrition.
* Organic food.

Get Smart

Eating Disorders

"You can never be too rich or too thin," says the old saying. However, you can be too thin. In fact, it can kill you.

Eating disorders are illnesses marked by an abnormal relationship with food. They are very dangerous. They are most common in young women in their teens and early twenties, but young men can get them, too. Here are three eating disorders to watch out for in yourself and in your friends:

* **Anorexia nervosa**. People with this disease starve themselves. Symptoms include significant weight loss, continuing to "diet" even though very thin, and preoccupation with food.

* **Bulimia**. A person suffering from bulimia binges, or eats large amounts of food in one sitting, and then purges by vomiting, using laxatives, or even exercising extremely vigorously.
* **Binge-eating disorder**. A binge eater uses food as comfort. The distinction between a person with a real problem and someone who may just need to improve his or her diet is that the binge eater has a crisis in self-esteem that underlies the destructive behaviors surrounding food.

If you suspect that you or a friend has an eating disorder, it is very important to get professional help.

Budgeting/Affordability

What food you buy depends a lot on how much you can afford to spend on food. Do you know how much your family spends on food each week? Do you know how much you spend personally? Average Americans spend about 16 percent of their weekly income on food. People with more money spend a lower percentage, while those with less money spend up to 30 percent or more of their income. It's a mistake to assume that you need to spend a lot of money to eat tasty, nutritious meals.

Knowing how to plan menus that give you good nutrition and fit your budget is a valuable skill. The least expensive way to eat is to buy basic ingredients and prepare meals from scratch. Many people feel they don't have time to cook that way, so they pay more to buy processed, packaged food. When you do that, you're paying extra for the time and energy the manufacturer spent to process the food.

EXAMPLE: You could make mashed potatoes by cooking potatoes and mashing them, or you could buy processed mashed-potato flakes in a box. Five pounds of potatoes may cost $1.79, whereas one 13 oz. box of brand-name mashed potatoes may cost $3.49. That's nearly 12 times as much! Cooking with fresh ingredients clearly saves a lot, and the food usually tastes better and may be more healthful.

Food Preferences

What is your favorite food? Do you like fatty, salty foods like potato chips and bacon? Or do you prefer sweet, creamy items like banana splits and milk shakes? Perhaps you love your fresh fruit and veggies. Your tastes and preferences for different foods greatly influence what you choose to eat. Be aware, however, that your preferences are continually being influenced by cultural forces, such as advertising, that aren't concerned with your health.

Nutrition

The slogan "You are what you eat" sounds funny, but it states an obvious fact that we seldom think about. We are physically composed of what we consume. The food we eat builds our bones, muscles, and organs. If you don't eat right, you can damage your body. A lack of certain nutrients often shows up first in the condition of your skin, hair, and nails.

EXAMPLE: A steady diet of junk food, such as pizza, hamburgers, chips, and fries, will give you a bad complexion and oily hair.

Nutrition should be a major factor in determining how you select the foods you eat. Although you don't want to discount the importance of good taste and you should certainly make a point of eating food you enjoy, you definitely want to eat food that will contribute to your good health.

The Role of Fat

Fat has been getting a lot of attention over the past several years. Fat gives food an appealing taste and texture. Also, we are attracted to fat because it is the way our bodies store energy. In the past, when food containing fat was less available and people had to work hard physically, people needed to eat fatty food to survive. Today, fat is plentiful—and we are stuck with our fat-loving genes.

Nobody wants to be fat, and some people mistakenly think they should avoid all fat. That just isn't true. Your body needs some fat in order to function properly. Try to limit the percentage of fat in your diet to below 30 percent or—even better—20 percent. More importantly, choose the right kind of fat. Oils, such as olive oil or peanut oil and certain fish oils, are better for you than solid fats, like butter or the fats in meat.

Nutritional requirements vary from person to person. Factors that affect nutritional needs include:

* Your age.
* Your size.
* Your gender.
* Whether or not you are still growing.
* How active you are.

The United States Department of Agriculture (USDA) has developed a Food Guide Pyramid that outlines general

USDA Food Guide Pyramid

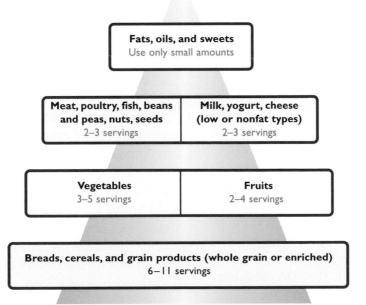

Fats, oils, and sweets
Use only small amounts

Meat, poultry, fish, beans and peas, nuts, seeds
2–3 servings

Milk, yogurt, cheese (low or nonfat types)
2–3 servings

Vegetables
3–5 servings

Fruits
2–4 servings

Breads, cereals, and grain products (whole grain or enriched)
6–11 servings

"I try to eat right, but huge chunks of raw meat are all you can find these days."

recommendations regarding which foods you should eat every day to stay healthy.

Nutritional Supplements

What about nutritional supplements? There is much controversy about they're benefits. Some health experts feel they're essential to getting all the nutrients we need. Most feel that supplements are not necessary if you eat a healthy, well balanced diet.

That "if" is the problem. Many people don't eat a diet that provides all the nutrients they need. Most people don't eat enough fresh fruits and vegetables.

The Food and Drug Administration recommends that you get most of your nutrition from food. The FDA publishes nutritional guidelines called the

Recommended Dietary Allowances (RDA). Daily vitamin and mineral supplements that contain ingredients at or below the RDA are safe but are rarely needed by people who eat a variety of foods, as recommended in the Food Guide Pyramid.

Sometimes supplements are needed to meet specific nutritional requirements. **EXAMPLE:** Iron supplements are recommended for pregnant women.

Organic Food

Organic food is grown without lab-made chemicals. Pests are picked off by hand, or crops are sprayed with substances like soap to discourage insects. Plants are fertilized with animal waste, like horse manure, and protected from weeds and sun with straw, vegetable peelings, and similar materials. Organic methods employ chemicals found in nature.

Most vegetables—fresh, frozen, and canned—are grown with fertilizers and pesticides created in laboratories. Most meat and dairy products come from animals that have been fed hormones and antibiotics—as well as commercially grown feed. These methods produce larger crop yields and build meatier animals. There is very little evidence that lab-made chemicals can make you sick, but many people fear it.

Organic food costs more because it is more expensive to produce and a lot spoils before it reaches the consumer (organic farmers don't use preservatives). If you want to eat organic food, you may need to shop more carefully.

Shopping Strategies

To get the most for your food dollar, you'll need to learn how to be a smart grocery shopper. These are strategies smart shoppers use:

* **Always shop from a list.** Plan your meals ahead of time. Make a list of what you'll need and what basic items you need to replace. Then stick to it.
* **Shop on a full stomach.** When you're hungry, it's hard to resist all the enticing sights and smells you encounter in a grocery store. Eat before you go shopping.
* **Compare prices.** Within a store, compare the costs of one brand against another. Compare prices from one store to another. Keep a list of the prices you pay for given amounts of items you buy frequently. It's the only way to know if a "sale" is really a bargain.
* **Buy what you like to eat.** Don't go overboard on price and nutrition. Tofu is cheap and nutritious, but if you don't like it, it will just go green and fuzzy in your fridge. Then it's a waste.

Fresh vs. Packaged

When you shop, you'll face choices between buying the ingredients for a dish or buying the dish already prepared. How will you decide?

Food Made from Scratch:

* Tastes better.
* Costs less.
* Takes time.
* Is limited by your skill and know-how.

Prepared Foods:

* Are convenient. You don't have to buy quantities of different ingredients you may not use.
* Are quick.
* Are easy.
* Provide variety. You can buy dishes you don't know how to prepare.
* Are expensive.

Food Grown Close to Home

Another set of choices you face as you shop involves where the food comes from. There are good arguments to be made for choosing food grown in your local area:

* Locally grown food is fresher.
* Locally grown food often tastes better.

Fruit that is transported long distances is picked before it is ripe. It may look ripe, but it doesn't have the full fragrance and taste of ripe food. You will need to experiment to discover which out-of-season food is worth buying.

Food Prices

Food prices are influenced by many of the same factors that affect other commodities:

* **Supply.** An early frost in Florida may kill much of the orange crop, making oranges more expensive nation-wide.
* **Demand.** A surge in the popularity of a certain kind of food will mean suppliers can, and will, charge more for it.
* **Transportation costs.** Imported foods generally cost more.

Using Labels

Almost all packaged foods in stores today have labels that describe what they contain. It is important to learn how to read these labels and choose foods that contain lower amounts of fat, sugar, and sodium.

The Nutrition Label

* *Serving size.* Be sure to note the serving size indicated and adjust the information to the amount you actually eat.
* *Calories.* Calories are all about energy. A calorie is a unit of measurement that expresses the heat-producing or energy-producing value of food when it is oxidized in the body. How many calories you need depends on your age, your size, and how active you are. An average-sized active woman needs about 2,200 calories a day, while an average-sized active man needs about 2,900 calories a day.
* *Calories from fat.* Fat is essential, but don't overdo it. Try to keep fat calories down to below 30 percent of total calories for a day.
* *Total fat.* Recommended fat intake for a diet of 2,000 calories a day is 65 grams with no more than 20 percent as saturated fat.
* *Cholesterol.* Try to keep your intake below 300 mg a day.

* *Sodium.* Sodium may be in the form of regular table salt (sodium chloride) or other additives such as monosodium glutamate. Aim for fewer than 2,400 mg a day.
* *Total carbohydrates.* Carbohydrates provide energy. Most of your carbohydrate intake should come from complex carbohydrates, such as whole grains, bread, fruit, and vegetables. Avoid simple carbohydrates like sugar.
* *Fiber.* Try to maximize your fiber intake. You should get about 11.5 grams of fiber per 1,000 calories.
* *Protein.* Protein helps build your bones and muscles. Most Americans get plenty of protein in their diet without even trying.
* *Vitamins and minerals.* These are the essential micronutrients. Labels will indicate which of these nutrients are in the food and the percentage of the RDA.
* *Daily values.* The RDA's values are based on a 2,000-calorie daily diet. These percentages indicate important nutritional information. Use them to tell how nutritious the food is. Look for high percentages for total carbohydrates, dietary fiber, vitamins, and minerals. Look for low percentages of fat, saturated fat, cholesterol, sodium, and sugar.

Anatomy of a Nutrition Label

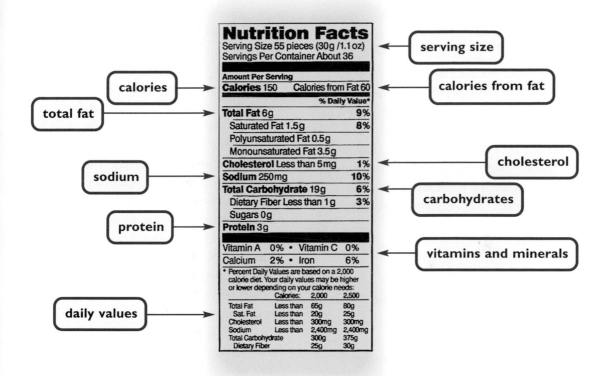

Comparing Prices

One way to be a smart food shopper is to shop around. Of course, most people shop at stores that are located in their neighborhood. You probably don't want to go too far away to buy groceries on a regular basis, because then any cost advantage of a particular store will be cancelled out by the transportation cost of getting there. However, if you're stocking up on a lot of items, it might pay to travel occasionally to a store that has significantly lower prices.

Convenience Stores vs. Grocery Stores

Convenience stores are those small stores, often located at gas stations, that keep late hours and carry a few basic food items, such as milk and bread, along with lots of snack items and newspapers. Such stores are relatively expensive to operate. The rent they pay, the people they pay, and the prices they pay are all higher than other, larger stores. So their prices to you are higher than the price of these same items in standard grocery stores.

Take Your Own Bags

Some stores offer up to a nickel or a dime off of your purchase price when you bring your own shopping bag. This may not sound like a lot, but it adds up over time. Taking a cloth or plastic bag with you when you shop also helps the environment because it conserves resources and produces less garbage.

Brand Names vs. Store Brands

Many supermarkets have their own brand versions of certain basic items, and these brands usually cost less. Depending on what kind of food you're looking for, store brands may be just as tasty and nutritious as more expensive national brands. It is certainly worth it to try store-brand versions of items that you usually buy. If you find that you prefer the brand name, you can always go back to buying it.

Bulk Buying

Bulk buying means that you buy items in large quantities, which generally means that you pay a lower price per unit. Bulk buying can save money, but it doesn't make sense unless you have a lot of storage space and a large enough family to eat the food before it gets too old and goes bad.

Coupons and Weekly Specials

Newspapers, store circulars, and Sunday paper inserts advertise weekly specials and provide coupons that give discounts on specific items. In fact, the average American household receives about 3,000 coupons every year.

If you're very organized and willing to make the extra effort, checking for weekly specials and clipping coupons can help you save money on groceries. The smart use of coupons can cut about 15 percent off of your food bill. Be careful, however, to clip coupons only for items that you would buy anyway. Don't buy the particular brand you have a coupon for if another brand is cheaper.

Also, be aware that specials and coupons are designed to get you into the store where you'll be tempted to buy more. Pay attention to your shopping list and don't give in to the temptation to buy items you don't need.

Frequent-Shopper Cards

Many supermarkets offer "frequent-shopper" or "preferred-shopper" cards, which provide automatic discounts at the checkout counter on specific items. Discounted items are identified on the shelf, but you don't need a coupon to get the discount. Instead, you need a card, which you get by filling out an application at the store.

The card has a bar code that identifies you and thus provides the store with information about what you buy and how often. This trend in the supermarket industry is made possible by computer technology.

The supermarket hopes that these cards will increase customer loyalty and keep you coming back for added savings.

Shopping "Clubs"

Shopping clubs are large, industrial-sized stores that tend to sell items in large-quantity packages. Sometimes, these stores cover an entire city block. You pay an annual fee to belong to the "club." Items are stacked in huge, open warehouses. These places can be fun to shop in, and sometimes you can find some pretty good deals. As with bulk buying in general, however, shopping at these clubs may save you some money if you choose wisely, but it doesn't really pay unless you have enough storage space. Still, you might want to shop with two or three friends in your neighborhood and divide up the bulk items in order to take advantage of the cost savings and still take home a reasonable amount of food.

Food Co-ops

If farmers can avoid wholesalers, they can sell at a price that includes only their price and a fair profit. This helps keep prices relatively low. Many early cooperatives in the U.S. were farm co-ops. Co-op food growers may collect, process, sell, and ship their products out of member-owned facilities.

CASE STUDY

Honeysuckle Farm

Food cooperatives can be as creative as the people involved. Honeysuckle Farm offers a whole farm "experience" for its members. Co-op members pay in advance for a bundle of fresh produce from the farm. The produce is preselected depending on availability. Members pay a flat fee for

twelve months. Orders are delivered to each house once a month.

As part of the co-op arrangement, families help plant, pick, and weed. They also bring their children out to experience "a day on a farm" by gathering eggs, grooming or riding animals, picking fruits and vegetables, braiding lavender, or making apple cider or fruit leather.

Eating Out

Eating out is a major form of entertainment, and it is often more convenient than eating at home. Think of the last time you ate out at a restaurant. Was it a special occasion with your family or just stopping for a burger with friends after a game? Americans eat out more now than they ever have before. The pace of modern life and the availability of good, interesting restaurants contribute to this trend.

Reasons

There are several reasons that eating out is so popular. In many families, both parents work, and it is easier to go out to eat than to come home after a long day and fix dinner. When you eat out, you don't have to spend time preparing food yourself and cleaning up afterwards. Eating out saves you time and labor. However, it costs more than making your own meals.

Nutrition

Nutrition may be one of the first areas to suffer when you eat out. Restaurants don't supply a nutritional content label when they serve you your plate, so you don't know the nutritional content of the food prepared in restaurants. Because really good restaurants make a point of buying the freshest, highest-quality food they can, the nutritional value of their food can be quite high. On the other hand, many restaurants will try to spend as little as possible on ingredients so they can increase their profits.

Cost

The cost of eating out can vary dramatically. Generally, whenever you pay for food, you want to look for the highest-quality food at the lowest price. Sometimes, of course, you just want to have a really great time and, if you have the money, you may be willing to splurge so you can enjoy a special occasion without the effort of cooking the food yourself.

Fast Food

The fast-food industry has a lot of clout in our economy. Americans spend $103 billion a year on fast food. Every day, about 20 percent of Americans eat in fast-food restaurants. Approximately half of all the money spent eating out in America is spent in fast-food restaurants.

Four out of five times when children eat out, they eat fast food. This fact goes far in explaining why there is currently an epidemic of overweight children—double the number in 1980. Fast food tends to be high in calories, fat, cholesterol, sodium, and sugar, all of which contribute to heart disease, high blood pressure, cancer, and obesity.

Fast-food companies have a lot of buying clout. Because they purchase food in such large quantities, they're in a position to exert a lot of influence over the suppliers they deal with and get low prices.

By the Numbers

Eating In vs. Eating Out

When you go to your favorite restaurant, what do you order? How much does it cost? Don't forget to include tax and tip!

Now, consider that meal. What ingredients are in it? Make a shopping list and take it with you to the grocery store. How much would it cost to cook that meal?

How much would you save on that meal if you made it yourself instead of eating it at your favorite restaurant?

Food Safety

Food is wonderful, and we can't live without it. But bad food can make you sick, or even kill you. Smart consumers know the basic rules of food safety:

* **Buy fresh ingredients.** Check the dates on food products. These will tell you when you can no longer use a product.
* **Buy only firmly sealed packages.** Stay away from anything that shows signs of damage or tampering. Don't buy or use canned goods that show dents or bulges.
* **Store food carefully.** Keep flour and cereals secure from bugs. You will want to keep perishable food in the refrigerator.
* **Wash your hands before and after handling food.** This simple precaution can help you avoid getting or spreading disease.
* **Prepare food in a clean area.** Wash countertops and cutting boards before and after every time you put food on them. Scour and disinfect the sink regularly. Empty the garbage daily. Keep shelves and storage areas clean.
* **When in doubt, throw it out.** Don't try to save money by buying or eating anything that doesn't look or smell right.

Storing Food

Proper food storage is important for food safety. Food naturally contains bacteria that may grow to produce food poisoning if food is not stored properly. Bugs pose another problem you can solve with proper storage.

Meat, Poultry, Seafood, and Dairy Products

These foods are at high risk of causing food poisoning. The right temperature, however, can greatly slow the growth of bacteria. So, these foods should always be refrigerated at temperatures below 41° Fahrenheit.

Flour, Mixes, Cereal, Spices, and Dried Fruit

These foods attract beetles, weevils, and moths. Some are not harmful, and you can sift them out of flour. But you still wouldn't want them. Store such foods in tightly closed containers. Use glass, plastic, and metal containers with tight-fitting lids.

Leftovers

Leftovers should always be refrigerated. Store them in containers with tight-fitting lids, or wrapped securely in plastic wrap. Eat leftovers within a few days after they've been cooked.

Sources of More Information

Some foods can be kept for longer periods of time than others. Some need to be refrigerated, and others don't. You can find out more in such sources as:

* Basic cookbooks.
* State colleges of education.
* State agriculture departments.
* The Internet.

Search This

Feeding the Hungry

Most communities have special food kitchens set up to help feed hungry people who can't afford to buy their own food. Go online and find out about ways to help feed the hungry in your community. You might try looking in your local or state government sites that have lists of special programs. Also look for sites for local charities such as the Salvation Army or your church, synagogue, or mosque.

Preparing and Serving

How you prepare and serve food can have a big effect on food safety. This is especially true when handling food such as chicken, which is known to be frequently contaminated. Always pay special attention to sanitation when preparing chicken. Rinse chicken in cold water and pat it dry with paper towels before preparing. Don't cut chicken on wooden cutting boards or other porous surfaces that will be used to prepare other food. Use a plastic cutting board when you cut and handle chicken, and wash the board and your knife and hands in soap and hot water immediately afterwards.

Raw eggs can also contain harmful bacteria and require special handling. Follow the tips below to make sure that eggs are safe to eat:

* Check the date on the egg carton and buy the freshest eggs you can.
* Refrigerate fresh eggs immediately and use them promptly.
* Refrigerate cooked egg dishes within two hours.
* Cook eggs thoroughly—until both the white and the yolk are firm.
* Don't taste raw cake batter or cookie dough after eggs have been added.

How you cook food is also very important. Frying is the least healthy way to cook because it cooks food at high heat with added oils and fats, which you do not want in your diet.

It's important to cook meat thoroughly. Meat that is cooked at too high a temperature or for too long will become tough.

Cooking meat at lower temperatures maintains the moisture content and nutrients. Always check a cookbook to find recommended cooking times and temperatures for various cuts of meat.

It is especially important to cook ground beef thoroughly. Bacteria grow on the surface of meat, and since ground beef has a lot of exposed surface area, it is more likely to be infected. Never eat hamburgers that are red and raw in the middle. Chicken also must be cooked well to avoid salmonella poisoning.

In addition to cooking your meat thoroughly, be careful how you prepare it. Never use the same knife or cutting board to cut vegetables after they've been used for meat unless you wash them in hot, soapy water first.

In Public Places

Have you ever gone into a restaurant that didn't appear to be very clean? If the area of the restaurant you're sitting in doesn't look clean, you can imagine what the kitchen might be like.

Pay special attention when you're eating food that is prepared for the public. Because public eating establishments prepare so much food, they need to be especially sanitary and careful about how the food is handled. It's not like fixing food at home where there are only a few people, all of whom you know.

Public establishments feed a lot of people every day and the food is handled, prepared, and served by many employees. There are strict health department rules that require food service employees to wash their hands and observe other sanitary procedures.

Whenever you're eating out, look for places that are clean and well maintained.

Salad bars and buffets present special problems, because the food is sitting out where it can be handled by the public. There is no way to know if people who eat at these exposed counters have washed their hands to avoid spreading disease. Never eat at a salad bar or buffet that doesn't have a glass shield protecting the food from the people who are serving themselves. Also, avoid food that looks like it's been sitting out for a long time.

Food is one of life's absolute necessities, and eating is one of life's greatest pleasures. As a consumer, you will be making choices about how to spend your food dollars. Understanding the factors that influence your choices of what to eat will give you freedom to make good choices. Your family and culture, the advertising you are exposed to, your education, and your personal preferences all play a part. When you make plans for spending food dollars, you'll consider your budget, your preferences, and the knowledge you've gained about nutrition.

Smart consumers use strategies when they shop for food. You'll plan your meals and shop from a list. You'll carefully weigh the choices you face in a grocery store. You'll read labels to assure you get nutritional value for your food dollars.

When you get food home, you'll store it safely. You'll prepare it safely. You'll be aware of safety issues when you eat out.

Purchasing, storing, and preparing food are truly essential life skills. Choose food that promotes good health. Pay attention to how food is produced and prepared. Pick restaurants that provide good value and a pleasant atmosphere. Learn how to cook some of your own favorite dishes. Cooking food from scratch can be a wonderful way to spend your time, and it can also save you a great deal of money.

Bon appetite! Enjoy your meal!

Consumer Economics

anorexia nervosa—eating disorder characterized by an abnormal fear of being fat, avoidance of food, and extreme thinness. *p. 141*

binge-eating disorder—illness characterized by out-of-control eating. *p. 141*

bulimia—eating disorder characterized by eating a lot, then purging so that what was eaten won't be digested. *p. 141*

comfort food—food that makes you feel better because you associate it with positive memories of family life. *p. 138*

cuisine—French word that literally means kitchen, but is used to refer to a style of cooking and the food prepared in that style. *p. 138*

eating disorders—illnesses marked by an abnormal relationship with food. *p. 141*

Smart Shopping for Clothing

In this chapter, you will learn about:

- why we wear what we wear
- how to plan your wardrobe
- how to shop for clothes

Al-Malik looked in his closet, which was full of clothes. "I have nothing to wear!" he thought. His favorite shirt was dirty, and most of his clothes didn't fit him anymore. Besides, he just didn't feel like wearing most of them.

He took a bright red jacket out of the closet. "When I bought this jacket," he recalled, "I thought it was so cool. Now, I feel embarrassed when I wear it. I wish I had picked something else."

Although the jacket was in style when Al-Malik bought it, it was out of style now. The jacket turned out to be a fad, a style that is really popular for a short time but quickly becomes dated. Having a few trendy items in your wardrobe is fine, but Al-Malik's problem was that most of his clothes were so trendy when he bought them that they went out of date very quickly.

When building a wardrobe, it's wise to buy classics.

Why We Wear What We Wear

"Never judge a book by its cover," goes the old saying. But in fact, we judge people—fairly or unfairly—by their appearance all the time. How you look says a lot about your personality, attitude, occupation, and social status. **Four** factors influence why we wear the clothes we wear.

① Social and Cultural Factors

How you dress reveals a lot about you personally. Social and cultural factors influence your clothing choices. So, while you may think you dress in a style that is unique to you, the chances are very good that the world sees the groups you belong to when it looks at you. Some of these factors include:

* Age.
* Gender.
* Region.
* School or occupation.
* Friends and coworkers.

Next time you are in a public place, look around you. How much information can you figure out about the people you see based on what they are wearing?

Sometimes, schools, workplaces, and other organizations have formal dress codes. These organizations let their members know how to dress. Stores and other businesses sometimes display signs requiring customers to wear shoes and shirts. They are saying it's not appropriate to come in here dressed as if you were at the beach. If you want to be taken seriously, you wear clothing appropriate to the place and occasion.

Your family probably takes an interest in your appearance. That's because they know that what you wear will influence others. That influence will bring respect or disrespect. It may cause people to like you, or to make fun of you. They want you to be well received in the world. Your family is a major influence on you.

Making it REAL

Play Sherlock Holmes

Pretend you're the famous fictional detective Sherlock Holmes for a day. Pick a spot that's good for people watching, perhaps a seat in a public park, shopping mall, or school cafeteria, and watch the passersby. Pay attention to what people are wearing. Can you learn anything about them based on their appearance? Do you think it's right to judge people on what they're wearing?

❷ Advertising and Media Influences

Clothing manufacturers and retailers spend millions of dollars every year to influence what you wear. They change styles and colors frequently so consumers will feel the need to keep their wardrobes up-to-date. Clothing makers place ads in magazines and newspapers to influence fashion. Television shows, movies, and the music industry also influence what clothes are seen as trendy.

It's fun to see the new styles and to know what's the latest thing. But be aware that businesses are trying to get sales. They want you to believe that your old clothes are no good and you have to have new ones. That's where their profits come from. Don't let them "pull the wool over your eyes."

"Why have we come? Because only Earth offers the rock-bottom prices and wide selection of men's, women's, and children's clothing in the styles and sizes we're looking for."

❸ Affordability

What you can afford to spend on clothes is a major factor in how you dress. Still, no matter what your clothing budget, you can learn how to get the most for your money by being a smart clothes shopper.

You need to know the territory. What shopping options do you have in your community? Are there good second-hand stores? What about discount stores and factory outlets? Which stores carry the styles of clothes that you prefer? Which stores give you the best value for your money?

❹ Personal Style

Personal style is something that develops as you mature. For many, it begins in the grade-school years. It grows out of how you think and feel about yourself. Some common styles of dress include:

* Classic.
* Dramatic.
* Trendy.
* Sporty.
* Western.

Pay attention to how you want to look and start to consciously create your own personal style. Over time, you'll discover what colors, fabrics, and styles express your own unique personality.

Planning a Wardrobe

The smartest way to make decisions about clothing is to consider your entire wardrobe at one time. Your **wardrobe** is all of the clothing you own. It includes:

* Outerwear—coats and jackets.
* Underwear.
* Everyday clothes.
* Clothes for special occasions.
* Nightwear.
* Footwear—shoes, boots, slippers.
* Accessories—belts, hats, gloves, scarves, and jewelry.

It is a good idea to evaluate your wardrobe once a year. Then figure out what you need, and make a plan to get those things. You'll want to follow these **six** steps:

1. Take an inventory.
2. Get rid of clothes that no longer work for you.
3. List what you need.
4. Add items you would like to have.
5. Work with your budget.
6. Plan your purchases over a year.

Taking Inventory

An **inventory** is a detailed list of current goods, in this case your clothes, on hand. It tells you exactly what you have. It takes a little time to take an inventory, but it is worth it.

You will need to look everywhere that you have clothes. That could include:

* Your closet.
* Your dresser drawers.
* Coat closets.
* Laundry hamper.
* Basement or attic.

Make a List

You'll need paper or a notebook on which you put these headings:

* Coats and jackets.
* Tops—sweaters, shirts, blouses, T-shirts, sweatshirts.
* Bottoms—slacks, jeans, pants, skirts.
* Suits or dresses.
* Underwear.
* Nightwear.
* Active wear—running shorts, swimsuits, any clothes for sports activities.
* Shoes and boots.
* Special—evening gown, tux, holiday sweaters, anything worn only for special occasions.
* Belts, gloves, hats, purses.

Now, write down the clothing you have in each category. Next, consider each of the seasons, and where it matters, list it beside the item.

EXAMPLE: Blue coat—winter. Raincoat—all year round.

Evaluate Your Wardrobe

Have you grown taller in the past year so that most of your pants have turned into "flood pants"? Are you having a hard time buttoning that shirt or blouse? Did you suddenly discovered that purple is not your color? Are your socks full of holes?

How do you decide what to keep and what to toss? Some things are obvious, while others require some thought and judgment. Key to your evaluation are these **four** factors:

1. **Fit.** Does it still fit you?

2. **Condition.** Is it whole or full of holes? Can it be repaired? Is it bright or faded? Stained?

3. **Style**. Will you feel comfortable at school or work wearing it? Perhaps it was a mistake to have bought it, or it was just a fad that has now gone.

4. **Taste.** Your taste changes. Perhaps you liked something very much last year, but this year it's just not "you."

Get Rid of Some Clothes

Now go back to your list and cross off anything that you feel is too worn or really wrong for the way you live today. These are items you should get out of your wardrobe. You need the room for new clothes. Clothes need room to "breathe." They look better and last longer if they are not crushed in a too-tight closet.

Throw away anything that is badly worn, torn, or broken. If you won't wear it for those reasons, neither will anyone else. If it still has good wear in it, then you should let someone else wear it. You've got several options for disposing of clothing. You can:

* Swap clothes with friends.
* Sell them at a yard sale.
* Sell them to used clothing stores.
* Give them to family members.
* Give them to friends.
* Give them to charities.

Figuring out What You Need

Your inventory told you what you had. Your evaluation was the beginning of your discovery of what you need. Consider these things:

* *Basic needs,* like a winter coat or jacket.
* *Your life in the year ahead.* Will you be going to a new school or starting a job? Are you going to take up a new sport that requires certain clothing?
* *Your heart's desire*. Perhaps you just really want a certain something very badly. That's fine. You can find room for it if you plan carefully.
* *How clothes in your closet go together.* Do the colors and patterns of different items in your wardrobe work together?

Start with the Basics

The basis of your wardrobe will probably be a small collection of tops and bottoms that go together and a jacket to dress them up. Here are some tips:

* *Neutral colors.* When your pants or skirts and jacket are neutral, many different tops will go with them. Black, navy, brown, and taupe (a beige gray) are neutral. Pick one.

  EXAMPLE: Suppose you pick navy blue because you already have a good pair of navy slacks. Then, next time you need shoes, you'll get navy shoes. Soon, you'll look well put together.

* *Classic styles.* Some **classic** styles never go out of fashion. Trendy clothes look great in the season you buy them, but can look very old hat the next year.

* *Quality.* Buy the best clothes you can afford. It makes good sense to pay more for something that will last several years, or that is extra special, than to buy cheap clothes that don't hold up.

Build Outfits

Look at your list of the clothes you have that fit well and look good on you. How many different ways can you combine them?

EXAMPLE: If you have one skirt or pair of slacks that goes with three T-shirts, a pullover sweater, and also a shirt and jacket, you have five outfits—and one of them is more formal than the others.

Get Smart

Accessorize!

Using **accessories** creatively is an inexpensive way to personalize and expand your wardrobe. You might not be able to buy a new outfit for every special occasion that comes along, but if you have good basic pants, skirts, shirts, tops, and shoes, you can dress them up with the right accessories.

One or two really nice items such as a great jacket and a nice tie or a beautiful scarf can dress up less expensive basics such as black pants or skirts and simple shirts. Some clothing experts suggest that you spend 20 percent of your clothing budget on accessories.

Accessories include:

* Hats.
* Scarves.
* Ties.
* Belts.
* Jewelry.
* Hair ornaments, such as clips and ties.

See how it works? Follow these **three** steps:

1. List your outfits and the kinds of times you would wear them: every day, for dinner out, to a party or club, and so on.

2. Consider what's missing. Perhaps you don't have anything to wear if you get invited to a certain occasion. Perhaps you've got to have a new warm sweater before it gets any colder.

3. Plan to purchase items that will work with what you already have.

   EXAMPLE: Let's say you have a favorite pair of black slacks that is in good condition. You know that many things go well with black. Will you buy a brown sweater? Probably not. You would stay in the same color family, in this case black, charcoal, or gray. You might also jazz it up with a color or pattern you like.

Prioritize Your List

What clothing item is your greatest need? If your only pair of shoes is falling apart, then that is probably it. If winter is coming and your jacket is so old that six inches of arm stick out of the sleeve, that may be number one. Rank every new item you think you need or want. The list of new items you want to buy will now have a number beside each one, from 1, the most important, going up to the least important.

Work with Your Budget

The annual budget you worked out for yourself is your starting point. Remember, it has a figure in it for clothing. Let's just say that amount is $600. That's how much you'll have to spend for the whole year. You probably don't even have it all now. Your budget is expecting you to accumulate it at the rate of $50 a month. So you won't rush right out and spend $120 on the new shoes that you said were your highest priority. Neither will you go out and buy a new T-shirt you found on sale for $15—more T-shirts are way down on your list. You need that $15 toward the shoes. You'll need to wait until you have enough money for shoes. In the meantime, you'll do some serious shopping—but not any buying.

Shopping for Clothes

You don't have to buy something every time you go shopping. Smart shoppers look around a lot before they buy. Why? Because then when they decide to make their purchase, they know these **two** important things:

1. Where to find the item in a style they like.
2. How much they'll have to pay for it.

Smart shoppers don't stop the first time they discover where they can buy the clothes they like. They keep looking. Another store may have the same or a similar item for much less, or the same store may reduce the price on this item later in the season.

Also, by looking at lots of choices, you may find that your idea of how to meet the particular wardrobe need you're addressing has changed.

EXAMPLE: You think you can get one more outfit for knocking around on Saturdays by buying a pair of shorts. You look and look for the shorts you have in mind. The more you look, the more you see these jogging pants. They grow on you. You think it over, and decide you can meet this need for a casual outfit with the jogging pants instead of the shorts.

Fashion Considerations

How fashionable you want to be is up to you. If you want to follow fashion closely, there are a couple of things you should be aware of.

Store Brands vs. Designer Clothing

Many large **department stores** have their own special brand names. Clothing with their labels is sold only in their own stores. It is usually of a decent quality, because the store would not want to put its name on an inferior product. However, such stores also sell some "designer" labels alongside their own brands.

Designer clothes are created by well known fashion designers. Designer clothes almost always cost more than department store brands. Sometimes, it's because the clothes use high-quality fabrics and have a superior cut. Often, however, it's because the manufacturers spend a lot of money on marketing and merchandising.

If you like the look of designer clothes, look for them in special **discount stores**. Some shopping malls specialize entirely in discounted merchandise. You need to shop carefully in them, though, or you could get ripped off.

Here's where your smart shopping comes in. If you've done your shopping well, you know how much you'd have to pay for a certain style in a department store. So you'll know if the markdown indicated on the price tag is a real bargain or not.

Fad vs. Classic

Fads can be fun, but classic clothes are always in style. A **fad** is a fashion sensation that lasts for only a relatively short period of time—perhaps only a single season or a couple of years at most.

EXAMPLE: Low-rise jeans. It may seem daring to walk around in clothes that show off your bare skin. But in another year, these may look ridiculous and no one will be caught dead in them.

Classic clothes, on the other hand, are clothes that may still look good and feel right many years into the future.

Here are some clothes considered classic, or timeless:

* Black slacks.
* Skirts no shorter than just above the knee.
* White dress shirts and blouses.
* Navy blue blazers.
* Trench coats.
* Black lace-up shoes for men and pumps for women.

These items will be in style for a long time, and you can make them look up-to-date by changing the shirt or blouse you wear with them, or adding funky accessories.

Practical Considerations

Visual appearance isn't the only consideration when choosing clothes. There are practical considerations, too.

Durability and Longevity

Well made clothes that use good fabrics will last longer and provide better service than poorly constructed clothes made with cheap fabrics. **Durability** is determined by how well clothes are constructed, or sewn, and by the kind and quality of fabric used. Here are some tips for learning to recognize durability:

* Look at the labels in clothes you own that have lasted well. What are they made of?

* Look at the hems. You should not be able to see the threads of a hem on the outside of a garment. Also, if the hem is beginning to unravel while the item is still on the store rack, you know it will pull out about the second time you wear it.
* Check the buttons. Are they sewn on tightly, or are they already loose?
* Is the jacket, skirt, or pants lined? A lining makes a garment last a lot longer.
* Is the sweater starting to "pill" just from the wear of other people trying it on? Look carefully.
* Learn about fabrics and what to expect from them. Some are much more durable than others.

Get Smart

Look Before You Buy

Closely examine any item of clothing you're considering purchasing.

Before you buy clothes, follow this process:

* *Always check the seams* to make sure that the stitching is thorough and strong.
* *Check the fabric in seams* to be sure it is symmetrical and evenly matched.

* *Check threads at the ends of seams* to see that they are neatly clipped.
* *Pay special attention to high-wear areas* such as collars and underarms in shirts and jackets.
* *Check the crotch of pants* to look for complete and reinforced stitching.

Safety Issues

It's very important to choose clothes and shoes that are comfortable and safe. Pay attention to the following safety issues when you choose clothes:

* Children's pajamas should be made from fabrics that will not catch fire easily.
* Clothes that are too tight can impair circulation.
* Cotton is absorbent and can help draw moisture away from skin. It can help prevent infections and is a good choice for socks and underwear.
* If you've discovered that some dyes, perfumes, and materials cause you to have allergic reactions such as rashes, avoid them.

Fabric Selection

Fabric is fundamental. Good fabric is essential to good clothes. Fabric gives clothing its **texture** and its **drape**. *Texture* is how the fabric feels. It may be:

* **Soft.** Flannel is soft.
* **Rough.** Some wools are rough.
* **Smooth.** Satin and polished fabrics are smooth.
* **Nubby.** Some weaves have a bumpy texture.

Drape refers to how the fabric hangs on your body. The fabric can be:

* **Lightweight** and moves as you move.
* **Heavy.** It holds its shape well.

Natural Fibers

Natural fibers come from plant and animal sources. Many people prefer fabrics made with natural fibers because they allow your body to "breathe," and they feel good to the touch. The fabric's ability to breathe, or let air circulate around your body, helps to disperse moisture and provides greater comfort in both hot and cold weather than synthetic fibers do.

Natural fibers can require special care. Cotton shrinks in heat. If you wash cotton clothes in hot water or dry them with a high heat, you may not be able to wear them. For this reason, cotton is often mixed with another fabric. Cotton clothes may also need to be ironed more often than

Natural Fibers		
Fabric	**Source**	**Characteristics**
Cotton	Seed pod of cotton plant.	Soft, absorbent, versatile, easy to wash.
Wool	Sheep hair.	Durable, warm, variety of textures.
Silk	Created by silk worms.	Soft, smooth, lightweight, warm, fluid drape.
Linen	Flax plant.	Crisp, nubby texture, cool in warm weather, absorbent, dries quickly, wrinkles easily.
Leather	Animal skins.	Smooth, protective, rugged, wind-resistant.

some synthetics that can be dried and worn without ironing. Most wool clothes can be washed, but very carefully. They need cool water (because wool also shrinks) and gentle soaps. They need to be laid out flat to dry and gently pulled into their original shape. Silk is another natural fiber with wonderful qualities, but often it cannot even be hand washed. Many silks have to be dry-cleaned.

Synthetic Fibers

People who like **synthetic fibers**, or man-made fabrics, are often attracted by their ease of care and their lower cost. Many synthetics can be machine-washed and dried and can be ready to wear without any ironing. Usually, however, these fabrics don't "breathe" as well as natural fibers.

Synthetic Fibers	
Fiber	**Characteristics**
Acetate	Soft, silky, drapes well, wrinkle-resistant.
Acrylic	Similar to wool, not itchy, shiny, blends well with other fibers.
Nylon	Strong, silky, slippery, stretchable when knitted.
Polyester	Shiny, silky, wrinkle-resistant, warm.
Rayon	Silky, fluid texture, nice drape, versatile.

Natural and Synthetic Blends

Lots of clothes are made from blends of natural and synthetic fibers that aim to provide the best traits of both. These blends can reduce cost and compensate for some trait of the natural fiber.

EXAMPLE: Polyester blended with cotton makes the cotton more wrinkle resistant.

Generally, synthetic blends are more comfortable than 100 percent synthetics. Look for fabrics with a higher ratio of natural fibers—for example, 70 percent cotton to 30 percent polyester.

Color

Along with good construction and quality fabric, color is a major factor to consider when buying clothes. Obviously, everyone looks better in some colors than others. Your own personal coloring determines what colors work best for you.

EXAMPLE: People with darker skin and hair often look much better in bright colors than people with light skin and hair. Bright, vibrant colors may overwhelm and fade the lighter person. A darker person may look a bit dull in pastels, which would look good on someone with blond hair and blue eyes.

Experiment with colors. Ask your friends which colors they think look best on you.

Neutral colors such as black, gray, and navy provide a good foundation for your wardrobe. You can then use accessories in brighter and trendier colors to provide variety and style. Remember that some colors, such as bright ones like fuchsia, go in and out of style.

Fit

So, now you've found an item that's well made with good quality fabric. The color works well for you, too, but when you try it on, something isn't quite right. Clothes that don't fit properly look bad and are often uncomfortable.

Look for the following elements when judging the fit of clothes:

* Make sure jackets can be buttoned and still look and feel comfortable.
* Check that jackets have enough room in the shoulders. Having a tailor adjust the shoulders is expensive and very difficult—often impossible.
* Avoid jackets, sweaters, and shirts if the sleeves are too short. Conversely, long sleeves can be hemmed easily.
* When buying shirts, jackets, and coats, cross your arms in front of your chest to make sure there's enough fabric to prevent the garment from binding across your back.
* Make sure pants are long enough. You can hem pants if they're too long, but you can't fix pants that are too short.
* Look for pants that can be buttoned or zipped up comfortably.
* Remember to sit down when you try on pants or skirts, to make sure they aren't too tight or too short.

Cleaning and Care

The care required by different types of fabric is an important consideration when purchasing clothes. Clothes that can be washed and dried with minimal effort can be worn more regularly and still look good. Clothes that must be dry-cleaned continue to cost more money even after you have paid the initial purchase price. You may find that you won't often wear clothes that have to be hand-washed, because you aren't willing to put forth the extra time and effort to wash them by hand.

These days, most items of clothing come with a label that explains the best care for the garment. Often, care instructions are written in English and say things like "Wash in warm water. Tumble dry—low." However, because of international commerce, visual symbols have been developed to explain fabric care to people who speak many different languages. Five basic symbols make up the **International Textile Care Labeling Code**.

It's important to follow the care instructions on your garments. Treat your clothes well, and they'll last longer.

International Textile Care Labeling Codes		
Symbol	**Variations**	**Meaning**
Wash tub	With the number 40 inside.	Washing instructions—Wash in lukewarm water.
	With X through it.	Do not wash.
Triangle	With CL inside.	Bleaching instructions—Use chlorine bleach.
	With X through it.	Do not bleach.
Square	With three vertical lines inside.	Drying instructions—Drip dry.
	With circle inside.	Tumble dry.
Circle	With A inside.	Dry-cleaning instructions—Use any solvent.
	With X through it.	Do not dry clean.
Flat iron	With one dot inside.	Ironing instructions—Use cool iron (225° F).
	With two dots.	Use warm iron (300° F).
	With three dots.	Use hot iron (400° F).

Clothing Care Tips

"Wash with similar colors" is one of the most important instructions you'll ever read. If you've ever washed all your white clothes with a new, red T-shirt and ended up with an all-pink wardrobe, you know why. Here are some other laundry tips:

* Separate light and dark clothes and wash them in different loads.
* Delicate clothing, silk, and wool should be hand-washed using a gentle soap.
* Bright colors should be washed in cold water to prevent fading.
* Fabric softeners help prevent clothes from clinging due to static electricity.
* If you have sensitive skin, use laundry products without dyes or perfumes.

Where to Shop

If you want to get the most for your clothing dollar, you'll need to learn where to shop and how to recognize the best values when you find them. Where you shop for clothes makes a big difference in what kind of clothes you'll have to choose from.

Most communities in America today offer a wide range of possible places to shop for clothes. You need to know the territory. Survey the shopping places in your community. You'll be able to tell rather quickly which places appeal to you and which ones you never want to visit again.

You can buy clothes at the following places:

* Department stores.
* Discount stores.
* Specialty stores.
* Catalogs and online stores.
* Factory outlet stores.
* Used clothing stores.

The **markup** on clothes varies greatly, depending on where you shop. Markup refers to the additional cost that wholesalers and retailers tack onto what it cost to manufacture the clothes.

What if you find a great winter coat at a department store? If the coat costs $100, that probably means that the store paid about $40 for it. The store's markup on that coat is $60, or in this case, 60 percent. The manufacturer took about $20 in profit over what it cost to make the coat. The fabric may have cost only $5, and labor was $15. Now, you may feel that you don't want to pay $60 over wholesale to buy that coat.

What are your options? Let's consider the advantages and disadvantages of the different places to shop.

Types of Stores

Type of Store	Advantages	Disadvantages
Department stores	* Wide variety of items available. * Wide variety of brands and styles available.	Big markup on clothes, up to 60 percent.
Discount stores	Lower prices than department stores.	Often lower quality.
Specialty stores	Carry a wide variety of a specific type of item.	Don't offer especially good prices.
Catalog and online stores	Shopping from home.	* Can't touch or try on the clothes before buying. * Shipping time and cost.
Factory outlet stores	Prices often low because the manufacturer is selling its own clothes.	Products may have defects or didn't sell well in retail stores.
Used clothing stores	* Frequent shoppers may find great deals. * Proceeds often benefit charities.	* Clothing may be in poor condition. * Selection varies greatly from day to day.

Vintage Clothes

Used, or "vintage," clothing shops, like thrift stores and consignment shops, can be great resources if you're trying to stretch your clothing budget. Look here for items such as:

* business suits
* winter coats and jackets
* formalwear
* purses, scarves, and hats
* designer clothing

The Price of Jeans

How much can you pay for a pair of jeans? Jeans have become very prestigious items in some quarters during the past 20 to 30 years.

American jeans are very popular in Europe and some other parts of the world. Interestingly, European-made jeans fetch pretty high prices in the United States.

Go online and see if you can find out how much you can pay for a pair of jeans. What's the most you can pay? What is the least you can pay?

Buying Grooming Aids

Clothes aren't the only products you buy to enhance your appearance. There are also cosmetics and grooming aids.

Cosmetics include all the various kinds of products that you use on your face, skin, and nails, including creams and lotions and makeup, such as lipstick, eye liner, and nail polish. Americans spend about $30 billion (yes, billion with a B) a year on cosmetics.

Grooming aids are items that help you keep clean and neat. Examples include: combs, hair brushes, hand soap, shampoo, scissors for nails and hair, razors, and shaving cream.

Determining Your Needs

What's your look? Are you the neat and natural type? Are you more into mystery and high drama? If you basically want to look clean and well groomed, a good bar of soap, some shampoo, deodorant, toothpaste, and a decent haircut will meet your needs. If you're going for a more dramatic look, you'll require more supplies and funds.

Skincare is one of the most fundamental aspects of grooming, and cosmetic companies make a lot of claims about how their products can improve your skin. Their creams and cleansers will make your skin "softer, smoother, younger, firmer, brighter, and clearer." Most of these claims are, of course, not true. Most lotions and creams contain very similar ingredients, but the prices for these items vary greatly. You can save a lot of money by understanding the truth about cosmetics.

Getting the Most for Your Money

The major factor in the pricing of cosmetic items has to do with packaging and promotion. Both of these factors cost money—and that cost is passed on to you, the consumer. Never assume that more expensive is better when it comes to buying cosmetics. Learn what to look for when purchasing cosmetics.

Read the long lists of chemical ingredients in different cosmetic lines. You'll find that they are much the same. The major difference in many cosmetics is the smell. Different companies add different scents to their products. Find low-cost products that smell good to you, and don't be fooled by fancy packaging or outrageous claims.

Chapter 9 Wrap-up
SMART SHOPPING FOR CLOTHING

Your clothes tell the rest of the world about you. Your family, your friends, and other social factors affect your clothing choices. So too do advertising, affordability, and your personal style. When making clothing decisions, consider your wardrobe as a whole. Take an inventory of your clothes, evaluate what you have, and figure out what you need. Work within your budget.

Shop before you buy. Consider fashion, but remember that some clothing fashions come and go. Choose classic clothes that will stay in style for years. Consider also such practical things as durability and longevity.

Clothing involves many choices. Learn about fabrics and how they wear. Understand what colors suit you best. Consider how you will have to take care of an item before you buy it. Shop where you'll get the most for your money.

Finally, grooming aids and cosmetics have a place in your budget. Investigate ingredients and know what you're paying for.

Consumer Economics

accessories—small items of clothing or jewelry that add personal style to your clothes. *p. 161*

classic—traditional or timeless. *p. 161*

cosmetics—products aimed at beautifying the face or body. *p. 172*

department stores—stores that sell merchandise in different departments according to type, such as sportswear, shoes, or ties. *p. 163*

discount stores—stores that offer merchandise at reduced prices. *p. 163*

drape—manner in which a fabric hangs on your body. *p. 166*

durability—ability to withstand wear and tear; sturdiness. *p. 165*

fad—style of clothing that comes and goes very quickly. *p. 164*

grooming aids—products aimed at cleaning the face or body or making them neat. *p. 172*

International Textile Care Labeling Code—code of visual symbols that explains how to care for clothes. *p. 169*

inventory—detailed list of current goods on hand. *p. 159*

markup—amount added to the cost of an item to figure its selling price. *p. 171*

natural fibers—threads made from plants or animal hair. *p. 166*

synthetic fibers—man-made fibers. Most are made from petroleum-based chemicals, or petrochemicals. *p. 167*

texture—appearance and feel of a surface. *p. 166*

wardrobe—all the clothes you own and wear, considered as a group. *p. 159*

Smart Shopping for Entertainment

In this chapter you will learn about:

- **developing your lifestyle**
- **planning entertainment purchases**
- **making wise vacation and travel decisions**

Jenna is trying to decide what to do with her spring break coming up. She's lucky in that she has a lot of invitations from people who want to spend time with her. Jenna's friends want her to go to an amusement park with them. Her sister thinks it would be fun to go out to the movies every night of spring break. Her boyfriend would like to take some cycling day trips with Jenna. Her grandmother would like to take her to the symphony one evening.

She's considering all these options. But she is also tempted just to stay home and relax, take a few bubble baths, watch a couple of old movies, and read a novel. Perhaps planning nothing at all would be the most relaxing vacation.

Whether you prefer crowds or country roads, cozy quiet evenings or late-night bashes, there are millions of ways to have fun. One of the most important ingredients of happiness is knowing what you enjoy doing and doing it!

Developing Your Lifestyle

Everyone wants to have fun! It's very important to be able to follow your interests and enjoy time with friends. Dashing off to a movie with a friend or deciding to go with friends to the beach for the weekend sounds great—especially after a hard week of work or studying. Having fun, however, does take some planning just like anything else for which you spend time and money. It's important to make entertainment choices consciously with your interests, time, and budget in mind.

In order to make smart entertainment shopping decisions, it will help to keep in mind the following:

* Know yourself.
* Know your budget.
* Know your options.

If you spend some time understanding the basics of entertainment shopping, you will end up doing things you really enjoy, with people you like, and without a bad case of budget blues after the fun is over!

Lifestyle Preferences

It probably isn't often that you've sat down and tried to define or describe your own lifestyle. You can turn on the television and view programs that describe the lifestyles of the rich and famous, but what about your own? Your lifestyle preferences include the choices you make about the following areas:

* Hobbies and interests.
* Use of private time.
* Vacation and travel.
* Health and fitness.
* Religious preference and activities.
* Stress-reducing activities.
* Self-improvement activities.

Entertainment preferences can overlap and fall into many of the areas above.

EXAMPLES: You may choose to reduce stress by mountain biking with friends several times a week because you love being outdoors and doing physical activity. If music is your highest interest, then your lifestyle might include monthly concert tickets rather than new video games. If you don't enjoy long-distance travel, then, as a lifestyle choice, it's likely you will plan vacations close to home.

My Notebook

What I Like to Do

To help you identify your personal lifestyle, take a quick survey of your current interests and entertainment preferences. Ask yourself the following personal choice questions—and add a few of your own. Write down your answers.

* Would I rather go on a hike or raft down a river?
* Would I rather read a book or see a movie?
* Would I rather exercise on a treadmill or take a fitness class?
* Would I rather go to a huge party or share pizza at home with some friends?
* Would I rather play cards or play softball?
* Would I rather do a crossword puzzle or work in the garden?

* Would I rather go window-shopping or take a walk on a nature trail?
* Would I rather exercise or watch a video?
* Would I rather go to a gym or go for a run?
* Would I rather play a team sport, such as basketball or soccer, or go for a long walk by myself?
* Would I rather sit and talk with a friend or hang out with a crowd at a coffee shop?
* Would I rather ride a horse or walk a dog?
* Would I rather buy a music CD or a magazine?
* Would I rather go to a rock concert or a basketball game?

Write some thoughts about how the answers to these questions might affect the entertainment choices you make.

Budget Limits

Entertainment choices rely on time and resources. You may have plenty of time to see a movie each weekend but your budget doesn't include enough money for tickets, popcorn, and soda each week. Check that your activity choices, time availability, and budget realities line up. Until you add financial resources to the picture, it will be difficult to develop a plan for your free-time entertainment and to shop wisely.

Entertainment Plan

Having fun shouldn't require a detailed action plan. But it is important to sit down and develop a plan for how you want to spend your free time and your precious few entertainment dollars. Both time and money are valuable resources. A plan will help you make choices based on your strongest interests, make sure you make time for those interests, and ensure that you can keep within your budget.

As you develop your plan, ask yourself the following **four** questions:

1. **What are my top three entertainment preferences** for my free time?
2. **Am I following my interests** or spending too much time on things I don't care about?
3. **How much time do my interests require** each day? week? month?
4. **Do I have sufficient funds** in my budget to follow these interests?

Community Work

Lee S., a recent college graduate in Salt Lake City, Utah, decided to use his free time to give something back to his community. In a newspaper, he read about the **Special Olympics** (an athletic competition held for people with physical and mental challenges) and signed on to help at the event held on the university campus.

You may not think of volunteer work as entertainment, but Lee found that his volunteer experiences helping children with their athletic events was entertainment with a plus. It was fun, it was heartwarming, it didn't hurt his budget, and it made a difference to very special young people.

Enjoying Yourself

Don't assume that because you are on a limited budget, you can't enjoy yourself. You can still make entertainment purchases, plan vacations, and even travel. You just have to shop wisely and keep your budget in mind.

From CDs to Concerts

The trick to buying entertainment products is to plan each purchase carefully. There is such a wide variety of choices on the market, it is tempting to buy on an impulse. All the choices sound like fun.

Before making an entertainment purchase, ask yourself the following questions:

* Do I really need to buy this right now?
* Is this a budgeted purchase or an impulsive purchase?
* Is there a less expensive alternative?
* Can I buy it used?
* What will I have to give up in order to buy this?

Search This

CD Shopping Online

Like many entertainment costs, the prices of CDs can vary widely. Use the Internet to find some bargains.

Think of five CDs you'd like to buy, and search for them on the Web. Do some sites offer them for less? Is one CD more expensive at one site while another CD is less expensive? What's the lowest price you can find?

* Will it last so I'll get long-term enjoyment from it?
* Is it is something I can enjoy with friends?

Think about your lifestyle to determine if this purchase really fits your interests.

Often, entertainment choices involve a trade-off. You know you'd love to go to a concert that costs $60 to $80 for a ticket. With closer consideration, you realize that you'd rather have new running shoes to enter a race coming up soon.

Saving Money on Entertainment	
Entertainment Purchase	**Lower Cost Options**
Music CD	Buy used or discounted titles or check out a library copy.
Concert Tickets	Take advantage of free concerts available in your community. If you must pay for concert tickets, go to less expensive weekday or afternoon performances.
Videos or DVDs	Rent videos instead of buying them. In addition to video stores, most local libraries have movie videos to check out at no or low cost. Trade movies with friends.
Movie Tickets	Instead of going to a newly released movie on a weekend night, select budget movie theaters or go to matinees. Don't buy tickets on the phone or online because you'll pay extra fees.
Performing Arts Tickets	Book ahead and go to matinees. The best deal of all is to volunteer as an usher and see the performance for free.
Sports Events	Professional sporting events are the most expensive. Minor league and college games are less expensive, as are women's professional events.
Computer Games	Check out online shareware games on web sites. Consider the non-tech board game versions.

Vacations and Travel

The trick to planning a vacation is to plan ahead. Early planning will help you develop a vacation that fits your budget. Regardless of budget, it will also enable you to have the time to get the best reservations and the features you want. The Internet provides a wealth of information, but reading all of it to make an excellent vacation plan takes time.

Planning ahead also gives you time to save up funds for the trip. Remember that last-minute travel almost always comes with a higher price tag.

If you need help planning your vacation, you may want to contact a **travel agent**. Travel agents are experts who can help you design a vacation that suits your particular needs. While most travel agents don't charge for their services because they receive a commission from the services they sell, be sure to ask your agent about fees before you consult with him or her.

You may find that a vacation package is your best choice. Packages usually offer transportation, accommodations, meals, and tours at one flat rate. Not all packages are money savers, however. Be sure you investigate all the options before deciding on a particular package.

The following are general guidelines for budget-conscious travel:

Transportation

There are almost as many ways to lower the costs of transportation as there are vacation alternatives. Here are some options to consider:

* Train and bus travel are, on average, about 30 percent cheaper than air travel. If you have time, take advantage of the savings.
* If you're going to fly, do so during **off-peak times** and days—when fewer people are flying and fares are cheaper. Off-peak times are on Tuesdays, Wednesdays, and Thursdays. Business travelers dominate and raise the rates on weekday mornings. Consider staying over a Saturday to take advantage of lower fares.
* Pick airports that are close to your destination but smaller and less crowded. Instead of Los Angeles International, try Long Beach. Instead of Chicago's O'Hare, try the city's Midway Airport.
* Always make reservations more than 14 days before your departure date.
* Comparison shop using travel agent price quotes, online ticket promotions, and airline reservation clerks price statements.

* Take advantage of frequent flyer mileage programs to earn free tickets and upgrades.
* Book flights that are close to full. Arrive at the airport in plenty of time, and let the ticketing agent know you would be willing to be bumped if the flight is overbooked. Being bumped can earn you a free ticket and other bonuses.
* Check out all student discount travel packages. There are many resources online that focus on low-cost travel for students and young adults.
* Plan a four- to seven-day **cruise** on a ship. Cruising is one of the best vacation options available. Cruise costs include food, entertainment, lodging— everything in one blanket price.
* If traveling abroad (outside one's country), investigate the low-cost Eurail or Rail and Drive packages.

Get Smart

Ask Away

When booking a flight, always ask these questions:

* Would it be cheaper if I flew at a different time or on a different day?
* Do you know any special fares that could save me money?
* Do you offer a student discount?

Road Trips

Traveling by car can be cheaper than other modes of travel. The money saved will depend on the condition of your car, how far you are traveling, and your time constraints. A car-camping trip can be very affordable because it covers both transportation and lodging. Even for a short driving vacation, don't forget the following:

* Make sure your car has been thoroughly serviced.
* Pack a roadside emergency kit with flashlight, flares, and jumper cables.
* Assemble a first-aid kit, which should include bandages, gauze, tape, band-aids, disinfectant, and pain relievers, such as aspirin.
* Pack lunches and snacks in a cooler in the car rather than pay high-cost convenience store and fast-food prices.

Lodging

There are many ways to lower the costs of **lodging** (rented rooms for temporary housing). Here are some ways to spare your budget:

* Consider staying with friends or family.
* Consider camping: A tent is the cheapest option.
* If you can't afford luxury, go for the budget motel corporate chains. Make sure they have an AAA or Mobil Travel Guides stamp of approval to guarantee safety and cleanliness standards. Call the specific motel directly instead of the corporate chain's 800 number to get a lower rate.
* Never use a hotel's phone service if you have a phone card or cell phone option. Make sure you know the hotel's system of phone fees before you decide to use it.
* Investigate **youth hostels** (low-cost hotels, often with big shared rooms for young adults traveling on low budgets) both within the United States and abroad.
* Consider trading living space with a friend or family member in another part of the country you would like to visit.
* Scour magazines, read from online budget travel centers, and get tips from friends to find affordable lodging.
* Check local colleges in the area you plan to visit to see if they rent empty dorm rooms during the summer.

Vacations at Home

What do visitors to your area do? Be a tourist in your home town.

* Take day trips to local places of interest.
* Read the information your community provides to tourists.
* Check out the activities listed in the weekend section of your newspaper.

Taking a vacation close to home can be easy on your budget and still be fun. What do you consider a vacation?

* A night on the town?
* A day-long getaway?
* A day at an amusement park?
* A day going to museums?
* An overnight stay in a lovely hotel?
* A chance to stay in bed and read all day?
* An overnight slumber party with your best friends?
* An overnight camping trip in a local state park?

Your vacation close to home might include a variety of things you love to do. Because expensive travel costs are eliminated, you will likely have money to spend for a higher-quality local vacation experience. Treat a vacation close to home like any other vacation. Research various options that match your interests, time available, and funds.

Your Life

Vacation at Home

Doesn't a vacation mean getting away from it all? Think about what you could do if you stayed home but only did your favorite things instead of work and chores. Here are some suggestions for planning a wonderful housebound vacation.

* Have friends over.
* Play board games or cards.
* Make pizza from scratch.
* Rent your favorite movie videos.
* Buy or check out a stack of magazines and books for vacation reading.
* Turn your bathroom into a spa with bath and shower extras.
* Take the phone off the hook.
* Work on an art or hobby project for which you never have time.
* Use your imagination!

Entertaining Friends

Friendship involves having fun together. Sometimes, as a friend, you should take the lead in entertaining. You can entertain your friends informally in a variety of ways, from unexpected pizza parties at your house to hiking on a local trail.

Making Friends

There are people who seem to have a wealth of friends, and there are others who are more comfortable with just a few close friends. People have individual needs and styles of making and developing friendships.

It is easiest to make friends when you meet people while doing things that you enjoy. It is likely you will have shared interests to start a conversation and see where it takes you. But you can also make friends anywhere if you have an interest and willingness to interact and initiate a conversation. Making friends requires putting yourself out there.

Sometimes you meet a person and you feel like instant friends. Other times, a friendship is slow to form. A close friendship is usually built over time on warmth and caring. It is based on shared values and interests.

Being with a good friend feels like being at home. You can take your shoes off. You can be yourself. You can relax in the comfort of the friendship, and it works both ways. Friendship relies on a shared positive and giving relationship.

Keeping Friends

Keeping a friendship requires attention and time. There is a difference between a casual friend and a close friend. Close friendships require more of you. You will have to make your friendship a priority and be conscious of doing the following things for the sake of a valuable friendship.

* **Make time.** Good friendship is built on attention, not neglect. Keep in touch frequently and set aside time to do things you enjoy together.
* **Listen.** Being a good listener is essential for maintaining friendships. Sometimes just listening without giving advice is all that is necessary.
* **Show respect.** Share your feelings honestly and also respect your friend's point of view. It isn't always necessary to agree on everything to be good friends.
* **Be trustworthy.** Do not betray a friend's trust. Lack of trust can ruin even the best friendship.
* **Offer support.** Let your friend know that in any way possible, you will provide him or her with support and assistance. You will be there when it counts.
* **Celebrate successes.** Celebrate with friends when they experience success. Admire achievements rather than feeling or showing resentment.

* **Handle conflict.** Even in the best of friendships, conflicts can arise. Talk out problems by expressing how you feel rather than making accusations and assigning blame. Take the initiative in making up.
* **Be flexible.** A long-term friendship changes over time just like anything else. Roll with the changes and identify ways to keep the relationship strong in spite of change.
* **Be thoughtful.** Friendships require thoughtfulness. Giving gifts, sending cards, and doing favors are all part of attending to an important friendship. Showing up to help your friend clean the house before a party is a thoughtful gift of time.

Setting Limits

Sometimes it's necessary to set limits with friends to keep the friendship strong. Setting limits in certain areas will avoid conflicts if the limits are clear and consistent. It's important to remember and make clear to your friends that setting limits is not the same as rejection. If you limit financial loans to friends to a certain amount and stick to it, you are supporting the friendship but not going over your comfort level. Doing more than you can reasonably offer can breed resentment, not friendship.

Coworkers

Usually it's better to have casual friends at work rather than intimate close friends. With our closest friends, we want to share our work experiences from our own point of view away from the office. Close friends working together can too easily get caught up in work-related conflicts and politics. The friendship can evolve into a constant dialogue about work, and the other important values and interests you share get lost.

If you meet someone at work and you want to develop a closer friendship, it's important to start doing things together that build on interests outside the work world. A work-based significant friendship requires careful dialogue about loyalty and limits in order to keep the friendship strong.

Making it REAL

The Dinner Party

Imagine you are throwing a party for your friends. What kind of an evening do you want to give your friends?

* Do you want a potluck dinner or picnic for 20 people?
* Or would you prefer a more formal sit-down dinner for six?
* Maybe you'd rather have a big bash with music and snacks but not a full meal?
* Perhaps you have your heart set on a different kind of party.

As you try to decide which type of event to throw, think about how your decision will affect the cost of the evening. Also, think about what the evening will say about the kind of friend you are.

Ways to Enjoy Friends Using Little or No Money

When you are with good friends, simple things can be fun. Just sitting around hanging out together can be great. It's easy to get into the habit of equating fun with things that cost money. Check out the following ways you can have fun without hurting your wallet:

* Go to a free concert in the park.
* Pack a picnic lunch and find a lovely spot for it.
* Watch a sporting event or movie on TV.
* Take a walk or go on a run together.
* Have a potluck dinner at home.
* Play cards or board games you already own.
* Go to local-area tourist or historic sites you've never visited.
* Hike on a local trail.
* Bike to another friend's house.
* Volunteer in a community service project.
* Try the lost art of conversation!
* Tell a progressive story—everyone gets a chance to add to the action.
* Read a one-act play, with people taking the various roles, or have your own poetry night.
* Attend a free lecture.
* Play cards.
* Play charades.
* Have a **progressive dinner** with a different course at each friend's house.
* Listen to music. Have a CD-trading party.
* Play instruments and make music together.

My Notebook

Group Activities

For one month, write down everything you do with your friends. This log will help you discover what you and your friends like to do together.

Ask yourself if these are really your favorite activities, or if you are just in the habit of doing the same things.

Do these activities fit your budget, or are you over-extending yourself to keep up?

What other activities would you like to do with your friends?

Community Newspapers

One of the best ways to find free and low-cost entertainment choices is to read your local newspaper. Most communities have not only a primary newspaper (at least one), but also smaller events- and arts-based publications that come out weekly.

Collect several newspapers on Friday and read through them, making a list of everything of interest that is free or of minimal cost.

Progressive Dinner

A progressive dinner, in which each course is served in a different house in the neighborhood, can be a fun and inexpensive way to entertain a large group. Nobody has to produce an entire meal, just one course.

In Dummerston, Vermont, one neighborhood has an annual progressive dinner in December to celebrate the winter holidays.

Each of the following courses is served at a different home:

* Appetizers.
* Salad.
* Soup.
* Main course.
* Dessert.

The main course is usually cooked by more than one family. Another family volunteers to place lighted candles in paper bags weighted with sand along the road and up the driveways. It's a beautiful effect that doesn't cost a lot. Each year, the neighbors rotate, so nobody has to do the same task two years in a row.

Shopping wisely for entertainment involves a personal understanding of several factors. You need to know what you most like to do in your free time. Prioritizing your entertainment preferences is the first step in matching your lifestyle with your interests, free time available, and budget.

You also need to look carefully at how you manage your time to ensure that you make time for fun, relaxation, and fitness. Your entertainment activities should allow for time alone and time with close friends.

Shopping for entertainment products and travel requires planning ahead and planning wisely. Use research and creativity to identify bargains and entertainment opportunities that cost nothing at all.

Consumer Economics

cruise—vacation onboard a large ship. Cruise costs include food, entertainment, and lodging in one blanket price. *p. 181*

lodging—temporary place to live or stay; rented room or rooms. *p. 182*

off-peak times—times of day, days of the week, and seasons when fewer people are flying or vacationing and airfares and hotels are cheaper. *p. 181*

progressive dinner—meal that is served in courses at different people's homes. *p. 187*

Special Olympics—athletic competition held for young people with physical and mental challenges. *p. 178*

travel agent—professional who helps tourists make travel plans and who makes their reservations and purchases tickets. *p. 180*

youth hostel—low-cost hotel, often with big shared rooms, for young adults traveling on low budgets. *p. 182*

Smart Shopping for Health and Fitness

In this chapter, you will learn about:

- planning for a healthy lifestyle
- getting appropriate health care
- paying for health care

Last week, Greta and her family moved her grandfather to a nursing home because his health was very poor. He was overweight and had trouble breathing, in part because he had smoked cigarettes his entire adult life. The doctors were very worried about his blood pressure. It just wasn't safe for him to live on his own anymore.

Greta knows that a lot of health problems run in families, and she's scared that she will end up like her grandfather when she's old. Her friend Miguel says the problem is that her grandfather never took good care of himself. Now his body has worn out after all those years of neglect. Miguel says the human body is like a machine. Just like a car, the body needs to be taken care of properly. Miguel certainly knows a lot about cars. He has restored several beat-up old cars that run beautifully now, and they look good too!

Lifelong Health

While factors beyond your control, such as your genes and your environment, play a large role in your overall health, factors within your control do, too. Does it surprise you to know that avoiding certain behaviors can improve your odds of being healthy and active your whole life, even in old age?

Dr. Lester Breslow, a healthy, active physician in his seventies, should know. He has been studying what makes people healthy for more than three decades. He's followed thousands of people for years and looked at which ones remained healthy as they aged. The more habits people had from the list below, the more likely they were to die young or become disabled as they aged.

Dr. Breslow's Seven Bad Health Habits

1. Being physically inactive.
2. Being overweight.
3. Smoking.
4. Drinking too much alcohol.
5. Skipping breakfast.
6. Sleeping more or less than seven to eight hours a night.
7. Eating between meals.

If you think of your body as a machine, as Miguel does, it looks like there really are some pretty simple things you can do to keep your body running well, right into old age.

When you're young, it's hard to imagine a time when you'll be older and your body won't work well. However, you can simply look around at many elderly people to see how a lifetime of poor habits can mean an early death or years of living with health problems and pain.

Yet, much of this suffering can be avoided. The habits you develop now can mean the difference between a long, healthy, active life or a life of illness and restricted activities.

Keeping Fit

Research shows that being fit improves your overall health and sense of well-being. Here are just a few of the benefits of being fit:

* Helps you achieve and maintain a healthy weight.
* Increases your energy level.
* Reduces the incidence of depression and anxiety.
* Improves self-esteem and confidence.
* Helps reduce blood pressure or maintain a healthy level.
* Helps build and maintain healthy bones, muscles, and joints.
* Reduces the risk of heart disease, diabetes, and colon cancer.
* Recent research shows it probably revs up brain power or, in other words, makes you smarter!

What does it take to be fit? It's possible to reap fitness benefits from as little as 30 minutes of moderate exercise a day. A brisk walk, dancing, washing windows, or biking to school can all provide fitness benefits.

There are **three** parts of a well-rounded fitness program:

1. **Aerobic exercise**—such as running, walking, swimming, or biking—that improves the ability of your heart and blood vessels to deliver oxygen to your cells and organs.
2. Exercise that strengthens your muscles and builds bone density, such as weight lifting.
3. Exercise that increases your flexibility through stretching or practicing yoga.

Building a Fitness Plan

Whether you are 15 years old or 50, you need to stay fit to maintain your health. The question is not whether to exercise but how, when, and at what cost. Your exercise plan should be based on resources available, your lifestyle, and personal interests.

Physical Factors

Basing your fitness program on a single interest, such as playing basketball, is not enough. Evaluate your fitness choices based on their aerobic, strengthening, and flexibility potential.

Matching Fitness Activities to Your Budget

Not all fitness choices are equal—at least not where budget is concerned. You may be passionately interested in kick-boxing and spinning, but your budget may not accommodate the health club membership and class fees these activities require. Fitness and sports activities vary widely in cost depending on the following **four** items:

1. **Equipment.** Make a list of three fitness activities that you enjoy or would like to try. For each, develop a list of the new equipment you would need to buy to participate.
2. **Clothing.** Think carefully about the clothing and gear requirements and how often they will need to be replaced.
3. **Location.** If your fitness activity of choice requires driving, the cost of gas and auto wear and tear need to be factored in.
4. **Special Fees.** If you own the equipment, the clothing, and have transportation costs under control, the final thing to consider is special fee costs.

In the world of fitness activities, there are lower-cost and higher-cost choices. Sometimes a particular fitness interest can have both a high-cost and a low-cost choice. Biking can be of physical benefit whether on a street bike on a neighborhood route, on a high-cost mountain bike on wilderness trails, or in a health club spin class. To make your fitness choices, consider a broad range of cost options.

Free Ways to Stay Fit

For some reason, when we have a problem, the first solutions we think of usually cost money. That's because throwing money at a problem feels like the easiest route to take. However, with creativity and common sense, a problem like keeping fit without a big budget can be solved without using any money (not even gas money). Consider the following ways that you can stay fit that cost little or no money.

* Take a power walk in the neighborhood.
* Go for a run.
* Jump rope.
* Work in the garden.
* Watch a fitness program on TV and join in.
* Go up and down stairs (forget elevators).
* Take your dog for a jog.
* Dance to your favorite music.
* Clean the house and do 20 jumping jacks every five minutes.
* Ride a bike everywhere you go.

My Notebook

Exercise Log

Plan to exercise and track your fitness activities in an exercise log. Each day, make a note of whether you followed through on your planned exercise for the day. If you did, make a note about how you feel as a result. If you didn't, make a note about why.

In addition to your planned exercise, jot down all your unplanned exercise for the day. Did you go rollerblading Saturday afternoon? Did you help wash windows on Sunday or rake the yard? All these activities provide aerobic exercise and should be counted since they contribute to your fitness level.

Avoiding Addictions

Americans have relatively easy access to legal and illegal substances that can impair their judgment and damage their health. As a young adult, you need to be aware of what these substances are and how they can affect your health now and as you age. Some substances, such as alcohol, might not damage your health if used responsibly when you're an adult. Others, such as tobacco, can cause cancer and other diseases even when used in small amounts.

In addition, many of these substances are **addictive**. In these cases, quitting can be very difficult. Often it requires professional help, and even then, might not be successful.

Drugs

When you first hear the word "drugs," you might think only of illegal drugs. In fact, each of the following types of drugs needs to be handled cautiously:

* Over-the-counter medications, such as aspirin.
* Prescription drugs.
* Illegal drugs.

Over-the-counter medications can be purchased without a prescription. However, this does not mean that they don't have health risks or are not addictive. Read the ingredients carefully and talk with your doctor or the pharmacist where you purchase them if you have any questions.

A prescription drug is one that is given to you by a doctor for a specific purpose. Pharmacists fill the prescription according to the doctor's instructions. Some prescription drugs, such as pain killers, can be very addictive. It is important to follow the physician's instructions carefully when taking prescription medications, and make sure they are used only by the person for whom they were intended.

An added danger of prescription drugs is that they can interact with other drugs or alcohol. This can make them much more dangerous than when they are taken on their own.

Illegal drugs can be very dangerous for **four** main reasons:

1. **They can have serious side effects,** such as organ damage.

2. **Many, such as cocaine and heroin, are highly addictive.**

3. **They might not really be what they are described to be.**

4. **It can be very difficult to control the amount taken.** Some batches might be weaker or stronger, so they cannot be measured accurately like prescription medications.

Many young people and sports and entertainment celebrities have died from taking illegal drugs. Others have spent years in and out of recovery programs trying to overcome an addiction that got started out of curiosity. One fact is definite: The only sure way to avoid the problems associated with drug use is to avoid taking them in the first place.

Alcohol

Alcohol produces serious health risks and is very addictive. Yet drinking it is portrayed in our culture as a common, socially acceptable activity. Early use and abuse of alcohol are associated with many problems. Financial, social, and health problems can begin as soon as someone's judgment and daily functioning are impaired by frequent alcohol use.

EXAMPLE: Four hundred teenagers are injured *daily* in alcohol-related car accidents. Eleven of them die.

And the problems only get worse. Long-term abuse of alcohol is associated with:

* *Brain damage.*
* *Liver damage.*
* *Heart disease.*
* *Malnutrition.*
* *Stomach, colon, and liver cancer.*

In addition, alcohol use is associated with the use of other drugs, particularly tobacco, a known **carcinogen** (cancer-causing agent).

Alcohol affects unborn children. When pregnant women drink, their babies can be born with **fetal alcohol syndrome**, a combination of conditions that includes:

* Low birth weight, which is associated with illness and poor growth and development.
* Low brain weight, which is associated with development and cognitive (thinking) problems.
* Learning disabilities.

Fighting Peer Pressure

The pressure to conform to others like yourself, or **peer pressure**, often leads people, particularly teens, to make choices they might otherwise not make. Here are **seven** tips that can help you resist peer pressure:

1. **Consider the consequences of your actions.**

2. **Ask yourself what decision you would make if you had a choice,** and remember that you do have a choice.

3. **Don't believe that "everyone is doing it."**

4. **When you are asked to do something that makes you uncomfortable, don't be afraid to say no.**

5. **Avoid situations in which you'll be asked to do something that makes you uncomfortable.**

6. **Look for friends who share your values and who will exert *positive* peer pressure**—the kind that helps you make good choices.

7. **Don't pressure others to do things that make them uncomfortable.**

Tobacco

In the U.S., tobacco-related illnesses cause a death every 13 seconds, and kill nearly 418,000 Americans per year. If you don't want to be one of those statistics, your best bet is to stay away from cigarettes as a teenager. Why? Because 90 percent of smokers begin as teenagers.

As addictive as heroin, tobacco kills four times the number of people who die annually from all the other drugs, car accidents, suicides, homicides, and AIDS combined!

In addition to causing cancer, lung disease, and heart disease as you age, tobacco also makes your teeth and nails yellow, causes wrinkles, and decreases sexual ability and fertility in women. Does this sound like the future you want? Furthermore, young adults who use smokeless tobacco can look forward to the possibility of getting cancer of the mouth, cheek, gums, and throat while still in their teen years.

Smoking is expensive and destructive. The best strategy is never to start. However, if you do start and then quit, there is a bright spot. As soon as you stop smoking, your chances of getting cancer or having other smoking-related problems go down. They continue to go down as long as you remain a nonsmoker.

As **cardiologists** (doctors who specialize in the heart) will tell you, if you smoke, quitting smoking is the most important thing you can do to improve your health.

How to Stop

If you smoke and now realize it was a bad choice, there is help. First, visit your doctor and tell him or her that you want to stop smoking. He or she will be able to give you advice and refer you to a smoking cessation program. (*Cessation* means to cease or stop something.) Often, your doctor will also recommend or prescribe devices to reduce your craving for cigarettes, like chewing gum that includes nicotine or skin patches that release nicotine into your system slowly.

Obtaining Health Care

Good health and dental care are important components of living a full, healthy life. If you are fit, manage your weight well, avoid too much **stress**, and avoid substance abuse, you can reduce your need for health care. Still, you will want to get regular check-ups and have access to health care when you become ill or injured.

As you become an independent adult, you will be choosing health-care providers.

Health-Care Options

There are many types of health care to choose from. There are many more medications, treatments, and procedures available. On the one hand, the range of choices and treatments means many diseases and conditions can be treated effectively. On the other hand, it means that you, as a health-care consumer, must take responsibility for being informed.

Standard Medicine

Standard medicine in the United States focuses on diseases or abnormal conditions and treats those conditions specifically. Medication and surgery are common treatments. Physicians specialize in a particular field, such as orthopedics (the treatment of the skeletal system) or neurology (the treatment of the nervous system).

Standard medicine offers many effective options for **diagnosis**—the identification of an illness through tests and examination, or in other words, figuring out what is wrong—and treatment of all kinds of medical conditions. Technologies such as laser surgery improve the quality of millions of lives a year. Medications such as antibiotics and vaccines have made many deadly diseases a thing of the past.

In addition, traditional medicine's focus on research and scientific data helps prevent many diseases. **Preventive medicine** saves lives by stopping diseases from developing in the first place.
EXAMPLE: Many doctors prescribe a baby aspirin a day to help prevent their older patients from having heart attacks.

Alternative Medicine

While standard medicine offers many health-care benefits, some consumers and health-care practitioners look to **alternative medicine** to meet their health-care needs. Alternative medicine includes:

* Chiropractic treatment.
* Acupuncture.
* Relaxation treatment.
* Vitamin treatment.
* Herbal treatment.

About one-third of all Americans use some form of alternative medicine. Many standard medical practitioners see value in some alternative practices and incorporate them into their practice.

Holistic Medicine

Holistic medicine is the practice of looking at all aspects of a person's life in treating disease. In holistic medicine, a person's diet, stress level, exercise habits, and attitudes are all considered as factors in treating disease and maintaining health. This approach is based on the belief that the mind and body affect each other, and that a person's health can be improved by taking this into account. Examples of this approach in action include:

* The use of relaxation techniques for people in chronic pain.
* Diet and exercise programs for people with heart disease.

Avoiding Quackery

Medical **quackery** is the use of an ineffective or unproven treatment by people who are not trained medical professionals. Unfortunately, people who suffer from a disease or debilitating condition are vulnerable to untruthful claims. They may have received standard medical treatment without improvement and are desperate for a cure or improvement in their condition.

The Food and Drug Administration defines medical quackery or fraud as the promotion, for profit, of a medical remedy known to be false or unproven. However, sometimes a person who promotes a false cure believes it really works. Is this person a quack? To complicate matters more, not all unproven treatments are quackery. **EXAMPLE:** Legitimate medical researchers conduct studies with unproven treatments to determine if they are effective.

If quackery is not clearly defined, how can you protect against it? Here are some things to look for:

* You're told the cure is secret but very effective.
* The person you deal with has credentials that you've never seen or heard of before.
* The treatment claims to cure many conditions or diseases.
* Anecdotes and testimonials—not scientific facts—are used to support the claims of success.

If you have questions or are considering trying some kind of treatment, check it out:

* Ask your doctor if he or she recommends it.
* Check with the Department of Health in your state government.
* Click on http://www.hhs.gov/ to see what the U.S. Department of Health and Human Services suggests.

Exercising Your Options

When you make choices among the various health-care options, you will want to:

* Research thoroughly. Use the library and the Internet. Read widely about the health issue you face.
* Get recommendations from trustworthy individuals.
* Use only licensed health-care practitioners.
* Ask for references.

Health Care Providers

Most health care falls under one of the following **two** categories:

1. **Routine Care:** visits to family or general practitioners for regular check-ups and minor ailments or injuries such as colds and sprains.
2. **Specialized Care:** visits to specialists such as internists, gynecologists, neurologists, surgeons, physical therapists, mental-health therapists, and those who perform diagnostic tests.

Primary Care Physicians

A **primary care physician**, often called a PCP, is a general or family physician who serves as your main doctor and coordinates all of your care. He or she provides all your routine care and some specialized care. If you develop a serious illness or have a serious injury, your PCP will refer you to a specialist.

Since this is the doctor you will turn to first, it is important to select the right one. Ask friends, family members, and coworkers if they can recommend someone. Your local medical society can also give you the names of doctors.

In the Doctor's Office

Before a visit with a doctor, write down on a piece of paper any questions you have and take it with you. It's easy to forget everything you wanted to ask once you're in the doctor's office.

Choosing Your Doctors

Here are some questions to ask about any physicians you're considering using:

* Are they board certified?
* Will care be covered by your insurance plan?
* How long will you have to wait to get in to see them?
* Are they affiliated with area hospitals? Which ones?

Once you've seen someone, make sure you feel that:

* You can communicate easily with him or her.
* You were treated respectfully.
* Staff were helpful and courteous.

Keep in mind also that you need to take responsibility for your health care. Always communicate clearly to your doctor, ask questions about anything you don't understand, and follow your physician's advice for treatment.

Specialists

Most of the time, your PCP will be able to handle your health-care needs. But when you are seriously ill or injured, it is necessary to see a medical **specialist**. Specialists have received additional training beyond that required to become a medical doctor. When you have a serious condition, it is a good idea to see two specialists. This allows you to get a second opinion to compare what two highly trained physicians say about your condition.

Medical Specialties

Area of Specialty	Specialist	What The Specialist Does
Cardiology	Cardiologist	Treats heart and blood vessel symptoms and diseases.
Dermatology	Dermatologist	Treats skin diseases and conditions.
Family Practice	Family Practitioner	Treats routine and some specialized conditions of children and adults.
Gynecology	Gynecologist	Treats female reproductive system disorders.
Immunology	Immunologist	Treats disorders of the immune system (including allergies and asthma).
Internal Medicine	Internist	Treats chronic, complicated diseases.
Neurology	Neurologist	Treats disorders of the nervous system, including the brain and spinal cord.
Obstetrics	Obstetrician	Supervises the care of pregnant women and delivers babies.
Oncology	Oncologist	Treats cancer.
Orthopedics	Orthopedist	Treats injuries or disorders of the skeletal system.
Pediatrics	Pediatrician	Monitors the healthy development of infants and children and treats childhood diseases.
Radiology	Radiologist	Uses specialized equipment—x-rays, sonar, magnetic imaging—to help diagnose diseases, treats some diseases with radiation therapy.
Surgery	Surgeon	Treats injury, deformity, or disease by physical manipulation or adjustment of the affected area, often involving the cutting and reattachment of body tissues. Most surgeons further specialize in an area, such as bones and joints (orthopedics).

Mental Health

Mental health and drug- and alcohol-abuse treatments play an important role in our society's health care. Modern life is complex and stressful. As a result, many people turn to therapists for help in dealing with difficult life circumstances and daily stresses. This is not something to be ashamed of. Seeking help can often make the difference between leading a full, happy life and experiencing depression or anxiety.

Seeking treatment for drug and alcohol abuse is also not something to be ashamed of. It takes courage to admit that a problem exists. In addition, current treatments provide a great deal of hope for people with addictions.

Treatment can be either of **two** kinds:

* Outpatient.
* Residential.

In outpatient care, you see a therapist, or attend group sessions, on a daily or weekly basis. During that time, you continue to live on your own and carry on with your regular life.

In residential treatment, you live in a hospital or other care facility for a certain amount of time. During that time, you are involved in an intensive daily treatment program. After residential treatment, you usually continue treatment in an outpatient program on a weekly or daily basis for a period of time.

Hospitals

In some situations, you may be required to go to a hospital or specialized medical facility for treatment or diagnostic tests. Hospitals are the most common facilities. They offer both in-patient care (when you stay in the hospital overnight) and outpatient care. For example, in a hospital, you might:

* Go for several hours to get a diagnostic test, such as an x-ray.
* Spend a day in outpatient or short-stay surgery.
* Be required to spend several days or longer for major surgery.
* Go to the emergency room for a critical or life-threatening injury or condition.

Hospitals should be accredited with the Joint Commission on Accreditation of Healthcare Organizations. In addition, the more experience the hospital you choose has with your procedure or treatment, the better.

If you are seeking unusual care, try to find a facility with much experience in that area. Research shows that the more experience a medical facility has in a particular area, the higher the success rate. Some magazines publish reports that rate hospitals. Check them out.

Outpatient facilities include such things as urgent-care centers, physical therapy clinics, and pain treatment centers. As with all other health-care facilities, it is important to verify that the facility is accredited and the people who practice there are licensed or certified.

Time for the Emergency Room?

Dr. Gary Young, medical director of an emergency room in a mid-sized Oregon college town, sees many young people who come into the emergency room when they shouldn't. Emergency rooms are not set up for routine medical problems. You should see your primary care physician for those. But if it's the middle of the night and all of a sudden you have chest pains, what should you do?

Dr. Young says deciding whether to use the emergency room or not depends on the situation. What kind of problem are you having, and what is your age and medical condition?

Dr. Young recommends first contacting your primary care physician. If it is not during regular hours, an on-call doctor will be available. If you don't have a primary care physician, he recommends getting one.

In addition, many cities now have urgent-care centers that are open 24 hours a day and are much less expensive than emergency rooms. Some communities and health insurance programs have a 24-hour line you can call to get advice from nurses about your symptoms.

Even though many people use the emergency room when they shouldn't, there *are* times when it is appropriate. In fact, there is a law in every state that says people with one of the following conditions must be treated if they come to an emergency room:

* Severe bleeding.
* Severe pain.
* Life-threatening symptoms.
* Labor.

Knowing this, what would you do if:

* You broke your arm, the bone is sticking out, and you're bleeding? *If you said go to the emergency room, you're right.*
* You tripped and now your ankle is very swollen? The pain is pretty bad. *If you said go to an urgent-care facility, good answer!*
* You felt nauseated all day, and now you're vomiting? If you're vomiting continuously, you could become dangerously dehydrated quickly. *Go to an urgent-care facility immediately, or an emergency room if an urgent-care facility is not available.* If you are vomiting occasionally, *contact your primary care physician or go to an urgent-care facility.*
* Your friend fell off a ladder and now acts confused and says his head feels as if it is going to blow up? *If you said go to an emergency room, good answer!* Your friend could be in shock, or have a hemorrhage, both of which can be life-threatening.

Dental Care

Preventive dental care plays an important role in a good personal health-care plan. A dentist who practices general dentistry can provide preventive care, fill cavities, and do restorative work, like crowns. (Crowns are permanent gold or porcelain caps placed over the tooth to prevent cracked teeth from breaking apart.)

Preventive care includes check-ups and regular cleanings. Brushing and flossing daily, and getting your teeth cleaned twice a year can help you avoid more costly dental care.

EXAMPLE: If you don't clean your teeth properly, you can develop gum, or periodontal, disease. This is an infection of the gum that requires treatment by a gum specialist, called a periodontist.

Just as there are specialists in the practice of medicine, there are also dental specialists. These include:

* Periodontists (specialize in diseases of the gums).
* Orthodontists (specialize in straightening teeth).
* Oral surgeons (specialize in removing teeth and other mouth surgery).

As with all health-care providers, it is important that you receive your dental care from licensed or certified practitioners.

Paying for Health Care

For decades now, the cost of health care has risen faster than any other essential living expense.

The Spiraling Cost of Care

Americans spend more than $1.2 trillion a year on health care. In the early 1990s, the figure was a little over $900 million. This trend of increasing health-care costs will undoubtedly continue. Why? First, people are living longer and receiving more health care during their lifetimes. In addition, diagnosis and treatment options are increasing and becoming more technologically sophisticated.

Insurance Coverage

With rising health-care costs, many people find it difficult or impossible to pay for the health-care services they need. This is especially true if you face a major illness, such as cancer. That's where **health insurance** comes in.

As with all insurance, you exchange a fixed payment for protection against the heavy costs of uncertain events. Insurance comes from the word *insure,* which means "to make safe or secure." With health insurance, you pay a certain amount, the insurance **premium**, in exchange for a guarantee of payment for health-care services described in the plan. Your health-care needs are secured.

Here's how it works. Many people pay premiums into one big pot, out of which the insurance company pays the costs it has agreed to pick up. Some people need very little health care. Others need more. As a result, the amount in the pot is enough to cover everyone's expenses. The insurance company makes its profit in **two** ways:

1. Premiums are a bit higher than the company's actual expenses.
2. Money taken in is invested and earns a return before it is paid out for medical expenses.

The second way is by far the largest source of insurance-company income.

Within this health-care insurance system, there are **three** main types of health insurance plans.

❶ HMO Plans

Within a **health maintenance organization (HMO)** are all the services you are expected to need, both to maintain good health and to receive treatment for illnesses and injuries. HMOs are **managed-care plans**. They manage, or control, your use of health-care services. Your doctor—your PCP—coordinates your access to services.

EXAMPLE: If you need a specialist, you must see your doctor and get a referral to one in the organization. If you go to a doctor without a referral, the HMO will not cover any of the cost of your care.

This approach allows the insurance company to control costs in **three** ways:

1. **One doctor is responsible for all your care.** He or she becomes familiar with you and can work with you to prevent and manage illness.
2. **Expensive procedures are not performed unnecessarily.** Plan doctors are discouraged from ordering expensive tests without good reasons.
3. **The insurance company must approve any nonroutine care** that your doctor orders.

In an HMO, you pay only a small fixed amount for visits, your **co-pay**, not a percentage of overall costs. So families with young children, who make frequent visits to the doctor, often choose HMOs.

2 PPO Plans

PPO stands for **preferred provider organization**. A PPO is a network of health-care providers approved by the insurance company. A PPO network includes primary care physicians, specialists, hospitals, and other facilities.

Generally, a PPO includes many more doctors and hospitals than an HMO. You have more choices. When you use providers in the network, you get the maximum amount of insurance coverage under your plan. Often, unlike in an HMO, you can see providers who are not in the plan and still get some insurance coverage.

In most PPO plans, there is an amount, called your **deductible**, that you must pay each year before the insurance company begins to pay. After that, you will continue to pay a percentage of the costs (often 20 percent) up to a maximum. It could be $1,000. After that, the insurance company will pay all insured costs. For people seeking protection from the costs of catastrophic illness, such as cancer, a PPO is a likely choice.

3 POS Plans

POS stands for **point of service**. This means your costs are determined by who provides the service. It is a plan that combines the way HMO and PPO plans work.

* Each time your care is coordinated by your doctor, the insurance company will pay the maximum amount.
* You can see someone who is on the preferred provider list without a referral from your PCP, but you will get a smaller amount of coverage.
* If you choose to see someone who is not on the preferred provider list, you will get an even smaller amount of coverage, perhaps nothing.

This approach gives you flexibility, but you pay more when you take advantage of it.

Maintaining Coverage

Once you get coverage, it is important to keep it because:

* Insurance companies usually refuse to cover conditions you had before you became insured with them. This is called a **pre-existing condition** exclusion. Asthma, diabetes, heart disease—all can be excluded from coverage when you get a new insurance provider.
* If you have a serious illness or injury, it can be difficult or impossible to find an insurance company who will sell you health insurance.

Rates for Individual Health Policies

The idea behind insurance coverage is that risks are spread across a diverse group of people. Some people have no or very few claims and some have a lot. It's all supposed to average out, and rates should stay low.

Unfortunately, insurance companies have a practice for individual health policies (not group policies) that prevents this from happening. Their premiums become more disproportionately high for people the longer they stay in the plan. What are insurance companies doing to cause this?

1. People are placed in a group when they first sign up, and the group is fixed. It never gets any new members.
2. As group members get older and have more claims, the premiums for that group go up.
3. Younger and healthier people in the group drop out, looking for lower premiums.
4. The sicker people remain in the group, and their premiums go up even more because there are more claims.

The result is that people who need insurance the most can afford it the least because the premiums are so high. Ultimately, they can't afford it at all.

Many people can afford health insurance only when it is provided as part of a job. More than 42 million people have no health-insurance coverage at all. Some of them feel they are healthy and don't need it, but most of these people are uninsured because they don't belong to a group—like a work group—that provides insurance. They can't afford to purchase individual health insurance. This is a serious issue facing our country.

"This patient has a rare form of medical insurance."

Shopping for Health Insurance

Dan Beltran has been an insurance agent for 15 years. He specializes in health insurance, and he has **five** useful tips for young adults looking for health insurance:

1. **Consider a short-term policy.** If you're just out of high school or college and you anticipate getting a job with health coverage, a short-term policy may be advisable. The premiums for short-term coverage are lower than regular policies, so you'll be covered but won't have to pay as much.

2. **Evaluate your health status.** Are you healthy? Do you rarely go to the doctor? Can you build up a good health-care savings account? Then a policy with a higher deductible and lower premium might be a good choice for you.

3. **Evaluate how often you visit a doctor.** Do you make frequent visits for routine care from a family or general practitioner? Do you have young children—or do you plan to start a family in the near future? If so, an HMO with co-pays and no deductible might be the right choice for you.

4. **Comparison shop for good premium prices.** Talk with an insurance agent. Get premium quotes on the Web. Be sure to carefully compare the coverage offered for each premium. If one premium looks much lower than others, check it out carefully. That policy might not cover as much as the other policies do.

5. **Check on the rating of the insurance company.** Before signing up, review Standard & Poor's and A.M. Best publications. Your public librarian can help you find these publications.

There are some federal laws that help:

* ***COBRA.*** This law guarantees anyone who leaves a job the right to continue the health-insurance plan for 18 months. However, now you must pay the whole premium—the part you've been paying plus the part your employer has paid.

* ***Insurance portability.*** If you don't have gaps in your health-insurance coverage, a new company can't exclude pre-existing conditions. When you end insurance coverage with one company, ask for a "certificate of creditable coverage" to show your new insurance company.

Prescription Drug Coverage

Coverage for prescription drugs is often included in a standard health-insurance plan. Depending on the type of plan (HMO, PPO, or POS), you will pay a fixed amount, such as $15, or a percentage of the bill.

If you don't have health coverage through an employer, you can save money on premiums by using a plan that does not cover medications. However, if you need prescription drugs, you will pay 100 percent of the cost. You need to evaluate your individual situation to decide what is appropriate.

One way to save money on prescriptions is always to ask for **generic brands**. These are non brand-name medications that have the same ingredients and properties as brand-name medications, but they cost less. It is also important to purchase all your prescriptions at the same **pharmacy**.

A **pharmacist** is specially trained to understand how drugs work before he or she dispenses prescription medications based on a physician's prescription order. When you have all of your prescriptions filled by the same pharmacy, the pharmacist can keep track of any medications you take to make sure they are not dangerous when taken with each other. When getting a new prescription from a doctor, be sure to mention any other medications you are already taking.

Catastrophic Coverage

Catastrophic coverage is coverage that pays for a medical situation that is very serious and expensive. This catastrophe might be a terrible car accident or cancer.

There are **two** kinds of catastrophic coverage:

1. Coverage that pays for costs at the point your regular plan runs out. This is usually a high number, $750,000 or $1 million. However, if you have a serious accident or get a disease like cancer, medical costs could go this high.

2. Coverage that takes over after you've paid a certain, fairly high amount of money.

If you don't have regular health insurance, consider a catastrophic plan. The premiums are low, and you have protection against the very worst situations.

Government Health Insurance Programs

Program	Sponsored by	Description	Issues
Medicare	Federal government.	A basic medical insurance program, paid for with payroll tax deductions, that covers: * People 65 or over. * Older adults who have certain qualifying disabilities but may not be 65.	* Coverage is very basic, so many older people purchase additional insurance called "medigap" insurance. * You may need to deal with Medicare when you are still young to help an aging parent receive appropriate benefits.
Medicaid	Federal and state governments.	A program that provides medical care for people who are: * Low-income. * Disabled.	* Helps people who cannot afford health insurance. * Offers a safety net if you fall on difficult times.
Workers' Compensation	State governments.	A program, paid for by employers, that helps cover the cost of on-the-job injuries. It covers: * All medical expenses. * Partial salary until you can work again. * Cash benefits for survivors in the case of a death.	A potentially work-related illness or injury must be reported immediately. If it is not, you may not be able to prove it was work-related. As a result, you may not be eligible for benefits.

Out-of-Pocket Expenses

As you can see, there are many ways that individuals are helped with the high cost of medical care. However, if you use health-care services, you will always have some expenses to pay yourself. These expenses are called **out-of-pocket expenses**. Your out-of-pocket expenses are all amounts you pay toward your own health care in addition to the premium you pay for health-care insurance. Such expenses include a deductible and co-pay amounts.

Noncovered Expenses

Health insurance never covers all medical expenses. It doesn't cover nonprescription medications. It may not cover eyeglasses.

It probably won't cover "elective" surgery, such as cosmetic surgery, that you want to have. You should read your plan carefully, to see what kinds of treatment are excluded. For noncovered expenses you must pay 100 percent of the cost yourself.

Limited Coverage

Many kinds of health-care coverage are limited. There may be a cap on how much a plan will contribute to the cost of certain kinds of medical care. Often, psychiatric treatments are limited to only a certain number of visits within a fixed time, and then payment is provided at a lower percentage than for other services.

By the Numbers

The Cost of Medical Care

There are many different kinds of health-care costs, from routine care and specialized treatments, to diagnostic tests, prescription drugs, and insurance premiums and co-pays. How much can you really expect to pay once you're out on your own or starting your own family?

To find out, interview a family about their health-care costs over a period of several months. Don't forget to ask about insurance premiums, co-pays, deductibles, and over-the counter medications in addition to direct expenses for health care.

From that information, find an average monthly amount. Next, develop a monthly health-care budget that would allow you to meet those expenses.

Self-Insurance

Self-insurance means that you choose not to carry health insurance. In this case, you take on all the risk of paying 100 percent of all your medical bills. Very wealthy people who have enough money to cover their own medical bills are probably the only people who can afford to be self-insured.

Chapter 11 Wrap-up

SMART SHOPPING FOR HEALTH AND FITNESS

Leading a healthy lifestyle pays off. It reduces your medical expenses and protects you from chronic illness and pain as you age. Research shows maintaining a healthy lifestyle is not complicated. In fact, it can be as easy as getting adequate exercise (as little as 30 minutes a day!), managing your weight and stress levels, eating and sleeping regularly, and avoiding tobacco, drugs, and excessive alcohol.

Even though a healthy lifestyle can protect you from medical problems, it is still necessary to receive good preventive medical care, like medical check-ups and dental cleanings. It is also necessary to have a way to pay for these expenses, and expenses for illnesses or injuries.

Medical insurance is the most common way to receive help in covering health-care costs. There are many options and issues to consider when purchasing insurance. For this reason, it is important to know about different types of insurance. It is also important to understand how to utilize the benefits properly, once you have chosen a plan.

Consumer Economics

addictive—causing an uncontrollable need and dependence on a substance; habit-forming. *p. 193*

aerobic exercise—form of exercise that improves oxygen delivery to the cells and organs. *p. 192*

alternative medicine—nonstandard medical practices, including chiropractic and acupuncture treatments. *p. 197*

carcinogen—cancer-causing agent. *p. 194*

cardiologist—doctor who specializes in the heart. *p. 195*

catastrophic coverage—health-insurance coverage that pays for expenses incurred when a serious and expensive medical situation occurs. *p. 208*

COBRA—federal law guaranteeing employees the right to continue with employer-sponsored health coverage for up to 18 months after leaving a job. *p. 207*

co-pay—in some insurance plans, amount paid every time you receive care. *p. 204*

deductible—annual amount you must pay before the insurance company pays anything. *p. 205*

diagnosis—identification of an illness through tests and examinations. *p. 196*

fetal alcohol syndrome—combination of conditions that babies suffer as the result of alcohol their mothers consumed during pregnancy. *p. 194*

generic brands—non brand-name medications that have the same ingredients and properties as brand-name medications but are less expensive. *p. 208*

health insurance—program that guarantees payment for certain health-care costs to individuals or group members. *p. 204*

health maintenance organization (HMO)—type of insurance plan that manages all of your health care in exchange for a fixed amount of money. *p. 204*

holistic medicine—medical practice of looking at all aspects of a person's life in treating disease. *p. 197*

managed-care plans—health-care plans that use a primary care physician to coordinate, or manage, individuals' care. *p. 204*

out-of-pocket expenses—amounts an individual pays toward his or her own health-care expenses in addition to the premium. These include co-pays and deductibles. *p. 210*

peer pressure—compelling influence of others like yourself. *p. 195*

pharmacist—specialist who dispenses prescription medications based on a physician's prescription order. *p. 208*

pharmacy—store where prescriptions are filled; drugstore. *p. 208*

point of service (POS)—medical plan in which costs are determined by who provides the service. *p. 205*

pre-existing condition—health condition you had before seeking coverage from or becoming insured with an insurance company. *p. 205*

preferred provider organization (PPO)—group of health-care providers who are approved by an insurance company to provide health care to people insured by the company. *p. 205*

premium—amount paid for insurance. *p. 204*

preventive medicine—medical care designed to prevent illness from occurring. *p. 197*

primary care physician (PCP)—general or family physician who serves as your main doctor and coordinates all your care. *p. 198*

quackery—ineffective, unproven, or fraudulent medical treatment provided by people who have not been trained to give medical advice. *p. 197*

specialist—physician who has received training in a particular branch of medicine beyond that required to become a medical doctor. *p. 199*

stress—pressure or strain. Humans seem to need some stress, but extreme pressure or difficulty causes our systems to fail. *p. 196*

CHAPTER 12

Smart Shopping on the Internet

In this chapter, you will learn about:

- **buying over the Internet**
- **protecting your privacy on the Internet**
- **using the Internet to comparison shop**

Brandon wanted to send a birthday present to his older brother Josh, who was attending a college in a different state. Josh was taking a French class, and Brandon thought he might like some books about France. "Why not use the Internet?" asked a friend, who pointed out that it would be fast and convenient to order some books online and have them shipped directly to Josh at school. Brandon went online to a bookstore recommended by his friend. The site was easy to use, and Brandon quickly selected two books about France for his older brother.

Josh received the books on his birthday, and he was delighted with them. Brandon was very pleased with his Internet purchase . . . until a few days later, when unexpected e-mail messages began to appear on the family's home computer. One message sold expensive apartments in Paris. Another promoted companies that rented cars in France. Brandon was annoyed by the unwanted e-mail messages. He didn't know that when he bought the books for his brother, he should have checked off the box saying, "Please don't reuse or resell my personal information." Internet shopping is great, but as with any other kind of shopping, you need to know how to go about it.

Why Shop Online?

How would you like to get locked in a room for a week with nothing but a credit card (with no credit limit) and a computer connected to the Internet? If your experience turned out to be anything like that of people who have really done that as an experiment, you wouldn't have any trouble getting everything you needed to survive and then some. You could order a phone in a matter of hours, and you'd probably have clothes and bedding the next day. By the end of the week you'd be living it up, surrounded by every imaginable product.

Despite its rapid growth, shopping online remains only a very small part of the $3 trillion annual retail market in the United States. Of this huge amount of money, less than two percent is spent online. Electronic commerce, or **e-commerce**, in which business transactions occur online, has become a significant way of selling some types of products. By 2000, almost one-fifth of all computer hardware and software was sold via e-commerce, and one out of ten books sold was purchased via the Internet.

Advantages of Online Shopping

The advantages of shopping online include:

* Convenience.
* Choice.
* Cost.

Convenience

In contrast to traditional **"brick-and-mortar" stores** that have physical locations, such as your local department store or discount store, Internet sites are open 24 hours a day, 7 days a week, 365 days per year. You can shop at an Internet site while wearing your pajamas or listening to your favorite music. When you order a gift for someone via the Internet, you don't have to wrap it or stand in line at the post office to mail it. The web site handles those services for you.

Mail order and catalogue merchants offer many of the conveniences of Internet shopping, but not all its advantages. On the Internet, you can shop at sites located around the world and be notified within seconds when a sale occurs.

Physical safety is also part of the convenience of online shopping. You don't have to drive your car on slippery or crowded roads. You don't have to walk through dimly lit parking lots. Nor do you have to worry about pickpockets or other criminals you might encounter in brick-and-mortar stores—although there are online criminals to watch out for.

Choice

In addition to convenience, the Internet greatly expands your choices. The whole world becomes your shopping mall when you search for items on the Internet. The expanded number of "stores" provided by the Internet is especially helpful to people living in small communities with a limited number of retailers.

Even if you live in a big city with lots of different stores, what if you are looking for a CD by an obscure group or a clothing item in an unusual style, color, or size? The stores in your city may not carry the precise item you want, but the Internet likely will.

The Internet is particularly useful for people who like to collect rare items. Imagine that you collect old comic books. At some point, you may have bought all the comic books in your neighborhood. On the Internet, you could get in touch with collectors located around the world.

Cost

Shopping on the Internet can also save you money. Fierce competition on the Web often results in low prices.

There are web sites that help you locate the best deals among Internet stores, among online auctions, and even among some of the stores in your neighborhood. You can print discount coupons from web sites. Often, you can avoid paying sales tax on an Internet purchase. When buying an expensive item, this can be a big savings.

Last-minute sales are perhaps one of the most impressive ways to save money on the Internet.

EXAMPLE: Consumers can take advantage of last-minute sales of airline seats, hotel rooms, rental cars, or any other item that must be sold by a given date.

The travel industry is full of products that aren't sold out, such as seats on planes that aren't full. Airlines, railroads, and resorts sell such products on the Web at a discount. Thus, travel companies can sell something that otherwise wouldn't have sold at all, and consumers get great bargains.

To get the best travel bargains on the Web, you need to be flexible. If you're willing to be flexible about when you travel, your exact destination, and the hotel you'll stay at, the Internet can offer inexpensive travel options.

You don't have to buy a product on the Internet to get the advantages of using the Internet. You can simply use it as a tool in the buying process.

EXAMPLES: You can find out the amount an automobile dealer pays for a particular car and use this information when you are in the showroom negotiating a price.

Also, you can search for the least expensive or most convenient flight between two cities and then buy the ticket via the phone or at a travel agency.

Or, you can use the Internet to find out which television, camera, or computer is best for your needs and then buy it at a local store.

What Kind of Internet Shopper?

Some people love shopping on the Internet. They can't get over the ease, speed, and convenience of it. Other people are petrified of shopping online. They fear that their credit card number will be stolen, their privacy invaded, or their money taken by a company that doesn't really exist.

If you have tried Internet shopping, what are your feelings about it?

* Were the benefits as great as you expected?
* What about the dangers?
* Were any of your fears justified?

If you haven't done any shopping on the Internet, give it a try. You don't have to actually buy anything. Just pretend. At each step of the process, jot down your reactions or questions.

Disadvantages of Online Shopping

With all the potential benefits of buying online, why doesn't everyone with a computer and a credit card do it? Most of the reasons why people choose not to shop online have to do with:

* Preferences for the traditional, offline shopping experience.
* Resistance to paying shipping charges.
* Uncertainty about the safety of sending credit card information over the Internet.
* Concerns about delivery, returns, and how to handle problems if they occur.

Preferences

If one advantage of e-commerce is being able to shop while wearing your pajamas, a disadvantage is that when buying a pair of pajamas, you can't examine the softness, color, and workmanship of the garment! Some kinds of information can't be adequately conveyed through a photograph on a web site.

This is no different from shopping through a mail-order catalogue. If you prefer to be able to touch and examine a product before you buy it, shopping online may not appeal to you.

Many people enjoy the traditional offline shopping experience. The sights, sounds, smells, and personal service can be sources of pleasure.

Shipping Charges

Another disadvantage of buying online is shipping charges. Although the cost of shipping is often balanced by the savings of not having to pay sales tax, many consumers still object to the idea that they are paying something for an online item that they don't pay in the offline world. In general, consumers dislike shipping charges, even though they typically have to spend money on gas when they buy from a brick-and-mortar store.

When considering an online purchase, don't forget to include the shipping costs in your calculation. If you want the item delivered within a few days, you'll pay even more for shipping than if you can wait the standard seven to ten business days.

Security

When it's time to pay for an item purchased online, many consumers are concerned about the security of their credit card information. Fortunately, this concern is generally misplaced. Most online sellers have taken steps to insure the security of data transmission. As a result, there have been few documented cases in which credit card numbers have been stolen in communication between buyers and sellers.

Still, the fear of having a credit card number stolen and misused prevents many people from buying online. These same people are unconcerned when they hand their credit card to a waiter in a restaurant or to a clerk in a brick-and-mortar retail store. In general, the risk of using your credit cards online is no greater than in those situations.

Delivery, Returns, and Other Problems

If customers have worries about placing an order online (and many do), they are also concerned about what happens after the order is placed. Consider delivery time. Can you wait seven to ten business days for the merchandise to arrive? If you can't wait that long, are you prepared to pay an extra fee to get the item overnight?

Another drawback of online buying involves returning goods that are defective or unsatisfactory. You can't just jump into your car, drive to a store, explain your problem, and get a replacement, refund, or store credit. Some online companies have brick-and-mortar stores to which goods can be returned, but in most cases you have to mail goods that need to be returned—sometimes at your own expense. If you want to exchange an item, you have to wait for the item to be shipped in two directions.

Finally, if you have a problem with an online purchase that cannot be readily resolved with the company involved, it may be difficult for you to assert any consumer rights or bring legal action. This is especially true if the seller is based in another country.

Making it **REAL**

What Kinds of Products?

The Internet seems well suited to the sale of some products but not others. So far, the products most frequently purchased online are:

* Books and CDs.
* Computers and software.
* Clothing.
* Airline tickets.

Think about the items listed above, and then answer these questions about online shopping:

* What is it about these types of products that makes them attractive to buy via the Internet?
* In the next few years, what additional types of products do you predict will become popular to buy online? Why?
* What types of products do you think will never be well suited for sale online? Why?

Is Shopping Online Safe?

All methods of payment carry some risk. Cash can be lost or stolen. A check sent through the mail can be intercepted or misdirected. A credit card number can be copied by a dishonest waiter or sales clerk. But because online shopping is comparatively new, people are very concerned about **Internet security**—the level of protection given to data collected online and sent over the Internet.

Buying by credit card over the Internet entails the same risks that exist when you use your credit card anywhere else, but it remains a convenient and secure method of payment. In addition, consumers enjoy certain protections with credit card purchases that they do not have with other payment methods.

Buying by Credit Card

The vast majority of Internet purchases are made with credit cards. You are typically asked to enter the type of credit card, your credit card number, and its date of expiration. Sellers generally ask for your address as well and check that it is the same address to which the credit card statement is sent.

Some consumers who are worried about the misuse of their credit card number use a clever strategy. They get an additional credit card and dedicate it solely to Internet purchases. This allows them to notice any unexpected or suspicious charges more easily.

If you are uncomfortable sending your credit card information via the Internet, many online merchants allow you to fax, phone, or mail your credit card details to them. Other merchants will accept a check or money order sent by regular mail. Both methods slow delivery, because sellers will wait to receive payment before sending out your merchandise.

Security Policy Statements

Most web-based companies make great efforts to ensure that transmission of your payment information via the Internet will be secure. These companies explain their efforts through privacy statements, privacy seals of approval, or both. Many sellers explain their use of special systems that encrypt, or code, any data you submit. They may also guarantee that if your credit card information is somehow used fraudulently, the seller will cover your share of any loss ($50 for a credit card).

Some companies provide logos, such as a picture of a key, to assure customers that high levels of security are being employed. In addition to increasing consumer confidence in a site's security policies, the logos allow site visitors to verify a site's identity.

Note that there are **two** potential threats to the security of any information you provide online:

1. Data transmitted via the Internet might be intercepted.
2. Someone might gain unauthorized access to your personal data after it has safely reached its intended destination.

The second threat may be the greater one. For example, criminals are more likely to "hack" into a company's records, gaining access to thousands of credit card numbers, than they are to intercept one transmission over the Internet. Careful consumers look for companies that explain what they do to minimize both types of security threats.

Consumer Recourse

Consumers can take advantage of special protections when they use a credit card online. According to the Fair Credit Billing Act, you are protected by **two** safeguards:

1. **You can challenge charges** that you believe you did not make.
2. **You will only be held responsible for $50** when a lost or stolen credit card or credit card number is used by someone else.

Is Shopping Online Private?

Think back to a recent trip to a mall or shopping center. You probably went from shop to shop, examining many items, and buying some of them.

Now imagine that during this shopping trip there was someone following you. This person recorded exactly which shops you entered, how long you spent in each one, every item you picked up or even looked at, and what you ultimately bought.

Furthermore, imagine that this spy sold the information collected about you to someone else to be used however the buyer of your personal information wanted. If this happened at the mall or shopping center, you would feel like your privacy was being invaded; yet this is exactly what can and does happen when you shop online.

Loss of privacy has become a major issue for consumers, not just for online shoppers. Concerns about your ability to control the collection and use of information that is gathered about you while you are online are why e-commerce growth has been slow.

Collecting Personal Information

Even when you buy something offline, say at a department store, a certain amount of personal information may be collected about you. If you buy with a credit or debit card, the store has your name and card number. If you use a check, your name and checking account number will be recorded. Only if you pay with cash can your transaction be totally anonymous. Even then, you may be asked for your name and address in order to receive a receipt.

If you shop through mail-order catalogues, much more information about you is gathered automatically—your name, address, the amount you purchased, and the sorts of products you buy are all recorded with each transaction.

Companies collect this information for several reasons. One is to tailor their product offerings to suit a particular type of shopper. Another is to be able to sell their lists of customers to other interested merchants. **EXAMPLE:** If you buy a sleeping bag from a catalogue that specializes in camping equipment, other companies that sell outdoor goods will pay the catalogue company for your name. They want to send you a catalogue of their products in the hope that you will buy, for instance, a tent from them.

When you shop online, additional information is typically gathered. The purchased item will generally be delivered to you, so you need to provide the details of your address. Even if the item is a gift to be delivered to someone else, you will have to give your address if you want to pay with a credit or debit card.

It is also typical to provide the web site with your e-mail address so that you can be sent a purchase confirmation and be notified when your item has been shipped. At least you are aware of giving out this information, because you typically type it in.

A great deal of information may be collected about you without your knowledge, and this can occur even when you don't buy anything on a web site.

How is all this information about you gathered? Programs called **"cookies"** do a lot of the legwork. A cookie is a small text file that is sent to your computer's hard drive from a web site (for example, that of a business, government agency, or educational institution). It is sent back to the web site each time you contact the site.

One purpose of cookies is to identify users so that web pages can be customized for them.

EXAMPLES: If you are buying CDs from a web site, cookies help the site remember the first CD you selected while you are shopping for additional ones.

Once you have purchased something from that web site, cookies might retain your name, address, and even musical preferences for your next visit. If you tend to buy a certain type of music, the groups featured on the site's home page will magically correspond to your musical taste.

You have the right to refuse cookies, but then you won't enjoy the conveniences they bring. Also, some sites won't provide you information or allow you to buy something unless you accept their cookies.

Selling Personal Information

A great deal of the information collected about you by web sites is used to serve you better, whether at the time of your Web visit or in the future. So, for example, once you buy clothes from a web site, don't be surprised if you receive e-mail messages announcing sales and other special offers.

Making it REAL

Opt-Out or Opt-In?

Businesses and consumers often agree on the principle of choice but differ on the method of providing it. Businesses prefer a system called "opt-out," in which your personal information can be reused by the original business or sold to another business unless you opt out, or say no to their sharing your information.

Consumer and privacy advocates want an "opt-in" system. Under opt-in, your information cannot be reused or resold unless you give your permission in advance.

What are some of the advantages and disadvantages of the two systems? Can you think of any problems with an opt-in system? Can you think of any benefits of an opt-out system?

This isn't very different from what happens in the offline world. It's common to receive mail from companies with which you have already done business. As consumers, then, we expect a certain amount of re-use of the information we give to companies.

We may not expect our personal information to be sold by one company to another. Imagine, for example, that a close friend of yours is stricken by a life-threatening disease such as leukemia or AIDS. You want to understand the course of the disease and help your friend in any way possible, so you get on the Internet and start researching the disease. How would you feel if you started getting e-mail messages from companies selling miracle cures or discounts on funerals? You would probably feel shock and anger, and you would wonder how these sites got your e-mail address.

There may be situations in which you would appreciate the unsolicited e-mail offers, but you might still resent the sharing or sale of your personal information from one company to another.

Overall, consumer and privacy advocates believe that web sites should follow **four** privacy principles:

1. **Notice.** Consumers should be told what information is being collected and why.
2. **Choice.** Consumers should be allowed not to have their information reused or sold.
3. **Access.** Consumers should be able to see, correct, and delete information kept about them.
4. **Security.** Firms should secure data held about consumers from unauthorized use.

Weighing Privacy Concerns

Unfortunately, the solution to a lack of privacy isn't necessarily giving consumers more privacy. The reason is that privacy is only one of many values that consumers want from Internet firms, and these values sometimes are in conflict. When making

repeat purchases from an Internet company, consumers may find it burdensome to fill out name, address, e-mail, phone number, and credit card numbers each time. They prefer that this information be kept by the merchant. But keeping this information increases the probability that it will be reused or misused.

Consider a second example of how privacy can collide with other things consumers want. Most consumers prefer to buy with credit cards at Internet stores. Yet, how is a merchant supposed to make sure that a credit card hasn't been stolen without asking the consumer for additional information with which to verify the identity of the buyer? Thus, providing consumers with privacy during their Internet experiences requires a delicate balancing of privacy against other consumer values. There can be too little privacy, but there can also be too much.

The greatest privacy concern of consumers, whether off- or online, is identity theft. This is the unauthorized use of another person's Social Security number, birth date, driver's license number, or other personal identifying information to obtain car loans, credit cards, or other services in the victim's name. When this happens, it is a nightmare for the victim. It can take years to clear up the financial mess identity theft creates.

As a rule of thumb, don't give your Social Security or driver's license numbers to anyone when you are shopping over the Internet or anywhere else.

How to Shop Online

Shopping in a store requires that you get there and have some way of purchasing items, such as cash, credit cards, or checks. Shopping online, however, requires a handful of other tools:

* Personal computer (or other device capable of connecting with the Internet).
* Online connection (usually a telephone line, but increasingly a cable line or even a satellite hook-up).
* Online connector (often a device known as a modem).
* Account with an **Internet service provider**, a company that sells access to the Internet.
* Credit card or debit card.
* Web browser, the software that finds and displays information, stores, organizations—anything stored on web sites on the Internet.

Where to Shop Online

In deciding where to shop online, some consumers shop only at companies that also have brick-and-mortar stores. Other consumers avail themselves of the full array of Internet merchants. What are some of the pros and cons of these two strategies?

Brick-and-Mortar Stores

Many of the most popular Internet retailers, or **e-tailers**, are also traditional retailers. Buying from companies that have both a web site and traditional retail outlets has several advantages:

* *Reputation*—the reputation a company has earned from years of selling the traditional way may indicate the quality of their performance in the online world.
* *Stability*—companies that have a track record as brick-and-mortar stores are likely to be more stable than companies that emerge with a splash. Many new e-tailers have gone out of business.
* *Ease*—returns may be easier when an online merchant also has traditional outlets.

Internet Stores

Consumers who confine themselves to companies that have both traditional and online outlets may feel safer. Yet, they may also be denying themselves most of the benefits of the Internet, especially choice and cost. Many popular Internet retailers don't sell any other way.

When choosing to shop with companies that only sell online, consumers are well advised to check one of the many Internet sites that rate the performance of Internet retailers. These provide detailed information on the quality of various web sites. The information on which these ratings are based often comes directly from other Internet consumers.

Search This

Shopping Bots

The term "bot" is short for "robot." On the Internet, bots are used to search through a large amount of data and then bring back an answer. **Shopping bots** search through Internet stores and provide information on the quality and prices of different products.

Most shopping bots are designed to help you find a brand at the lowest price. They assume you know what you want. Some shopping bots first help you decide which brand might be best for you and then help you find it at the best price.

Pretend you want to buy a particular pair of athletic shoes, a specific tennis racket, or a given set of golf clubs. Use at least two shopping bots to find the item at the lowest price. Do different bots yield the same buying recommendation? Do certain bots seem to favor certain stores? How do bots support themselves financially?

Warning: Not all shopping bots are independent. Before relying on a shopping bot, try to find out who created it. If the bot was sponsored by a seller of the products you're buying, double-check the information with other sources.

Online Auctions

Auction sites have been very popular on the Web. Because buying in auctions is unfamiliar to many consumers, it may take some time and practice before you master this method of online buying.

Internet auction sites offer an enormous variety of products from name-brand digital cameras to hard-to-find vinyl records and one-of-a-kind antique toys. Sellers range from full-time businesses with large inventories to individuals with a single item to sell, and the difference may not matter much.

What counts is a seller's record. Users of auction sites are encouraged to rate their experience with sellers, and this information is made available to potential buyers. The one problem with this form of feedback is that you can never be sure whether the testimonials are real or have been created by the seller's friends.

The heart of the Internet auction is the bidding process itself, and it can be very exciting, even addicting. Here are some of the highlights of the bidding process:

* In an online auction, there is a time limit and the exact amount of the bids is not known until the bidding ends. Sellers can set minimum bids, and individual buyers can set automatic and maximum bids for themselves. In between, there is a great deal of gamesmanship that occurs until the time limit on the auction expires. All of the "action" may occur during the last few minutes, leaving you exhilarated or disappointed.

* The bidding process takes place over a number of days, but the bidding becomes more intense as the auction deadline nears. As a potential buyer, you can see the initial bid and the current bid. You can also see the number of bids that have occurred but not their amounts. You don't have to be sitting by your computer to participate; you can preset your bids, including a maximum amount you are willing to pay.

* Often, two buyers will get locked into a bidding struggle, and the price is forced up. In other cases, there are only a few bidders, and you may end up getting the item at a great price. As with any bidding situation, the key is knowing how much an item is worth to you and not going higher than that amount.

Participating in online auctions can be a little intimidating. You can get a feel for the process without actually taking part in the bidding. Just watch the bidding and read about the performance history of sellers.

If you are worried that you might be buying from someone who is less than truthful, auction sites offer consumers a variety of ways to protect themselves. In addition to information about the past behavior of sellers, some sites offer a service in which your money is not released until the seller has delivered.

My Notebook

Bidding War

Observe an online auction and describe the bidding process.

Begin by selecting a product you might buy at an online auction. From the dozens or hundreds of auctions that might be going on, select four or five that will be ending in the next few minutes. For each auction, follow the bidding by looking at the bid history. Be sure to reload or refresh your screen every few seconds, especially during the last minute or two of the bidding.

What patterns did you observe? How many people seemed to be bidding at the end of each auction? Did new bidders appear at the last minute? Can a person win the bidding by only a few cents? What did you notice about your own reaction to the auction? Did you get caught up in the excitement?

"Just sign it 'To the Lucky High Bidder.'"

Instead of taking a chance on sending payment directly to the seller, you can send payment to the service, plus a fee (usually five percent of the purchase price). The service holds your payment until you receive the merchandise and determine that it meets your expectations. Some sites allow you to buy insurance, covering you in the event that a seller takes your money without delivering the promised item.

Get Smart

Auction Tips

The Federal Trade Commission, one of the primary government agencies in charge of protecting consumers from deceptive and unfair sales practices, is a great source of information and advice. In the area of online auctions, here are some of the FTC's suggestions:

* Find out who you're dealing with. Verify the seller's identity before you place your bid, and be wary of sellers you can't identify.
* Get a telephone number for the seller and use it to confirm that you have some way other than e-mail to contact the seller.
* Check to see how the seller has treated other buyers.
* Try to determine the approximate value of an item before you bid.

* Before you bid, find out what form of payment the seller will accept. If the seller accepts only cashier's checks or money orders, decide whether you are willing to take the risk of sending your payment before you receive the product.
* Find out who pays for shipping and delivery before you bid.
* Check on the seller's return policy. For example, if you return an item, are you required to pay shipping costs or other fees?
* Save all your transaction information. Print or make note of the seller's identification, the item description, as well as the time, date, and price you bid for the item. Print and save a copy of every e-mail you send or receive from the auction company or seller.

Gifts Online

Even if you are hesitant about buying online, you may find yourself drawn into the world of e-commerce. Along with an invitation to a relative's wedding shower, you may receive information about her gift preferences in an online gift registry. Or, you may receive a birthday present in the form of an Internet gift certificate. So, whether you are ready or not, it's important to understand how to give gifts online and what to do when you get a gift online.

Gift Registries

A gift registry is a list of items you would like to receive as gifts for a special occasion such as a wedding, birthday, or graduation. By specifying in advance the items you would like to receive, you make the shopping process more convenient for your friends. Plus, they have the satisfaction of knowing that you will need or want the present you receive. Gift registries have been used in the offline retail world for a long time, but online gift registries may represent an improvement on this traditional way of gift giving.

Traditional offline gift registries work like this:

* You begin by selecting a store, typically a department store, that carries a wide variety of products sold at a price and quality level you consider reasonable.
* You then tour the store, indicating the items that you would enjoy receiving as gifts. This list of goods constitutes your registry.

* Next, often with the assistance of the store, you notify potential gift-givers about the existence and location of the registry. They can then select a present from your list and avoid buying something that has already been selected.

Gift registries are particularly useful during times, such as a wedding or the birth of a baby, when you know you will be getting a lot of gifts. They also may help you receive items that are too expensive for any one person to purchase.

EXAMPLES: A set of high-quality dishes for 12 people might cost hundreds of dollars. With a registry, 12 different people can buy a single setting each. Or let's say you're having a baby. You want only one crib, one stroller, one changing table. A registry helps you—and the people giving you gifts—keep track of what's already been bought for you.

Online gift registries make a good idea even better. In this case, the list of items that are desired as gifts for special occasions is distributed and operated via the Internet. You can build and modify your registry—and gift givers can make their selections—without actually visiting the store. Online registries provide the exact price for gift items, whereas traditional registries often omit this crucial information.

One advantage of online registries is that you do not have to confine yourself to a single retailer. Whereas most department stores operate online registries, there are additional registry services that combine several merchants and allow you to specify which store you prefer for which items. Some web-based registries even allow you to specify charities to which you would like contributions made in place of presents.

Gift Certificates

Gift certificates are popular because they allow you to give a present without knowing exactly what a person wants. Traditionally, gift certificates have required both the gift giver and the recipient to visit a store. Although the recipient has many choices, he or she must still buy something from a particular retail outlet with the gift certificate.

Online gift certificates have a number of advantages over traditional ones. One is speed. If you are invited to a birthday party that starts at 7 p.m., you can go online at 6:30 p.m. and have the gift certificate arrive via e-mail before you do. Or, you can print the gift certificate on your own computer printer and bring it with you to the party.

Another advantage of online gift certificates is expanded choice. If you buy a gift certificate from a particular company, your gift recipient can choose anything available in either a brick-and-mortar store or a web site. There are also services that let you buy a web-based certificate that can be used at dozens of online stores.

The advantages of Internet shopping include the convenience of not having to leave your home, a wide variety of choices, and many opportunities to compare prices. However, you can't see, pick up, hold, and feel the merchandise the way you can in a brick-and-mortar store. You will have to pay shipping charges to send or receive goods.

Shopping online is just as safe as traditional shopping, maybe more so. You can't be responsible for more than $50 if a thief should use your card, and many sellers will not charge you this. Privacy is another issue for many consumers. Internet stores do track their customers to personalize their promotions, and many customers find they like it. However, you can insist that information about you not be sold or given to anyone else.

The Internet makes it easy to participate in auctions. Learn what's involved before you do. And finally, gift registries online offer many aids to givers and receivers.

Consumer Economics

brick-and-mortar stores—traditional retail stores that have one or more fixed physical locations. *p. 214*

cookies—small text files that travel between a web site and your computer's hard drive, used to collect information and customize web sites for individual users. *p. 221*

e-commerce—buying and selling of goods on the Internet. *p. 214*

e-tailer—company whose sales are made entirely or in part via the Internet. *p. 224*

Internet security—level of protection given to data collected online when it is transmitted on the Internet and stored upon receipt. *p. 218*

Internet service provider—company that sells access to the Internet to individuals or organizations. *p. 223*

online gift registry—list of items desired as gifts for a special occasion (such as a wedding, birth, or graduation) that is distributed and operated via the Internet. *p. 228*

shopping bot—service that searches a large number of Internet stores and provides consumers with information on the quality and prices of different products. *p. 224*

CHAPTER 13

Making a Home

In this chapter, you will learn about:

- evaluating housing needs
- renting vs. buying
- house hunting

Imagine you live tens of thousands of years ago in Europe. You're returning home after a day out hunting and gathering berries and fruit. Flames are flickering ahead. "Ah, home at last," you think. Home for you is a hillside cave.

Now fast forward to your home today. You probably think it's quite different from a hillside cave, but is it?

The basic purpose of housing is to provide shelter and protection from the elements. However, even caves used by early humans provided more than shelter. We know that early humans decorated their cave walls with paintings. They also used their caves to conduct religious rituals, prepare food, and make craft items for everyday use.

Housing Needs

While our houses might be much more comfortable than caves, we use many of the same criteria to evaluate our housing needs as cave dwellers did:

* Is the size appropriate?
* Is it located near things I need or want?

In addition, we are concerned about cost.

Space Needs

Most young people starting out on their own will probably not be able to afford a large place. This is because when you rent a house or apartment, you pay the owners for use of their space. Since it costs them money to maintain and manage the property, they want to make a reasonable profit from renting it. If you are buying, you'll find that large homes may also be out of your price range. Most young people can only afford small homes, often called starter homes. For this reason, you'll need to be realistic about the amount of space you will be able to afford.

EXAMPLE: If you're going to live alone, a studio apartment might be most realistic. Studio apartments have one main living space with a kitchen and bath, but no bedroom, and limited storage. In a studio, you'll need to be creative about how to use the space efficiently.

If you can afford it, or plan to have a roommate, you can look into larger apartments, townhouses, and even small houses. All of these living arrangements have bedrooms that are separate from the main living space. They may also have extra storage, utility rooms, small patios, balconies or yards, and garages.

The cost of an apartment or house will also be affected by its location. Rents will generally be higher in more desirable areas. The same rule applies when buying a home.

Making it REAL

Your First Place

Where we live and how our living quarters are arranged can have a dramatic effect on our satisfaction in life. Some people like the hustle and bustle of an urban setting and would be happy living in a studio apartment downtown. Other people prefer living in a quiet area surrounded by nature rather than cars.

What do you prefer? Think about these issues and others that will influence where you choose to live. For example, do you want a yard or patio? Extra space for hobbies? Lots of storage space?

Location

Real estate professionals love to ask, "What are the three most important things to look for in a new home?" "Location, location, and location," they answer. It's an old joke, but it has a kernel of truth. Where your home is located is very important.

Even though you might not be able to afford to live in a fancy neighborhood, where you live can affect your happiness and quality of life. Are the neighborhoods you're considering safe? Will you be able to meet your daily needs for things like shopping and transportation conveniently? How close to your place of employment—and your friends and family—is the home you're considering?

Safety

Fulfilling the desire to feel safe is a basic human need. Safety might be less tangible than the number of square feet you'll have, but it is just as important. Don't sacrifice safety by renting in an unsafe area because you can't afford a larger apartment in a safer location.

Neighborhood

In most towns and cities, there are always some neighborhoods that are more or less safe than others.

Here are some ways to evaluate a neighborhood's safety:

* Walk through it. How do you feel? Be sure to visit the area at night as well as during the day.
* Call the chamber of commerce to ask about the neighborhood.
* Discuss the neighborhood with property managers who are helping you find an apartment.
* Contact the police department for crime statistics.
* Ask coworkers, friends, and family members what they know about the area.
* Contact the student housing office if you are attending school.

Environment

In addition to safety issues, consider other aspects of the neighborhood that will affect your quality of life. Here are some questions to ask:

* Do you like the feel of the neighborhood? Does it feel like your kind of place?
* What is the noise level? Is it quiet?
* Is the neighborhood attractive? Are the buildings well maintained? Are there trees and shrubs?
* What is the traffic level?
* If you're looking at apartment complexes, are there desirable **amenities**, such as an elevator or parking spaces.

Schools

Access to schools for yourself or children, if you have them, is an important thing to consider—especially if you're considering a home you plan to live in for many years, such as a house. If you have children, it might make it hard to get to school or work on time yourself if their schools are not within easy walking or driving distance.

If you plan to attend school, your life will be less hectic if you can walk or bike to campus. Of course, rents might be higher closer to campus where the student population increases demand. If this is the case, you will need to balance the cost of rent against increased transportation costs and time spent traveling to and from school.

Convenience

Imagine you've found the perfect place. It has just the right amount of space. It's new and well maintained. There is a lot of light inside, and a great little deck where you can grow a few herbs and read a book on a sunny day. There's only one problem. Well, several, actually.

You don't have a car, and the closest bus stop is almost seven blocks away. The neighborhood shops where you can pick up groceries and other odds and ends are only four blocks away, but they're on the opposite side of your apartment from the bus stop. That means a 16-block trek on your way home from work or school to run errands. Not only that, your two best friends have decided to rent apartments much closer to campus. They've decided to do that because a bus route goes right by their apartment building, and one block over is a small shopping center.

If you rent the apartment you love, you might be happy when you're actually inside. The many inconvenient aspects of its location, though, could mean a tiring, frustrating, and even lonely daily life. When looking at housing, whether to rent or buy, it's important to find a place you like. It's just as important, though, to make sure the resources you need for daily life are available.

When thinking about a new home, ask yourself if these quality-of-life facilities are available in the neighborhoods you're looking at?

* Parks.
* Community centers.
* Libraries.
* Places of worship.
* Museums.
* Movie theaters.
* Restaurants.
* Shops.

Cost

Housing costs are influenced by size and location. This is true whether you plan to rent or buy. By the time you begin looking for housing, you should have a budget that includes a monthly housing expense.

With that information, how can you zero in on places that will fit your monthly housing expense? Here are **three** suggestions:

1. **Study newspaper ads** to get a sense of neighborhoods with housing options within your budget.
2. **Narrow down neighborhoods.** For example, if your research shows that in safe neighborhoods you can only afford studio apartments, look first at the ads grouped under "studios" or "efficiency apartments."
3. **Visit apartments for rent** that might interest you by contacting the landlord and attending open houses. When considering buying, start by going to open houses.

These activities will help you get to know the housing market in your community so you can get the most "home" for your housing expense.

Do you want to live alone or with a spouse or roommate? Does a single-family house with a yard appeal to you, or do you like high-rise buildings? These are just a few options you'll need to consider when you start living on your own.

Out on Your Own

The prospect of living on your own for the first time can be both exciting and terrifying. On the one hand, you have more freedom to live as you want. On the other hand, you have more responsibility. Bills need to be paid. Groceries need to be purchased and meals prepared. Laundry has to be done.

Do you want to share these responsibilities with others, or manage them on your own? Each approach has advantages and disadvantages.

Living With Roommates

Sharing your living arrangements, or having roommates, offers the advantages of companionship, shared expenses, and shared responsibility for tasks like shopping, cooking, and cleaning up.

No matter how well you know someone, it's best to have a written agreement. If you're the only person on the rent or lease agreement, and the roommate is renting from you, this is especially important. In this case, you are the one who will be held **liable** (responsible) if the apartment is damaged or rent is not paid on time.

Picking a Roommate

Many a friendship has turned sour once the friend becomes a roommate. Before you pick a roommate, consider these issues:

* **Compatibility**. Do you and your potential roommate have similar lifestyles? Remember the movie and TV show, "The Odd Couple?" You want more harmony than Oscar and Felix had. Is your would-be roommate a neat freak like Felix, while you're a slob like Oscar? Are you the out-going party animal, while your roommate is the quiet studious type? In a good roommate setup, personalities match—or at least mesh.

* **Reliability.** Can you count on your roommate to pay bills on time? Will your roommate wash dishes and dust bookshelves?

* **Willingness to communicate.** If problems arise, will you be able to talk them through and come up with solutions?

Before you live together, talk honestly about what you each expect from the other. Do you want to share groceries and some meal preparation, or would you rather be on your own for dinner? If one of you plans to come home late, should you call the other? How will household chores, such as cleaning the bathroom, get handled? How will you share expenses, such as the phone bill?

The Chore Wheel

During her senior year in college, Emily H. lived with four other seniors in a town house owned by the college. All five women were friends, with varying degrees of closeness. Each had made the choice to live in the town house because she had grown tired of life in a dormitory and craved an atmosphere more like home.

At the beginning of the school year, Emily and her housemates held a house meeting. In it, they talked over ways to share the household chores.

First, they agreed they wanted to eat a home-cooked meal together five nights a week (Sunday through Thursday, leaving the weekends free). Fortunately, there were five of them so each could cook one night of the week.

Next, they decided to divvy up the chores. They agreed on four important chores that needed to be taken care of each week: grocery shopping, cleaning the living room, cleaning the two bathrooms, and cleaning the kitchen. Since there were five of them, one person would get a "chore-free" week. To keep track of whose turn it was to do which task, one of them made a paper wheel with the name of each house-mate and the name of each chore. Each week, they would rotate the chore wheel to know who should do what.

Because Emily and her friends talked about their expectations and found they shared the common goal of wanting to live more like a family, their system worked very well for them.

Not everybody wants to be so formal and structured. Do you?

Living Alone

Living alone offers the advantages of being able to set up your living quarters as you like, spend your time as you like without worrying about disturbing a roommate, and arranging activities and chores to fit your lifestyle.

Of course, living alone also means that only one person's income is contributing toward housing, food, and utility costs. This might mean you'll have to live in a smaller place and budget more wisely in general.

Do you think you're the live-on-your-own or the roommate type? Why?

Living With a Spouse

Living with a spouse is another arrangement that takes special considerations. It is similar to and different from living with a roommate. Living with a roommate is generally seen as a temporary arrangement. Day-to-day and monthly planning and coordination are required, but long-term planning is usually not in the picture. In addition, while many expenses are shared, roommates manage their finances separately.

In contrast, setting up a household with a spouse involves long-term planning, including:

* Sharing chores and household responsibilities fairly.
* Arranging shared living space together.
* Sharing income and expenses beyond those used to manage the household.

Types of Housing

There are several different types of housing. The most common are:

* Apartments.
* Condominiums, co-ops, and co-houses.
* Houses.
* Low-income housing.

Apartments

For many young people, apartments will be the first place they live because they are economical. This is because more people can live on the same amount of land than when there is only one house. When many families live in one building, even though they live in separate living spaces, it's called **multi-family housing**.

An apartment can be a small studio or much larger with a number of bedrooms. An apartment building can be small or a large complex with many amenities like common rooms and recreational facilities. Shared laundry facilities are often found in apartment buildings.

When looking at apartments, consider:

* General up-keep of the grounds and building.
* Security.
* Availability of parking for yourself and guests.
* Laundry facilities.
* Extra storage options.
* Services, such as a doorman or superintendent.
* Recreational facilities.

Condominiums, Co-Ops, and Co-Houses

Condominiums are a form of multi-family housing. They often look like apartment complexes but differ in one important way. They are not rented. Instead, they are owned by an individual who is responsible for the interior of the individual unit. Upkeep of the grounds, shared facilities, and buildings are paid by each owner. Condominiums, often called "condos," have the advantage of home ownership without all the responsibilities of home maintenance.

When you buy a home or condo, you actually own the property. **Co-housing** and **cooperatives** , known as co-ops, are twists on the traditional approach to home ownership.

When you buy a co-op, you're actually buying shares in a corporation that owns the property. In a co-housing community, you own your own house and share ownership of common areas—grounds, recreational facilities—with other people.

Co-Ops, Condos, & Co-Housing			
Type	**Description**	**How It Works**	**Value**
Condo	Owner purchases a living unit and is responsible for the upkeep of the interior. Exterior upkeep is paid for by association dues.	Owners are members of a homeowners' association and vote on issues of concern to all owners.	Owners have many benefits of home ownership, but not the personal responsibility of maintaining the building and the grounds.
Co-op	Owner purchases shares in a corporation and is given a living unit to use in exchange. A board of directors holds the mortgage, not individuals.	Shareholders vote on issues that affect the property and other shareholders. The board is responsible for paying the mortgage, managing the property, making repairs, and handling similar issues.	Shareholders have exclusive rights to their unit, offering them many advantages of home ownership without all the responsibilities.
Co-housing	A combination of private home ownership and cooperative: 1. People own individual residences. 2. Common areas, such as recreation facilities, are owned jointly by all.	Individuals are responsible for their residences but vote on issues related to management of common areas and community issues.	The purpose and physical design of co-housing are to: * Bring people together. * Involve people in the process of managing the community. * Create small, friendly neighborhoods where people know and help each other.

Houses

In contrast to apartments, individual homes are called **single-family housing** because there is only one living unit on the property. An individual, a family, or a number of unrelated individuals can live in the house and share the same living space. Compared with most multi-family housing, individual houses often have the advantages of a private yard and more space, privacy, and storage.

In addition to traditional houses, other kinds of single-family units, like mobile homes, offer many of the same advantages of traditional houses at less expense.

Low-Income Housing

Government and private programs help low-income families rent and purchase homes.

Government-Subsidized Housing

The federal government offers programs to make housing more affordable for both renters and buyers. The U.S. Department of Housing and Urban Development (HUD), the main agency responsible for this assistance, offers:

* Rental assistance in which a portion of the rent is paid by HUD for qualifying renters.
* Loan guarantees for home buyers who would not otherwise qualify for conventional loans.

In addition to federal assistance, many states and local communities also have programs to help low-income families with housing costs.

Habitat for Humanity

If you wanted to own your own home but couldn't afford to buy one, would you be willing to help build one and apply the value of your labor to the cost of the home? Since 1976, over 30,000 Americans have had just that opportunity, thanks to the nonprofit organization, Habitat for Humanity.

With volunteer labor and donations, houses are refurbished or constructed. The prospective homeowner who helped build the house then buys the house through a no-interest loan. No profit is made on the house by Habitat for Humanity.

Across the country, Habitat for Humanity and similar local programs are putting home ownership within reach of low-income Americans. Potential homeowners are selected by a committee based on their need, their willingness to participate in the building project, and their ability to repay the no-interest loan.

Former President Jimmy Carter has been an enthusiastic supporter of Habitat for Humanity since 1984. In his first project that year, he helped renovate a six-story building in New York City with 19 families. Now, he and his wife work for one week a year on a Habitat for Humanity project.

To Rent or To Buy?

For many people, owning a home is the American dream. But home ownership does not suit everyone's needs and lifestyle.

Renting

Most young adults' first steps toward independence involve living in rented housing. Some people do so for a short period of time before buying, and others rent for many years or indefinitely.

It's likely your first place will be an apartment, because apartments offer the most affordable housing options. However, information on apartment renting also applies to renting other units like houses or mobile homes.

"It's a new rent concept—fifteen minutes for a quarter."

Rebuilding Lives and Communities

In 43 states across the country, 16- to 24-year-olds are building affordable housing for their communities, while rebuilding their own lives. It all started in 1978 in New York City when a group of teenagers asked the director of the Youth Action Program at East Harlem Block Schools to help them figure out how to renovate abandoned buildings in their neighborhood. The success of their first renovated building led to a national program that helps unemployed young adults complete their education and acquire job and leadership skills—all while making their communities more livable.

From this first success in New York, there are now 145 programs across the country. More than 2,000 low-income housing units have been built or renovated, many with housing rehabilitation grants from HUD.

Pros and Cons of Renting

Topic	Advantages	Disadvantages
Responsibilities	The landlord is responsible for maintenance and repairs.	You will not be able to make changes, such as painting or other modifications, without the landlord's permission.
Amenities	You might have access to some amenities, such as recreational facilities and parking, at no extra cost. Some utilities, such as water, might also be covered in the rent.	Your rent includes the cost of amenities, so unless you use them they are an expense with no benefit.
Freedom	As a renter, you have the freedom to move easily if you desire or if it's necessary.	You do not own the property and cannot benefit if it gains value.
Property Taxes	You don't have to make a separate tax payment.	Property tax amounts are included in your rent payment.
Equity (share in the monetary value of the property)	None.	Your rent payments are not going toward ownership, or equity, in the property.

Search Strategies

Imagine that you know in which part of town you want to live. How can you find the right apartment in that neighborhood? There are lots of good techniques:

* Look for "For Rent" signs in windows.
* Check the classified rental ads every day for your desired part of town.
* Let coworkers, friends, and family members know you're looking for something.
* Visit or call the property managers of apartment complexes or buildings in which you would like to live.
* Attend open houses.
* Contact property management firms.

Finding an apartment you like will take legwork and organization. Keep track of all your calls and appointments in a small notebook. If an apartment interests you, write down the address and a brief description, and request an application.

In large cities where competition is stiff, additional methods are available for finding apartments.

Paperwork

Applying to rent an apartment is a little like applying for a job. The **landlord** (the person who owns the property) or property manager wants to know you are a good prospect. This means he or she wants to know that you are responsible, will pay your rent on time, will treat the property well, and will abide by the rules. For this reason it is important to provide all information requested on the application. In addition, you should line up three people as references. These should not be relatives. An employer, a teacher, or a supervisor for volunteer work you do are all good choices.

If your application is accepted, ask to walk through the apartment again before signing a rental agreement. Evaluate its condition carefully and make sure it will meet your needs and standards. Keep a checklist of problems. If the apartment will meet your needs, you're ready to sign on the dotted line.

Before you do, though, review the agreement carefully. Ask questions if there is anything you don't understand. Ask that your checklist of problems be attached to the agreement. This way, you will not be responsible for paying for those problems when you move out because you will have proof you didn't cause them. Your rental agreement, or *lease*, should spell out the:

* Monthly rental amount.
* Rent due date.
* Penalties or consequences for late rent payment.
* Security and cleaning deposit amounts.
* Term of the agreement (month-to-month or annual).
* Utility payment responsibilities. (Are any included as part of the rent?)
* Tenant responsibilities.
* Landlord responsibilities.
* Occupancy restrictions. (Can you sublease? Can you get a roommate?)
* **Notice**. (How many days in advance do you need to notify the landlord that you're moving out? How much notice will the landlord give you if he or she wants you to leave or won't renew the lease?)

Costs

It takes more than one month's rent to get into an apartment. Typically, you will pay some combination of the following:

* First month's rent.
* Last month's rent. (This is applied to your last month's rent when you give notice.)
* Cleaning fee.
* Security deposit. (This fee covers out-of-the-ordinary repairs. The total amount or remainder after repairs will be refunded when you move out. If you treat the property well, you should get the entire amount back.)
* Key deposit. (This will be refunded when you move out and return the keys.)

Tenant Rights and Responsibilities

When you rent an apartment, you are paying for the right to use the landlord's property. Both parties in this agreement—you and the landlord—have rights and responsibilities.

There are state laws governing tenant-landlord rights. If a disagreement develops between you and the landlord, these laws will be used to resolve the situation. Public mediation services and legal assistance are available in many communities to help resolve these kinds of disputes.

Rights and Responsibilities

	Rights	Responsibilities
Landlord	The right to: * Receive timely rent payments. * Have property treated well. * Have tenant rules followed.	Responsible for: * Ensuring property meets legally required standards. * Providing other items identified in the rental agreement. * Getting permission from the tenant before entering the residence.
Tenant	The right to: * Use the property as specified in the rental agreement. * Privacy.	Responsible for: * Paying rent on time. * Observing tenant rules. * Notifying landlord of needed repairs. * Giving appropriate notice as specified in the rental agreement.

Rental Discrimination Is Illegal

A federal law, The Fair Housing Act, prohibits discrimination in the sale, rental, and financing of housing, based on race, color, religion, sex, national origin, family status, or disability. If you think you might have been discriminated against, contact your state HUD office or local legal assistance office.

Buying

Just as renting housing works well for some people at certain times in their life cycle, so can owning a home. Do you share the American dream of home ownership?

Advantages and Disadvantages

Owning your own home can be fun and satisfying. It offers many advantages over renting, but has disadvantages, too. Owning your home is a much bigger responsibility than renting it.

EXAMPLE: What happens if something goes wrong, like the roof starts to leak? If you rent an apartment, you call the landlord or super, and he or she solves the problem one way or another. If you own a home and the roof starts to leak, you've got to figure out how to fix it and pay the cost of fixing it.

Finding a Home to Buy

Throughout your life, your housing needs will change. At different phases of your life, the importance of different factors might shift.

EXAMPLE: If you have children or plan to start a family soon, nearness to good schools, playgrounds, and parks will probably be more important to you than when you were single and wanted to be near good restaurants and movie theaters.

To find a home you'll be happy with, you need to evaluate your needs for space, location, and amenities. Then you can use those priorities to help focus your hunt for a house.

How Much Should You Spend?

While the general rule for how much you can afford to pay for a home is two-and-a-half times your gross annual income, this can vary. If you are getting a conventional loan, the banker or mortgage broker will want your monthly payment, including the loan payment, taxes, and insurance, to come to no more than 28 percent of your monthly income. Interest rates and the amount of your down payment can influence this percentage. This in turn can affect whether or not you qualify to buy certain homes.

In areas where homes are very expensive, you may qualify for special programs that allow people to buy homes when their payment takes up more than 28 percent of their income.

Pros and Cons of Owning		
Topic	**Advantages**	**Disadvantages**
Responsibilities and Costs	You can choose how repairs and maintenance are done. You can make repairs yourself.	You have to save money for upkeep that a landlord would provide if you were renting.
Freedom	You can change and fix up the property according to your personal taste.	It might be more complicated to get away or move to another city if, for example, you change jobs.
Property Taxes	They are deductible from federal tax returns.	This is an expense that must be budgeted for in addition to payments.
Equity Issues	With each mortgage payment, you are buying the home from the mortgage holder. Over time, you gain equity, adding to your net worth.	If property values decrease, your home might be worth less than when you purchased it.

Financing a Home

Most people **finance** a home, or get loans to buy it. This is because homes are expensive, and most people don't have enough money of their own to pay for a home all at once. Buying a home is usually the biggest purchase a person makes. It is also often an excellent investment because home values grow over time.

There are **three** important financial factors you will need to consider when purchasing a home:

1. **Your down payment.**

2. **A mortgage.**

3. **Points, fees, and other charges.**

A *down payment* is a lump sum of money that you contribute toward the cost of the home. Generally, the buyer needs to make a 10 percent down payment to qualify for a conventional loan.

EXAMPLE: If you want to buy a house that costs $90,000, you will need to have $9,000 for your down payment.

To meet other requirements, such as a co-op board's house rule, you may have to put 20 percent down. Some banks will require you to take out mortgage insurance if you put down less than 20 percent.

A mortgage is a loan for the purchase price of a home, minus your down payment.

EXAMPLE: If you put down $9,000 on a $90,000 house, your mortgage would be $81,000.

When you buy a home with a mortgage loan, you do not own the property until the loan is paid off. You are buying the property from the mortgage holder and securing the loan with the property. This means the mortgage holder can take the property if you **default**, or don't make your payments.

The **two** most common kinds of mortgages are:

1. **Fixed Rate.** The interest rate, and thus your payment, remain the same for the term of the loan, usually 20 or 30 years. Having the same payment every month allows you to budget well. If interest rates drop, it can be worthwhile to refinance, or get a new loan. When interest rates are low, fixed-rate mortgages are popular.

2. **Variable Rate.** The interest rate goes up and down, depending on market interest rates. This means your monthly payment can change. This is an advantage if interest rates drop and a disadvantage if interest rates go up. When interests are high, variable-rate mortgages are more popular.

In addition to these kinds of loans, there are also low-down-payment and low-interest loans available through government programs for prospective homebuyers who qualify.

By the Numbers

How Much Down?

You've been saving toward a down payment for five years. You've finally got enough to begin looking at houses seriously. How much will you need to have saved for the following homes, assuming a 10 percent down payment? How much, assuming a 20 percent down payment?

$73,500
$85,000
$92,500
$103,500

What will the mortgage be on each after deducting the down payment?

Mortgage Calculators

The Internet is full of online calculators that can help home buyers figure out the costs of a mortgage. Find a mortgage calculator online. Pretend you're buying a $125,000 home with a 10 percent down payment. Type in the amount of your 30-year mortgage. How much will your monthly payment be if the interest rate is 6.5, 7, and 9 percent?

When you borrow money to buy a house, you will be charged points and other fees. In addition to the interest you pay on the loan, there are bank fees and other up-front costs to obtain a loan. The most common ones include:

* *Application fee.* A typical application fee is a few hundred dollars.
* *Points.* A point is one percent of the value of the loan. So, if you are charged two points by the lender on a $81,000 mortgage, you will owe $1,620.
* *Title insurance.* This requirement and its cost protect you from a lien, or claim, against the property that creditors of previous owners may have made.
* *Credit report.* Banks make you pay the cost of researching your payment habits.
* *Miscellaneous fees.* These pay recording, survey, notary, and other fees.

These fees and charges may be included in the loan amount, so you don't need to pay them out-of-pocket. The application fee is usually due at the beginning of the process, but most of these other charges come at the **closing**, when buyer and seller and/or their representatives come together to transfer the home ownership and "close" the deal.

Buying on Contract

Most property owners want buyers to get a loan. This is because the seller will get paid in full for the value of his or her property at the time of the sale. In some cases, though, an owner will offer what is called owner financing. This means you purchase the home directly from the owner over time. When this occurs, a legal document, or contract, needs to be written up. This is why this type of home sale is called "buying on contract."

There are two main reasons owners sell on contract:

* A seller wants to collect interest and make more money from the sale of the property.
* The property is not in good enough shape to qualify for a conventional loan.

Moving In

You've finally done it! Imagine you just signed loan papers or a rental agreement for your first place of your own. Now it's time to move in and set up housekeeping. What steps should you take to make the move go smoothly?

Preparing for the Move

Planning is the most important first step of moving. Here are issues you need to address before you begin the move:

* Contact phone and utility companies to have services started.
* Complete a postal service new-address kit.
* Decide if you will use a commercial mover or move yourself with the help of friends and family.
* Set aside money for moving expenses.
* Complete any painting or other fix-up projects.
* Gather boxes and packing material.

Packing How-Tos

Whether you're moving across town or 1,000 miles away, you want to arrive in your new home with everything in good condition. To ensure that this will happen, give yourself plenty of time to pack. Then, pack like items in the same boxes and label them. This way you can put all "kitchen boxes" in the kitchen as you move in, making unpacking much smoother.

Here are some tips:

* Pack breakable items carefully in newspaper or other material.
* Be careful not to over-pack boxes so they become too heavy to carry.
* Pack an overnight bag with clothes, toiletries, and other items you might need the first few days before you unpack completely.
* Label each box carefully so you'll know what's in it.
* Clean and organize as you pack. Recycle things you never use, or have a garage sale before you move.

Choosing a new home is a complicated process. There are many points to consider.

Location may well be the first. Many real estate professionals say it is the most important feature. Observe the neighborhood you're thinking of living in carefully—and at different times of day and night. Is it safe? Does it fit your personal style? Will you be near stores, parks, and schools?

The people you'll live with will make a big difference, too. Do you want to live alone or with roommates? Or perhaps you're newly married, getting your first home with your spouse.

You'll need to decide which type of home is best for you at this stage of life: apartment, house, co-op, condo, or co-housing arrangement? Are you planning to rent or buy your new home?

Getting a new home can be exciting and satisfying—especially if you take the time to think through all the decisions carefully before you fall in love with a home.

Consumer Economics

amenities—things that increase pleasure. In housing, these might include parking places, plants, even recreational facilities. *p. 233*

closing—the final step in the home-purchasing process when all the papers are signed and you become the owner of the property. *p. 248*

co-housing—community of single-family housing in which you own your own house or living unit yourself, and co-own common areas (park, meeting hall) with other co-housing owners. *p. 238*

cooperative—(co-op) multi-family housing in which each owner holds the purchase of shares in a corporation that owns the property. Your shares give you an exclusive right to your living unit. *p. 238*

condominium—(condo) multi-family housing in which the units are owned by individuals who are responsible for

their individual units and a share of the building. *p. 238*

default—fail to fulfill an obligation, such as making a loan payment. *p. 247*

finance—take out a contract or mortgage to purchase property. *p. 246*

landlord—owner of rental property. *p. 243*

liable—legally responsible for something, such as the damage to an apartment that occurred while you lived there. *p. 235*

multi-family housing—living facilities where several families or individuals have separate living units. *p. 238*

notice—written statement to a landlord stating the last day on which you intend to live in property. *p. 243*

single-family housing—living facilities where one family or group of individuals use the one living unit on a property. *p. 240*

CHAPTER 14

Furnishing Your Place

In this chapter, you will learn about:

- **basic furnishing needs**
- **buying guidelines**
- **making purchases**

When Amy moved into her first one-bedroom apartment, she made some bold decorating moves. First, she put the bed in the living room, because it was the largest room. Then she put the television in the kitchen because she liked to have the morning news shows on when she got ready for work. So she could drink tea easily while working at her computer, she put the electric kettle near her desk in the bedroom, which became her office.

She replaced the curtains with bamboo blinds and removed the out-dated light fixtures in favor of colorful paper lanterns. Since she didn't have enough closet space, she used large wicker baskets to store socks and sweaters. She found an old wooden table and chairs at a garage sale and painted them each a different color.

Everybody told her that her place was unusual, but cheerful and fun. As for Amy, she had never felt so at home in her life. Furnishing your living space isn't only an exercise in practicality, it is a chance for you to express who you are.

Basic Needs

It's easy to identify our basic needs for survival—water, air, food, and shelter. But once those basic needs have been met, what's next? In our vast array of consumer choices, American shoppers must constantly balance what they truly need, what they want, and what they can afford. Faced with furnishing your first independent living space, you will find yourself balancing your needs against a limited budget and a desire for all the exciting furniture products available.

To avoid being swept up in a tidal wave of spending, begin by creating a reasonable purchasing plan that will:

* Meet your basic furnishing needs.
* Keep within your budget.
* Create a comfortable living space that feels like home.

To determine your basic furnishing needs, ask yourself the following questions:

* What basic furnishings do I need to prepare food and eat?
* What basic furnishings do I need to sleep and rest?
* What basic furnishings and products do I need for personal care and hygiene?
* What basic furnishings do I need for relaxing, entertaining, studying, and working?
* What supplies do I need for cleaning and maintaining my place?

Review your list of items.

* Circle the items that you must have to meet your most basic needs.
* Star those you could live without now but will eventually need.
* Underline items you consider luxuries—desired but not essential.

My Notebook

Getting Started

Identify your basic furniture needs. Create a list that categorizes furnishing items and household goods into **four** categories:

1. What I already have.
2. What I can get from others.
3. Essential items that I have to buy now.
4. The first purchases I will make when I have more money.

Use the newspaper sales section or go online to create a preliminary budget for the essential items you need. Make phone calls to discount or department stores to get additional prices. Contact other shopping sources, such as local second-hand stores and catalogs, to complete your budget.

To complete your basic purchasing plan, consider your available resources:

* How much money do I currently have to apply to furnishing purchases?
* What furnishings and supplies do I already have and can take with me?
* What items can family and friends loan (or give) me?
* What items can I ask for as gifts during the upcoming year?

In the Bedroom

Let's start with the bedroom because you probably already have some experience with it. Perhaps you have or had your own room in your family's home. Maybe you helped furnish or decorate it. Draw on those experiences when it comes time to furnish your own home.

Entering your bedroom should help you make the transition from a busy, active world to sleep. It's your private getaway. Even if it is only a small space set off by a screen in a one-room studio, it should be a restful, private place. Basic bedroom furniture and supplies are tied to the activities of preparing to sleep, sleeping, and storing your personal belongings. Assuming you will have a closet, here are some essential elements:

* Bed.
* Dresser.
* Night table or shelf.
* Lamp.
* Alarm clock.

Beyond these basics, there's almost no limit to the extras people buy for their bedrooms, including entertainment centers and computer workstations. Think carefully about your budget, your needs, and your sleeping habits.

Getting Your Zzzz's

Getting a good night's sleep is critical to your health and sense of well-being. You may be able to spend a couple of nights in a sleeping bag on the floor, but eventually you need to make the investment in a comfortable bed.

Whether you slide under a **down** comforter—made from bird feathers—in a queen-sized bed, crawl into a sofa bed in your one-room studio, or curl up on your futon on the floor, you need support and comfort. Even if you give up another piece of furniture to stay within your budget, get the best bed you can afford.

All of the following sleeping options range in cost and quality:

* Traditional bed with frame, innerspring mattress, and box springs.
* Sofa bed.
* Daybed or trundle bed.
* Futon.

If space and funds are limited, it's wise to choose a bed that can serve more than one purpose. Trundle beds can be rolled away when not in use. Daybeds also function as couches, while sofa beds are couches that fold out into beds. All of these may be used for seating, storage, and sleeping. The **futon** is a Japanese innovation that is a thick pad for sleeping that can be rolled up and stored out of the way when not needed. If it's in a frame, a futon can be used as a couch during the day.

If you have the space and budget to buy a traditional bed, you will need a frame, mattress, and box spring. Typically, frame and box springs are included in the price of the mattress. Throwing a single mattress on the floor will not give you support or comfort, and it will shorten the life of the mattress. **Platform beds** are very similar to futon frames, providing support for traditional mattresses, without the need for box springs.

The size of your bed is a function of space availability, your body size, and your budget. Beds have the following size options from smallest to largest. The bigger the bed, the more space and funds you will need. Consider the following guidelines:

* *Twin,* comfortable for one person of average height.
* *Extended long twin,* suitable for a taller person.
* *Full or double,* a luxurious option for one, an economical choice for two people of average height.
* *Queen,* a practical choice for two people of any size.
* *King,* a more comfortable choice for two people of any size.
* *California King,* bigger than a traditional king, a luxurious choice for anyone.

Mattress Shopping Questions

When you head for the department or discount store to shop for a bed, pay special attention to the quality of the mattress. A reasonably good mattress is a necessity.

Take a friend with you when you go shopping for a bed. Assume you have a limited budget, and you want to get the best value for every penny you spend. Keep a comparison chart of costs and total budget. Decide which bed is the best value in quality and price.

Always "test-drive" a mattress before buying. The best way to test a mattress is to use it! Wear comfortable clothing. Take along a magazine and lay on each mattress for a while, changing positions as you read. It can tell you more about comfort than any salesperson's pitch.

Mattress Shopping Questions

Shopping Question	Possible Answers	Things to Consider
How many coils?	Coils range from 300 to 700+.	The higher the number of coils, the more body support.
What is the gauge (thickness) of the coils?	Heavy or light.	Heavy-gauge coils will offer more support.
How many turns in each spring?	Six to eight turns.	The more turns, the more bounce.
What kind of padding is on top?	Padding materials can include polyfill, cotton, wool, down, silk, and cashmere.	The more layers of padding, the more comfort. But don't spend extra money on expensive fabrics like silk.
Is there a warranty?	Warranties range from 90 days to a lifetime guarantee. Some stores offer a comfort guarantee that allows you to return the mattress after 30–60 days if you don't like it.	Don't buy a mattress without a reliable warranty. It's a good reason to buy from one of the well known mattress companies with years of experience.
What other services does the retailer offer?	Free delivery, free frame, removal of the old bed, free set-up.	Get as many free services as possible. This is often negotiable.

Linens

Bed linens are expensive, and the bigger your bed, the higher the price. Even at super-saver discount stores, queen-size sheets can still cost more than $40 apiece. Before buying high-ticket items like goose down pillows, comforters, or a **feather bed** (a separate thin mattress filled with feathers or down to fit on top of a regular mattress and make it softer), think about your basic needs. For example, if you really like the feel of a feather bed, you might find that it is more economical to buy a "pillowtop" mattress, which includes a soft layer on top of the firmer basic mattress. But when you consider your basic needs, before you buy the least expensive option, consider how paying more can save in replacement costs later.

Basic Linens

Basic linen needs for the bedroom and bath include:

* Sheets (1 or 2 sets).
* Pillow(s).
* Pillowcases.
* Blanket (1–3, depending on climate).
* Bedspread or comforter.
* Bath towels.
* Hand towels.
* Washcloths.

It's important to get a basic set of each linen item. The set should be of reasonable quality to withstand repeated washing. Adding items to your linen collection will give you more options and extend the life of your favorite linens.

Get Smart

Choosing Sheets

All sheets list a thread count—the number of cotton threads per square inch—that ranges from 150 to 350+. The lower the number, the cheaper the sheets. The higher the thread count, the stronger and softer the fabric.

You may decide to purchase sale sheets with a low thread count. After several washings, you may find the bargain price wasn't worth it. Over time, low-thread-count sheets begin to thin and sprout rough fabric balls that can feel like sandpaper to a tired body.

Bed linens come in a variety of fabrics. Pure cotton sheets are softer to the skin but are more expensive than blends. While 100-percent cotton sheets last longer than blends, many people prefer blends because they don't wrinkle as easily.

Pricier options, such as flannel, satin, and silk, offer both durability and extra warmth and comfort. A high–thread-count flannel is a lovely winter option. Satin is a more affordable alternative to silk.

Your Favorite Pillow

People get very attached to their pillows. The right pillow can mean the difference between a sleepless night and a good night's rest. It's likely you'll bring your own pillow to your new place. You can spend anywhere from $4 to $200 on a pillow. If you buy a new one, here are **four** things to consider:

1. **Material.** Pillow stuffing includes affordable cotton, pricey goose down, and synthetic fillers. Cheaper cotton pillows aren't as durable as down pillows. They sag and lose shape within a few months. However, you can't wash down pillows. They must be dry cleaned. So, you might decide to buy the less expensive cotton and replace them when needed. Down pillows can lose shape as they lose feathers. Some people feel that sinking into them is a bit too suffocating. Plus, some people are allergic to down. Synthetic fillers are a good choice as they keep their shape and are washable.

2. **Size.** No matter how pillows are filled, they come in the same shapes and sizes: standard, queen, and king. Beware: sometimes sheet sets come with standard size pillowcases even if the sheets you bought were for a queen- or king-sized bed.

3. **Firmness.** Pillows have a firmness label ranging from extra firm to soft. The stuffing material affects the degree of firmness. Test all pillows before buying. Take your time, just as you would with a mattress. Pillows can be expensive, so be sure you choose the firmness you find most comfortable.

4. **There are also special pillows:** neck pillows that support just your neck even if you use another pillow, knee pillows for those prone to lower back pain, and body pillows to hug through the night.

Bath Linens

How many towels do you need? Towels vary in fabric and quality. Look for towels made mostly of cotton, not acrylic fabrics. Acrylic can feel rough and unravel with repeated washing. Be wary of the cheapest towels, but steer clear of the most expensive ones. Middle-range towels cost between $8 and $12 and will last a long time if you treat them well. To prolong the life of your towels, avoid excessive and repeated bleaching. If you can afford it, start with two decent towel sets that include bath towel, hand towel, and washcloth.

In the Bathroom

While it may seem like the least important room in your home, a functional and comfortable bathroom is essential. You may find that you need to install conveniences such as towel racks, toilet paper holders, shower curtains, and clothes hooks in order to make your bathroom more efficient. If you have minimal storage space, you may also need to purchase small wall shelves, shower racks, or even simple baskets in which to store your hygiene products.

Other items that will make your bathroom more comfortable are: a bathmat, toilet seat cover, mirrors, toothbrush holder, soap dish, and wastepaper basket.

In the Living Room

Your living room is where you greet friends, entertain, and relax. It can be the busiest room in your home and serve many purposes. Since this is your first place, your living room might also be quite small. The living room might also double as a bedroom, a dining room, or an office.

Inexpensive Options		
Living Room Item	**Things to Consider**	**Lower Cost Options**
Sofa or Couch	Size, fabric, frame, sofa bed options.	Futon, smaller loveseat, used couch with slipcover, or two lower-cost chairs instead of a couch.
Chair	Size, fabric, frame, style.	Used chairs with new slipcovers, outdoor furniture, wicker.
Table	Size, material (glass, wood, plastic).	Trunk, or low-cost piece of wood with brick support and tablecloth covering.
Shelves	Material, height, shelf depth, durability for heavy objects.	Boards with bricks, stacked boxes, or plastic bins.
Lamps	Table, floor, or hanging.	Used lighting at garage sales and second-hand stores.
Desk	Size, computer use, storage requirements.	Board or door supported on two small file cabinets.
Television or Stereo Stand	Size of electronic equipment and number of shelves needed, storage options for tapes and CDs.	Sturdy table.

Good Things Come in Small Packages

Here are some tips for making a small living room look bigger:

* Hang a mirror.
* Paint walls a cool light color like a light green or blue.
* Paint the ceiling a lighter color than the walls.
* Add a screen to set off a study area.

Deciding on essential living room furnishings requires you to consider:

* Budget.
* Activities that happen there.
* Space available.

Further define and prioritize the furnishings you need in your living room by thinking carefully about the activities you do there.

* *Will I read and study there?* If so, you'll need good lighting and a desk area with sturdy shelving for books.
* *Will I have friends over often?* If so, you'll need more seating options. If you watch TV together or listen to music, furniture for the television set and CD player needs to be in this room.

* *Will I have a separate dining room?* If the living room will also be an eating space, then a good-size table becomes more important, especially when you have guests.

In the Dining Room

The dining room (if you're lucky enough to have one) is the place for friends and family to gather for holiday celebrations and festive occasions. Besides eating, it's a place to gather to talk, celebrate, and enjoy each other's company. Dining rooms used to be very formal and stuffy. Today you can create a dining room environment that's warm, festive, and informal.

Furnishing the Dining Room		
Item	Purpose/Considerations	Level of Importance
Table	To serve food to 4 to 12 people.	Necessity.
Chairs	To seat 4 to 12 people.	Necessity.
Sideboard or Buffet	A long, low cabinet with drawers and areas to store dishes and napkins.	Optional.
Hutch or Cabinet	A tall cupboard with open shelves at the top to display special dishes.	Optional.

Tables and Chairs

The table and chairs are the most important dining room furniture. Whether you buy an expensive, solid-wood matching table and chairs set or a less expensive option, it's important that people can sit comfortably and have room to eat. Your guests' elbows and knees need enough space to move around without bumping into their neighbor's or their neighbor's food. Remember these space tips:

* A **place setting**, or basic set of dishes, for one person is about 14 inches deep by 25 inches wide.
* Chair seats need to be 12 inches below the table height.
* You need about 36 inches from the edge of the table to pull your chair back.
* The table should be wide enough for each guest to have 20 inches of foot room.

Sets

At both high-quality furniture stores and discount marts, dining room furniture is usually featured as "sets." The emphasis is on matching all the pieces, including table, chairs, sideboards, and hutch. In some cases, you cannot buy a piece of a set, but only the set as a whole. However, used furniture purchased at resale shops, or from house or garage sales, can be very attractive.

Other Considerations

Price depends on the number of pieces and the quality of the materials used. Materials include wood, glass, **wrought iron** (crafted iron, often used in outdoor furniture), upholstered chairs, and synthetic materials. Styles range from modern to folksy country to classic formality.

Things to remember before you spend a fortune on a dining room set:

* Everything doesn't have to match.
* Consider buying unmatched wooden chairs at garage sales or thrift stores and painting them the same color (or each a different color if you want!).
* Buy folding chairs and add a tie-on pillow seat for comfort.
* Use long benches instead of chairs.
* Use less-expensive outdoor furniture—even a picnic table covered with a nice tablecloth.
* Visit a home improvement warehouse store and purchase an unfinished door to put on carpenter horses as your table. Throw an Indian bedspread over it, and you've got a table to seat six to eight guests.
* Flowers and candles add beauty and soft lighting.

In the Kitchen

You have to eat. The question is, do you like to cook? Do you spend a lot of time cooking for yourself and others? If the answer is yes, then the kitchen becomes one of the busiest parts of your home. It also means that your list of needed **appliances** (stoves, refrigerators, dishwashers), pots, pans, and accessories (nonessential items) is long. If you don't like to cook, but heat up frozen pizza or order frequently from Chinese restaurants, then your kitchen needs are minimal, and your choices less complicated.

Major Kitchen Appliances

You can't always assume when moving into an apartment that the major kitchen appliances will be in place. Study the major kitchen appliance list and related questions:

* **Stove:** Do I need a gas or electric stove? Should I get a free-standing range or a countertop with wall oven?
* **Refrigerator:** How much space do I have? How much food do I need to store or freeze?
* **Dishwasher:** Dishwashers save time, but how many dishes do I wash daily?

Purchasing Guidelines

Hefty guidebooks are written on how to buy stoves, refrigerators, and dishwashers. Whether you are buying used or new, appliances are major purchases and need careful and thorough up-to-date research.

Most rental apartments come with appliances such as stoves and refrigerators. If an apartment is not equipped with a dishwasher, you may not be allowed to install one. In this case, you will have to do without or buy a portable dishwasher. Because portable dishwashers can be rolled from place to place, and because they are finished on all sides, they cost $50 to $100 more than otherwise identical built-in dishwashers.

Energy Efficiency

In most American homes, about 20 percent of energy costs go to run appliances such as refrigerators, freezers, washers, dryers, dishwashers, and stoves. The more energy-efficient an appliance, the less it costs you monthly in utilities such as gas, electricity, and water.

Consider energy-efficiency features when purchasing a new or used appliance. New appliances are sold with a yellow Energy Guide Label to indicate their energy efficiency. An Energy Star label is awarded to appliances that significantly exceed minimum national efficiency standards.

Refrigerators

Refrigerators can be the most expensive appliance in the kitchen. However, a used, basic refrigerator may cost only $100.

Refrigerators are set up in **five** ways:

1. **Top mounts.** The freezer is in a separate compartment on top of the refrigerator section. This is the most common refrigerator.

2. **Bottom mounts.** The freezer section is below the refrigerator.

3. **Side-by-sides.** In these models, the refrigerator and freezer sections are next to one another with separate doors.

4. **All-refrigerator units.** As the name suggests, these appliances have no freezer section at all.

5. *Single-door refrigerators.* In these models, a small freezer section is included behind the single door.

Stoves

Stoves also vary widely in cost. Gas stoves cost more than electric models, but may be cheaper to run. Gas stoves offer more control

By the Numbers

Energy Efficiency

Traditionally, a refrigerator has been one of the most energy-consuming appliances in the home. Recently motivated by new federal standards, manufacturers have released new models that promise a wide range of energy efficiency.

It is often the case that the more energy-efficient, the higher the price of the refrigerator. However, in theory, savings in long-term energy costs can make up for the initial cost.

Conduct your own research by visiting stores and looking at shopping guides, such as the ones found in *Consumer Reports*. Find out which brands and models are the best value. Compare cost and operating expenses among refrigerators. What would you buy and why?

over heat than the fixed settings on an electric stove. When you turn a gas stove off, it stops immediately, while an electric element gets cooler gradually.

Stoves also come in a wide variety of sizes and models. A range includes both the **cooktop** (the burners for heating food) and the oven (or ovens). Ranges may be free-standing or built into the cabinets or countertop. Sizes for free-standing ranges go all the way from models that are just 20 inches wide to big, restaurant-style models that have side-by-side double ovens and are 60 inches wide. The most common range size is 30 inches wide. These typically have four burners or electric heating elements on top.

You can also buy a separate cooktop that is built into your countertop, with single or double built-in ovens that are installed in special cabinets on the wall. Ovens can be self-cleaning or manual cleaning. Of course, you pay more for automatic cleaning options.

Dishwashers

While not a necessity, dishwashers are very convenient. They range widely in price, starting at about $200. Most dishwashers are standard size, under-the-counter models. The higher the price, the quieter and more energy- and water-efficient your dishwasher will be.

Convenience features, such as loading ease, number of wash cycles including pots and pans, and delay start options, will add to the price. Also, remember that dishwashers need a water line hook-up. If there isn't a dishwasher hook-up in your kitchen, you will need to pay to have one installed.

Other Kitchen Appliances

Microwaves can be great if you want to defrost or cook in a hurry. They're great if you do a lot of cooking and entertain often. Using a microwave is a fine way to make a quick bowl of popcorn. Microwaves cost around $80 to $100 for a basic countertop model. Compare your cooking habits and style with the realities of your budget to determine if you can justify owning one.

If you're renting a single room, you may want to invest in less-expensive appliances that don't take up as much space as microwaves and can be easily stored out of sight:

* **Toaster oven.** This can toast bread or bake chicken, lasagna, and other food items. (Many store-bought microwave dinners may also be prepared in a toaster oven.)
* **Hot plate.** This can make grilled cheese sandwiches, fried eggs, and other meals.
* **Electric kettle.** This can boil water quickly to make tea, coffee, or soup.
* **Crockpot.** This cooks food slowly, at low heat over several hours. It is great for making stews and soups. You put the ingredients in it in the morning, turn it on, and when you come home in the evening, your dinner's done.
* **Electric wok.** This is a Japanese-style frying pan used for making stir fried vegetables and meat.
* **Rice cooker.** This is an electric appliance that makes it easier to prepare rice.

Many other small appliances are found in the kitchen. They include:

* Food processor or blender.
* Mixer.
* Toaster.
* Coffee maker.

In the beginning, if you can stick to carefully purchasing the basic kitchen essentials, you will have laid a foundation for a terrific functional kitchen. Start with only the things you need most, and buy the highest quality you can afford. If having things match is important to you, avoid items that are being discontinued. But if quality and price are your goals, discontinued items can be great buys.

Other Household Appliances

Whether to purchase a washer and dryer or go to a public **laundromat**—a business that lets you use washing machines and dryers for a fee—is a question of space, budget, and convenience. Here are some questions to help you figure out what's right for you:

* Does your place have room for a washer and dryer?
* Is there plumbing in place for a washing machine?
* Are there gas or electric dryer hook-ups? (Will your lease allow you to install such appliances?)
* Do you wash clothes frequently and in medium to large quantities?
* Do time and convenience factors outweigh the additional cost?

Kitchen Basics		
To Prepare Food	**To Prepare Baked Dishes**	**To Serve Food**
Pans: small frying pan, medium saucepan, deep pan for pasta.	Rectangular baking pan.	Four place settings of dishes.
Knives: a medium paring knife and larger butcher knife.	Cookie sheet.	Four cereal or soup bowls.
Cutting board for meats.	Covered, medium-sized casserole dish.	Four settings of cutlery.
Cutting board for vegetables.		Medium serving bowl.
Utensils: spatula, stirring spoon, whisk.		Salad bowl with salad utensils.
Mixing bowls.		Platter.

Washing Machines

There are two main types of washing machines: top-loading and front-loading. Although top-loading washers are more common, front-loading washers use less water and wear clothes more slowly. Because gravity draws the water through the clothes, front-loaders are said to clean the clothing more thoroughly as well. However, front-loading washers are also quite a bit more expensive.

Washing machines feature a wide variety of settings for washing different types of clothing, from delicate to super-dirty. The most important setting feature makes it possible to adjust water level and temperature. Washing machines come in a variety of sizes, including a small apartment size often sold as a vertical set with a dryer. There are even some small washer/dryer combination machines designed for use where space is very limited.

No matter which type of washer you buy, they all do a pretty good job of cleaning your clothes. As you spend more on the appliance, you get more features and different cycles for different fabrics.

Clothes Dryers

A clothes dryer is a very simple, basic machine. All the dials and features merely drive up the price.

There are both electric and gas dryers. The type you buy depends on the hook-ups available at your location. Initially, gas dryers cost more than electric dryers. However, in the long run, you will save money in energy costs with gas. For most people, the choice is driven by the type of hook-up that is available. It will cost a lot to install a gas line if one is not available.

As you spend more on a clothes dryer, you get more temperature and time controls. The most expensive dryers may feature moisture-sensors, which detect the amount of moisture coming off your clothes and shut off automatically when the clothes are dry. However, even inexpensive dryers have a setting for knit and delicate fabrics that dries the clothes with lower heat to avoid damaging the fabrics.

Other Essentials

Finally, almost everyone needs **two** more appliances:

1. A vacuum cleaner.
2. An iron and ironing board.

Like almost everything else, vacuums come in many different styles and prices. For a small apartment or studio, an inexpensive, small vacuum may be sufficient. For carpets, an upright vacuum is usually preferred, but it costs a bit more. Almost all vacuums come with attachments for cleaning carpets and bare floors, as well as a hose and attachments for cleaning furniture and crevices.

Inexpensive irons will do a good job on your clothes. Extra money buys more features, such as self-cleaning, bursts of steam for eliminating tough wrinkles, and finer temperature controls.

One tip for finding an ironing board: Check garage sales. You might find a perfectly good ironing board for less than $5.

Beyond Basics: Electronics

The world of electronic products is full of complex and expensive choices. There are few things you'll pay more for that will require more knowledge on your part to spend your money wisely.

To begin, decide what you need versus what you want. Do you need a computer because you're a student with limited access to a computer at school? Do you want a large-screen TV because you love to watch football games on the weekends? Make a list of needs and wants. Be honest and keep an eye on your budget.

Home Computer

The first question to ask is *what am I going to use it for?* Consider the following possibilities:

* *Word processing:* writing papers for school, letters, short stories.
* *Keeping in touch:* e-mailing friends and family.
* *Research:* surfing the Web for information for school, news, personal interests.
* *Entertainment:* playing computer games.
* *Personal finance:* keeping track of your budget and bank account and paying bills.
* *Creativity:* storing and manipulating photo images, composing music, creating newsletters, editing video.

As you consider what type of computer to buy, keep in mind the ways you'll be using it.

Mac vs. PC

One of the first choices you'll make is whether to buy an Apple Macintosh or an IBM-compatible PC that runs Microsoft Windows.

PCs are more popular than Macs (the market share of PCs is above 95 percent), but Macs have very loyal fans. In the business world, most people use PCs, except in the following fields, where the Mac rules:
* Graphic arts.
* Publishing.
* Education.
* Animation.

Ultimately, it's a personal choice. But before you make the final decision, find out what your family, friends, and coworkers are using. While it's possible to share files with the other type of computer, it can be tricky. Also, for the most part, you can't run software made for one type on the other type. Because PCs are so much more common, more types of software are available for that platform.

Desktop vs. Laptop

The next choice is whether to get a traditional **desktop computer** or a small, light **laptop computer** .

Miniaturization costs money, which means laptops are more expensive than desktops. If price is your biggest concern, go with a desktop. You'll get more "bang for your buck," or power for the price.

If price is less important than other considerations, such as space on your desktop or mobility, consider a laptop. One major advantage: A laptop can run on batteries, so you can use it on an airplane or at the beach!

Prime candidates for laptops include:

* ***College students*** who want to take their laptop with them to classes and the library.
* ***Business people*** who travel frequently and want to have their computer with them on road trips.
* ***People who live in small spaces,*** where the size of a laptop is an important advantage.

Before buying a laptop, do consider what you give up: The keyboard and the display (or monitor) will almost always be smaller than those of a desktop computer. Also, if you want a very powerful computer, desktop computers are generally less expensive than same-power laptops.

Other Considerations

The key to buying a computer is to do your homework. Computers are constantly getting faster and better. To keep on top of the latest technology, do some research. There are many sources of information about computers:

* *Consumer Reports* and other consumer publications.
* Computer magazines.
* Web sites about computers.

Because computers are always being updated, one rule of thumb is to spend as much as you can. That way, your computer will be up to date longer, which means it will be able to run new software programs longer.

Finally, remember that the machine is just your first purchase. Undoubtedly, it will come with software programs, but you are likely to want to buy more programs over time. And if you want to use the Internet—and you probably will—you need to get an Internet account (about $20 per month).

Making it REAL

The First Big Purchase

When Hari moved into his first apartment, his family gave him lots of help. His parents, grandparents, aunts and uncles, brother and sisters all gave him housewarming presents.

His parents gave him dishes and silverware, pots and pans. Plus, they loaned him a kitchen table and chairs from their attic. Hari's older brother and sister chipped in and bought him a queen-size futon that could double as both a bed and a sofa—perfect for Hari's studio apartment. His grandparents gave him sheets and blankets for the bed and towels for the bathroom. His aunts and uncles gave him a coffee table and a lamp.

He was pretty well set up with the basics, thanks to his large and generous family. In fact, Hari was in such good shape that his moving-in costs came in $500 *under* budget. He thought about what he could buy with that extra $500: an air conditioner, a TV set, a microwave oven, a dishwasher, or a dresser he saw at an antique shop. Or he could put the money into a savings account.

If you were Hari, would you buy yourself something nice but not absolutely necessary, or would you save the money? If you spent it, would you buy a home electronics product, a piece of furniture, an appliance, or something else? What steps would you take to make this decision?

Sound System

Knowing your budget limitations and conducting careful research are important when entering the complex world of audio sound system products. You may be able to afford a basic "boom box" with a CD player, radio, and tape player, or something more. Boom boxes range in price and quality and may be a good first purchase option. Their portability is a definite advantage.

If you decide to buy a stereo or digital sound system, prepare to research and compare sound quality, play modes (including CD, tape, vinyl, and radio), quality controls, and the number of preset automatic play features.

"This CD player costs less than players selling for twice as much."

TV—VCR—DVD

Walk into an electronics store and look at the walls of TV sets with flashing screens. The variety is enormous. It makes deciding on a TV purchase time-consuming and complicated. How much do you watch television or view movies at home? Your answer will determine how important it is to buy a high-end version with a big screen and great sound or a small portable to lug around the house. Consider these features:

* Screen size.
* Picture quality.
* Sound quality.
* VCR or DVD player included.

The VCR, which plays videotapes using a TV set, is a technology well established on the market. VCRs are widely available and range from low cost to expensive. You can buy videotaped movies to view and also rent movies. New features are being added to VCRs all the time, including the ability to record a movie without the commercials.

A DVD player, which plays movies on a disk that looks like a CD, is still a relatively new digital product. It's still in transition, and while the number in homes has increased, there are fewer titles available to buy or rent. DVD players are higher priced but deliver excellent picture quality. They can still skip, but eliminate the extra noise and picture-tracking jitters associated with VCRs. Some home-entertainment experts think it is wiser to invest in DVDs than in videos when building a film library.

Product Considerations

Since electronic equipment purchases are both expensive and complex, prepare to research carefully. Consider these issues as you explore options and match them to your budget:

* *Longevity of the technology.* Buying an electronics product is complicated by how fast the technology changes. You want to buy the latest and greatest. But you also don't want to spend your hard-earned money on a technology that is jazzy but not proven. Look for a product that's been around long enough to have a proven track record you can research to compare different brands and features.

* *Repair rates.* You don't want to purchase a piece of equipment with a dismal repair rate. Whether buying used or new, refer to electronic products magazines and other consumer publications to find out which brands and models have the best repair records.

Buying Advice

No matter what type of furniture you purchase, before buying, ask yourself the following questions. Answering each one with a resounding "yes!" will give assurance that you are getting a good value for your money.

* Do I really need this?
* Is it durable enough to last for the time I need it?
* Is it well constructed with quality materials?
* If it uses energy, will it be efficient and not overly drain my resources?
* Is it attractive so that I will enjoy having it in my home?
* Does the price match the value of the product *and* my budget?
* Is it backed by a manufacturer's or retailer's warranty?

The durability, energy efficiency, quality, materials, style, and price are important whether you buy from a department store, discount store, online catalog, second-hand store, or garage sale.

New or Used?

Buying new is usually considered the desired option. New furniture probably has better quality (no one has used it before), and you can get at least a short-term warranty. However, if you have a small budget or enjoy hunting for value in unlikely places, check out used furniture. A good used chair of high-quality wood is a better value in price and quality than a new chair made with flimsy materials.

After all, once it's been in your place a while, it will be "used." Look for used furniture from:

* Used furniture stores.
* Thrift stores such as ones run by the Salvation Army or Goodwill.
* Consignment shops.
* Newspaper classified ads.
* Estate sales.
* Garage and yard sales.
* Online auctions for used items.

If you look carefully, there are great furniture buys to be found that will be budget-friendly and meet your needs.

EXAMPLE: A well constructed couch with worn upholstery can last for years with an attractive slipcover. An oak table with a worn surface can be covered with a tablecloth or refinished. Be particularly careful when buying used appliances. It is advisable to purchase from a used appliance store that offers at least a limited warranty.

Durability

You should expect furniture you buy to last over a period of time. The durability increases if furniture is well constructed, made with high-quality materials, and backed by a warranty. In general, the higher the price, the more durable the furniture.

How long you expect each piece of furniture you buy to last is up to you as you juggle durability and budget. Review your purchasing plan. Next to each essential purchase, determine how long you want this product to last. You may decide to spend more to purchase a durable, high-quality bedroom set you can count on to last for more than a decade. You may also decide to pay a lower price for a dining room set. In this case, you may sacrifice durability because you plan to buy something of higher quality later when you are more established and have more income.

Treating even low-ticket items with respect will increase their **longevity**—their ability to last over time—and keep them looking attractive. Research how to best maintain your furnishings and appliances and keep instructions and warranty information close at hand in labeled file folders. Even before buying, make sure you understand what it will take to keep it in good condition. If you'll be eating on the couch, make sure you buy one with an easy-to-clean fabric.

Considering Materials

Furnishings are usually put into two categories: soft goods and hard goods. **Soft goods** include upholstered sofas, chairs, linens, mattresses, and so forth. **Hard goods** include tables, desks, chairs, and shelves. Each category requires different materials that affect the quality of the furnishing.

Wood Furniture

Wood furnishings are a good choice. They are very attractive, easy to maintain, and durable. Before choosing wood furniture, know your choices:

* Hardwoods include oak, birch, maple, cherry, mahogany, and teak.
* Softwoods include fir, pine, and cedar.
* Wood products include cheaper wood-based substitutes for solid wood, like particle board.

You can purchase furnishings made of *solid* hardwood or softwood. **Hardwoods** are dark-hued woods like oak, maple, mahogany, and cherry. **Softwoods** are lighter in color, and include alder, pine, and aspen. Hardwoods are generally more expensive than softwoods, but they are also more durable.

You can also purchase wood furnishings with a veneer. A veneer is a slice of wood attached to another piece of wood, or particle board. For appearance, an inexpensive material may be covered with a veneer of beautifully grained wood.

Avoid products that say "wood grain finish," which likely means a plastic top with a picture of wood on it. Finally, don't confuse wood construction with type of finish. The words cherry or oak can reflect the kind of color stain used—not the type of wood used to build it.

Upholstered Furniture

It is often very hard to judge the quality of **upholstered**—covered in fabric—furniture. You can wander through the furniture store and find you can't tell the difference between a $400 couch and one that costs over $2,000.

Besides the quality of the construction materials (custom or not), it is also important to look at the fabric itself:

* Is it durable and easy to clean?
* Does the pattern line up, especially back to front?
* Is the color likely to fade if placed in direct daylight?
* Does the warranty specifically include the upholstery fabric?

When Should You Shop?

Item	Best Time to Buy	Reason
Linens: Sheets, Towels, Comforters, Pillows	January, May, and August.	Traditionally, stores offer so-called "White Sales" during these months.
Clothing	At the end of the season.	Stores offer end-of-season sales to make room for the next season's merchandise.
Athletic Shoes	January and July.	Manufacturers introduce new product lines, so stores put the old lines on sale.
Computers and Home Electronics	December and January.	Manufacturers bring out new products for the winter holidays. Look for bargains on old and new lines before and especially after the holidays.
Holiday Decorations	Immediately after the holiday.	Shops can't afford to store the items for a year, so they reduce prices considerably.

Decorating Advice

Twenty-five-year-old Derek P. is a part-time student with a part-time job in Salt Lake City, Utah. He lives in a small apartment with a roommate. He's had more fun than he expected furnishing his place and decorating it in a style a guy could love.

On a very limited budget, here are Derek's tips for low-cost decorating:

* Define your style. Don't just see something cool and buy it. You'll end up with a bunch of junk that doesn't go together.

Mixing and matching styles is good. Chaos is not.

* When you finally buy your own television, save the box. Put a $4 leopard sheet over the box and add a phone, plant, and a candle. No one will ever know your table's a box!
* Watch for closeout paint sales at home improvement stores. There are dark interesting colors—not just soft pastels. You can get a $35 gallon of paint for $5! Then paint only a couple of walls for a striking contrast.

Style

When you buy furniture, it's important to get what you like! Besides fitting your needs and budget, you also want it to fit your style. You can use color, personal items like photos, and interesting furniture arrangements to add style to your place. Sometimes the desire for high style can stress your budget unless you know how to be creative.

Price

A good value is a furnishing that is durable, of reasonable quality, attractive, and fitting to your budget. Being a careful, informed shopper will help you balance these criteria to get good value for your money. People say "you get what you pay for." But a smart shopper who researches, takes time, and compares products can get more than he or she pays for. A not-so-smart shopper can pay too much and get too little.

Decorating Styles		
Style Name	**Description**	**Examples**
Country	Informal, warm, comfortable, with a lot of wood and traditional accents.	Maple or pine furniture, braided rugs, quilts, wooden boxes.
Contemporary or Modern	Formal or informal, but less warmth; geometric forms, chrome, glass, and leather.	Glass tables, metal chairs, bed low to floor, bold, white and red colors.
Southwestern	Eclectic, informal, and warm, based on styles from cowboy and Native American cultures.	Iron, cactus, Mexican or Native American blankets, iron lamps, tile mirrors.
Victorian	Inspired by Queen Victoria; ornate and formal, dark woods, overstuffed chairs, heavy frames, and mirrors.	Brass beds, chests, gold frames, china hutch, velvet fabric.

Whether you live in a studio apartment or a large house, your home is your castle. It is where you go to at the end of the day to rejuvenate and prepare for the challenges that await you. Furnishing your living space is a great opportunity to create an environment in which you feel comfortable, happy, and productive.

Prioritize your needs and wants, deciding what is a luxury and what is essential. You may find that your ideas about necessities differ from those of your parents, or even your roommate.

Since many of the things you will buy to furnish your home represent large purchases that will be with you a long time—a bed, a TV, a dishwasher—it's important to make wise purchases. Do your homework before buying.

Be resourceful. Explore uses for things before throwing them away. Finally, don't be afraid to experiment. Move your furnishings around until you find an arrangement that feels best to you.

Consumer Economics

appliance—household equipment, such as an oven or refrigerator, operated by gas or electricity. *p. 261*

cooktop—electric or gas burners for heating food; may be part of a range or a separate appliance. *p. 263*

crockpot—electric pot that cooks food at low heat over several hours. *p. 263*

desktop computer—traditional computer in three pieces: the central processing unit, keyboard, and display (or monitor). *p. 267*

down—fluffy feathers from a bird. *p. 253*

feather bed—thin mattress filled with feathers or down to fit on top of a regular mattress and make it softer. *p. 256*

futon—Japanese-style sleeping pad that can roll out on the floor or fit on a frame. *p. 253*

hard goods—furniture made of wood, metal, plastic, or other hard materials. *p. 272*

hardwood—dark-hued woods like oak, maple, mahogany, and cherry, more expensive and more durable than softwood. *p. 272*

laptop computer—all-in-one computer that is smaller and lighter than a traditional desktop computer; it is portable and can run on batteries. *p. 267*

laundromat—place to wash and dry clothing for a fee. *p. 264*

longevity—ability to last over time. *p. 272*

place setting—basic set of dishes for one person. It includes dinner plate, salad plate, soup bowl, cup, and saucer. *p. 260*

platform bed—structure that provides support for a mattress, without the need for box springs. *p. 254*

soft goods—household furnishings or goods made of fabric. *p. 272*

softwood—light-colored, porous woods like birch, alder, pine, and aspen. *p. 272*

upholstered—covered with cushions, springs, and fabric. *p. 273*

wok—Japanese-style frying pan traditionally used for sautéing vegetables and meat. *p. 263*

wrought iron—crafted iron, usually for outdoor furniture. *p. 260*

CHAPTER 15

Getting Around

In this chapter, you will learn about:

- **the different types of transportation**
- **how to choose the right mode of transportation**
- **how to buy a car**

In 1913, Henry Ford forever changed the way cars are made. Before Ford, they were pieced together by hand. Ford came up with the idea of using a moving assembly line to make cars. That made it possible to make many more cars than before—and to make them less expensively.

Suddenly, cars were cheaper than ever before. Within a few years, cars went from being a luxury only wealthy people could afford to something within reach of many American families. Today, owning a car—like owning a house—is built into the American dream.

But a car is just one type of transportation available to people today. Buses, trains, bicycles, and motorcycles make it possible for millions of Americans to get around every day.

Evaluating Your Needs

What you spend on transportation must be carefully considered in light of your overall budget. What do you need? What can you afford? One thing is for certain: It is a major financial decision. Unlike other purchases, if you make the wrong choice, you can end up paying much more than you ever expected.

When considering a means of transportation, take some time to think about where you must go each day, your lifestyle, safety, personal preferences, comfort and convenience, and cost.

Getting to Work or School

The primary purpose of transportation for many people is getting to school or work every day. This daily trek from home to school or work and back again is called a commute. Since most commuting takes place five days a week, it's worth thinking about the most efficient and economical transportation options.

When determining how to get where you need to go, consider these questions:

* How far away do you live from school or work?
* What convenient and reliable transportation options are there?
* How long does it take to get there by each option you listed above?
* What are the advantages and disadvantages of each one?

Of course, cost is a major factor in which transportation option you finally choose.

My Notebook

Exploring My Options

Think about every possible means of getting to school or work: car, bus, subway, riding a bike, or walking. How much time will it take to travel to and from school or work by each mode of transportation you listed? What are the advantages and disadvantages of each?

Write it all down. You may want to make a chart to see the comparison more easily. Which mode of transportation best meets your needs?

Lifestyle Considerations

Knowing your lifestyle will help you determine the best type of transportation for you.

Lifestyle considerations may not be important now, but in a few years, these and other questions may become relevant:

* Do you regularly drive two, three, or more friends to school or work? Do children or older people count on your car?
* Will clients, or potential clients, often ride in your car?
* Do you need to haul dirt, plants, animals, artwork, or tools?
* How important is it to conserve energy?
* Do you love to feel the wind blowing through your hair?
* Do you prefer to get your daily exercise in going to and from school or work?

How do you think the answers to these questions will affect your transportation decisions?

Safety

Safety is at the top of the list when choosing any mode of transportation. Picture yourself going to and from school or work using all of your transportation alternatives. Here are some examples of safety-oriented questions:

* Is this mode of transportation safe in all kinds of weather conditions? If not, do you have an alternate plan available?
* Can this mode of transportation safely carry the number of people you need to transport?
* Is available parking safe and would your car, bike, or other vehicle be secure?
* If you're considering public transportation, will it be safe for you to use it when you need it? If you get off work at midnight, the bus may not be the best option.
* Has your vehicle been carefully checked for safety?
* Does the walk from the subway to your school or workplace require you to walk through an unsafe area?

Talk to people who may know more than you about the pros and cons of different transportation modes from your school or workplace. Then pay attention to the information you have when making a final decision. The price of using an unsafe mode of transportation can be more than anyone would want to pay.

Personal Preferences

You've considered some of the basics: need, lifestyle, and safety. Now it's time to think about comfort and convenience.

* Are you tall? Do you need extra leg room?
* Will there be a baby or young child you need to get into and out of a car seat?
* Would you prefer to let someone else drive you to and from work in bad weather?
* Do you hate paying for the privilege of parking eight blocks away from school?
* Do you regularly have several stops to make on the way home from work?
* Does waiting in the rain on a busy street for the bus bother you?

* Do you like parking your mode of transportation indoors?
* Are you sure you could not walk home faster than the time it takes you to drive?

How would the answers to these questions affect your choice of transportation?

Cost

Cost is where the rubber hits the road, as the saying goes. You may have big transportation dreams with a very small budget. Check your monthly income. What can you afford for transportation?

By the Numbers

Car Costs

Say you just purchased a car. Your expenses are far from over. In fact, they've just begun.

Call around in your area. What might you need to budget for each of these categories?

* License and registration.
* Car insurance.
* Gas and oil.
* Routine maintenance and repairs.

* Unexpected repairs.
* Parking fees.

Some budget items are paid just once a year, others twice a year, and others as needed. Convert each amount to a monthly figure. For example, if your car insurance costs $800 per year, the monthly cost is about $67.

What's the monthly cost of owning a car?

Transportation Options

There are usually many ways to get to another location. Take a moment to think of all the public and private transportation options available in your area.

Public Transportation

Public transportation in the form of **mass transit** is available in cities. Mass transit delivers many people to set destinations in many parts of the city and the suburbs. Mass transit may be in the form of:

* Subways.
* Trolleys.
* Buses.
* Light rail.
* Streetcars.
* Trains.
* Ferries.
* Taxis.

All public transportation systems have advantages and disadvantages.

Pros and Cons of Mass Transit	
Advantages	**Disadvantages**
Inexpensive, compared with the cost of driving a car. You don't need a license or insurance and don't have costs of parking, repairs, maintenance, or parking tickets.	You must get to the station and walk from the station to your destination, which may be several blocks. If you drive to the station, you may have to pay for parking there.
Cuts down on the number of individual cars on the road, decreasing air pollution and saving energy.	Seating may be hard to find during busy times of day.
Takes you to and from the main areas in a large city conveniently and, often, more quickly than driving a car.	You must work around the bus or subway schedule, meaning you have less flexibility.
You leave the driving to someone else. No hunting for a parking place.	Traveling to and from certain areas can be unsafe during late-night hours.

Subways

Subways are like small trains. Some systems, like San Francisco's Bay Area Rapid Transit system (BART), run under and above ground and even underwater. In fact, they're called subways because they often travel below, or sub, ground. In Chicago, the subway is called the "El" because it runs on an elevated track above the street as well as underground.

Subways deliver people to set stops. You get off at the stop nearest your destination. You may need to connect with a bus line to get closer to your destination. You can buy tokens or transit cards in advance, which saves time standing in line to purchase a ticket. Subways run frequently, so you usually don't have to wait long for the train you want. However, during commuting hours in large cities like New York City, subways can be packed, with no room to sit or stand.

Trolleys

Some parts of Portland, Oregon, and San Francisco, California, use trolleys. Electrically powered cars that run on tracks, trolleys remind people of the old days, and many people like to ride them for that reason.

Sometimes trolleys have a circular route that transports people between several popular areas, such as a college campus, a shopping mall, an area with popular nightspots, and nearby neighborhoods. Sometimes they even operate as free shuttles!

Light Rail

Light rail trains are a newer source of public transportation. They are very quiet trains that run on small tracks down city streets. They help congestion by moving people quickly and quietly to different places within the city. Light rail trains are efficient, nonpolluting, quiet, and fast. Salt Lake City, Utah, San Jose, California, and Portland, Oregon, have light rail systems.

Buses

Buses are another form of public transportation. You wait at the bus stop for the correct bus. You ride until the stop nearest your destination and then get off. In big cities such as New York City, the bus is much slower than the subway. But some people prefer the bus because it travels above ground, just like a car, and you get a better view!

Some buses and trains have special commuter schedules. They make fewer stops at certain times of day to speed up the time needed to move people from one end of town to another. Buses are flexible. New routes or scheduled stops can be added to accommodate changing patterns in a city's growth and riders' changing needs.

Taxis

Taxis are probably the most expensive means of transportation. This is because a car with a driver picks you up and delivers you right to the door of your destination. In addition to paying the fee on the taxi's meter, you are also expected to tip the driver.

You can save money by sharing a taxi with other people going to the same destination. (The driver may charge you a flat rate of one or two dollars for each extra person, but only one fare will be charged, so it's usually cost-effective to share.)

Besides the cost, there are other drawbacks to relying on taxis as a primary mode of transportation. It's hard to get a taxi in bad weather (everyone wants one), during busy parts of the day (traffic is slow and use is high), and in some parts of town (taxi drivers don't like to go into unsafe areas at night)—in other words, when you need or want one the most! Still, taxis are useful:

* In an emergency.
* If the weather is bad and you don't want to drive or walk.
* When you are in a hurry to reach your destination.
* If you are sick or have a disability that limits your ability to walk, drive, or use a public transportation system.
* If you are new to an area or unfamiliar with the public transportation system.
* If your destination is not easily reached by public transportation.

Private Transportation

Private transportation options are ones you own, lease, or rent for your personal use. They include bicycles, scooters, motorcycles, electric bikes, and, of course, cars.

Bicycles

A bicycle can range from around $250 (a decent, basic mountain bike) to $4,500 (pro racing bike). There are many types of bikes to fit specific needs.

Bicycle Options	
Type of Bicycle	**Characteristics**
Commuter Bike	Made for easy, comfortable travel on paved city streets.
Travel Bike	Folds up to be carried in a suitcase or on an airplane.
Street-riding Bike	Grinds off curbs, jumps off walls; strong, heavy, 20-inch wheels.
Triathlon Bike	Very aerodynamic and streamlined, lightweight.
Mountain Bike	Cross-country racing model—for trail racing. Downhill racing model—made to go downhill fast; full suspension bike with front and rear shocks.
Road-racing Bike	Dropped handlebars, skinny tires.
Tandem Bike	Made for 2 (tandem), 3 (triple), or 4 (quad) people.
Specialty Bike for People With Disabilities	Has three or four wheels for balance; can be pedaled with arms if legs are paralyzed.

A commuter bike is used by students, professionals, and workers as a form of transportation. If you decide on this ecological and cost-effective mode of transportation, look for a bike with these features:

* Medium-width, strong, nonknobby street tires for a comfortable ride, even over potholes.
* Fenders (or the ability to have fenders added during the rainy season).
* Rear rack (to carry a set of bags or attach a plastic basket to carry items).
* Flashing rear red light and a good headlight.

You'll also need to budget for a helmet, a basket or saddlebags to carry your belongings, mirrors, and clothing to keep you safe, warm, and dry in different types of weather. In some areas, you are also required to buy a license for your bike.

Cars

A car can be very convenient. You drive it in and out of your driveway, parking space, or garage to work or school. You can stop anywhere on the way home if you need to run errands. It can usually hold several other people. But, cars can cost a lot of money and can be expensive to insure, drive, park, and maintain.

Motorcycles and Electric Bikes

Motorcycles and electric bikes are primarily one-person vehicles. Several million motorcycles and motorbikes are registered in the U.S. You may find that a motorcycle or motorbike is the best option for you. Buying one costs far less than buying a car, and the costs of running and maintaining a bike are much less than most cars. You can set your own schedule, plan your own route, and take what you can hold.

Remember, you must pass a test in order to get a license to drive a motorcycle. Insuring a motorcycle can also be expensive—nearly as much as insuring a car. Motorcycles can be uncomfortable or unsafe in bad weather and limiting in what they can transport.

Chances of injury are much greater on a motorcycle or motorbike than in a car. These vehicles can be hard for other drivers to see. Unlike car drivers, motorcyclists don't have a frame surrounding them in case of an accident. Hospital emergency rooms see many young people with head injuries, some permanent, as a result of failing to wear a helmet. Helmet laws have been enacted in many states to try to decrease the number of deaths and head injuries from motorcycle accidents.

Don't forget to include the cost of a helmet and other safety and weather items when budgeting for a motorcycle.

Get Smart

Riding Safely

Besides a helmet, required by law in many states, serious motorcyclists recommend the following for safety:

* Goggles.
* Boots.
* A leather or other heavy jacket and pants.
* Gloves.
* Rear-view mirror.
* Windshield and roll-bar (for long trips).

Renting a Car

If you don't have access to a car, it's possible to rent one for the day or week. When you travel, renting a car allows you to get to your destination and then pick up a rental car to use while you're there.

Many people take advantage of rental cars for vacation use.

EXAMPLE: A family visiting another part of the country can rent a car for the week. Having a car allows them to drive to other nearby destinations at less expense and with more flexibility than do other forms of transportation.

Although car rental dealers offer you the option of paying extra for insurance, most people don't need it. If you have personal car insurance, it often includes rental car coverage. If you pay with a credit card, car insurance is often a benefit of card use. When traveling for business, your company's insurance will provide coverage.

If you plan to rent a car in another country, check on the requirements and papers you will need before you go.

Beware! It often comes as a shock to many young adults that in many states you must be over the age of 25 to rent a car. You must also have a valid driver's license that has not expired.

Alternative Transport

There are many unusual ways to get where you're going! One small-town teacher uses a scooter to get to work. Many students find skateboards or in-line skates perfect for getting to school. People in snowy areas sometimes cross-country ski or snow-shoe to work. If you live in a watery geographic area, you just might take a ferry, kayak, or small boat to work or school. Some ranchers use small planes to oversee their property, while people in rural Alaska may travel primarily by dogsled. Of course, there is always plain old-fashioned walking.

There are also innovative programs using familiar forms of transportation such as bikes and cars.

Bikes for the Taking

Imagine walking a couple of blocks down the street to a rack of basic, no-frills bicycles. You take one and ride it to your destination, and then ride back. The bikes, hundreds of them, are free to everyone in the area on an as-needed basis. They are easily distinguishable and there is no reason to steal them.

In some cities in Europe and in this country, variations on this theme are taking place. The goal: to decrease pollution and traffic by keeping as many cars off city streets as possible.

Carpools and Vanpools

With a carpool or vanpool, people take turns driving private cars with two or three other people to the same location at the same time each day.

EXAMPLE: Four people who work in the New Hampshire state capital all live one hour away in another town. They regularly carpool to work, which means three fewer cars on the road, five days a week.

Vanpools are groups of people who take turns driving a small van to the same business each day. The van aids workers in getting to work without having to drive and park private cars. Sometimes the vans are owned and maintained by the business. Of course, there are advantages and disadvantages to carpools and vanpools. Still, for many people, the advantages far outweigh the minor inconveniences.

Pros and Cons of Carpools	
Advantages	**Disadvantages**
You save money because you pay only a share of gas, oil, repairs, and parking fees.	Requires you to stick to the group's agreed-upon schedule.
Lets you take advantage of carpool lanes for vehicles with one or more passengers, thus getting to work faster.	Leaves no room for spontaneity, such as stopping to run errands on the way home, unless everyone agrees.
Is better for the environment.	Depends on the habits of the others in the car pool.

Car Sharing

Designed to help people who can't afford a car and to cut down on private car use and the frustration—and expense—of paying for parking, San Francisco's CarShare program began as a federally funded nonprofit organization in March 2001. Geared to big-city living, the program allows you to reserve a Volkswagen Golf, Jetta, or Beetle online for time periods as short as fifteen minutes.

You pick up your car from one of nine garages located in various parts of the city.

A keychain attachment opens the garage, and a swipe card in the glove box allows you to get gas if needed. The swipe card electronically meters the time you use the car. At the end of the month, a bill neatly itemizes all your trips at a charge of $2.50 per hour plus 45 cents per mile plus the $10 monthly fee. One car owner's monthly bill was $71, far less than he would have spent driving and parking his own car. For people who don't have their own cars, CarShare can be an easy way to run errands.

Owning Your Own Wheels

Even with all the alternative transportation options available, owning a car is still Americans' overwhelming first choice.

For all the independence and freedom car ownership can bring, it's important to make sure your decision to buy a car is a wise one. If not, your decision can leave you financially strapped and feeling anything but free.

Selecting a Vehicle

What kind of vehicle do you want? What will be its primary use? Can you afford a new car? Will special requirements be necessary to drive in your climate? What options do you want or need? All of these questions and many more need to be asked and answered before you go shopping for a car. If you don't do your homework ahead of time, a car dealer may spot you coming and talk you into something you perhaps don't need and can't afford.

New or Used?

Most people would pick a new car over a used car if they could afford it. But there are advantages and disadvantages to new cars and used cars.

New cars start to **depreciate**, or lose their value, as soon as you drive them off the lot, and they continue to lose resale value each year. You may be able to take advantage of depreciation by buying a used car in good condition. Look for one with very low miles on it.

The chief benefit of buying a new car is that just about nobody else has driven it. Certainly, nobody has driven it for any length of time or distance. It's never been in an accident or poorly maintained. Also, it may include safety features that older cars lack.

The chief benefit of buying a used car is that it will cost significantly less than a new one. But, you can never be sure of how it was cared for before it came to you. It's wise to choose a used car from a dealer or individual who can provide a repair record. Have a mechanic you trust check it out before you buy.

Lemon Laws

Every state has **lemon laws** to protect consumers. A "lemon" is a new car that:

* Can't be repaired after three or four tries.
* Can't be driven for one month out of one year (or the warranty period).
* Has one major problem after another.

Keep all receipts and service records for any car, but especially for one you think is a lemon. Lemon laws require manufacturers to either replace a lemon or refund money paid for the car and the repairs.

When looking for a good used car, think about what you can afford and what make and model of car you want. Are there specific features you want, such as **manual transmission**—a gear shift mounted on the steering column or on the floor that you operate by hand? Here are some helpful hints:

* If you go to a dealer, make sure it has a reputation for honesty. Talk to people who may have bought a car there. How long has the dealership been in business? Have complaints been filed against it with the Better Business Bureau in the last three years? How were they resolved?

* Research the make and model of car you want in consumer magazines and on the Internet to see the repair record and overall performance.
* Check the "For Sale" ads in places such as your local paper, weekly shopper ads, company newsletter, or credit union bulletin board.
* Test-drive the car. Ask to see the repair records. Ask every question you can think of. (Make a list ahead of time.)
* Have the car you like checked out by a mechanic of your choice. It may cost a little money, but it's worth it.
* Pay attention to the **odometer**, which measures the car's mileage. Dealers are required by law to give you the true mileage of the car. If the odometer has turned over at 100,000, the dealer is required to give you that information.
* What warranty, if any, does it have?
* Be willing to walk away if the price doesn't meet your expectations.

Repossessions

Credit unions sometimes have repossessed vehicles for sale. These cars are often quite new with low mileage and are for sale at a reasonable price, since credit unions aren't in the car-selling business. Check them out!

Beware of any used car with these telltale signs:

* Excessive rust.
* Drips of fluid on the pavement under the car.
* Brakes that pull or seem weak.
* Car that seems hard to steer or turn.
* The paint doesn't match (indicates the car has been in an accident). Some people suggest sliding a small magnet along the body. Wherever the magnet won't stick, it means plastic or epoxy body repair has been added—the car was in an accident.
* Moldy, wet odor inside the car.
* Blue smoke coming from the tailpipe (usually means the engine is burning oil).
* Lights that don't work, or only work sometimes.

Good Sources of Car Information

Good information can come from many different sources, including:

* The first-hand experiences of family, friends, and neighbors.
* The Internet.
* Your insurance agent.
* A credit union car-buying service or recommended used-car-finding service.
* Daily newspaper columns that regularly review new cars.
* *Kelley Blue Book.*
* Magazines.

Your research should answer any questions about your year, make, and model of car related to:

* Overall performance.
* Gas mileage.
* Repair records.
* Safety.
* Comfort.
* Price, including new and used models and cost of options that interest you.

Makes and Models

Decisions regarding makes and models of cars may take some time to research. It's important not to have your heart set on one particular car. If you do, you might end up making a poorly informed purchase that you'll regret later. Keep your options open.

Your first decision may be about the size of car. If you regularly drive with kids you may want a minivan. If you take public transportation during the week, you may only need a mid-size car to take out of town on weekends. There are many categories of cars to choose from:

* Economy car.
* Mid-size car.
* Full-size car.
* Luxury car.
* Sports car.
* Sport Utility Vehicle (SUV).
* Minivan.
* Small or full-size pick-up.

Standard Equipment

Standard equipment includes features that are part of the car's base price. You do not pay extra for them. They may include:

* AM/FM radio and cassette tape deck.
* Air conditioning.
* 6-cylinder engine.

It's important to know what features come with the car and which ones you will have to pay extra for.

Options

There are many ways to increase the base price of a new car. One way is to add a lot of **options**, or added features, such as:

* Sunroof.
* CD player.
* Roof rack.
* Side airbags.
* An anti-theft package.
* Leather seats.

You can also pay extra for your car through dealer add-ons, options that come from the dealer's repair shop rather than from the manufacturer. These are not typically worth the extra money. Such add-ons include:

* Stain resistant spray for the upholstery.
* Rust-proofing.

Options are usually sold in sets, or packages, so in order to get, say, leather seats, you also have to get the more expensive sound system. Think carefully about the options you really want.

Energy-Efficient Vehicles

Vehicles that use gasoline create carbon dioxide, a greenhouse gas. Scientific evidence suggests that the rapid buildup of greenhouse gases in the atmosphere raises the earth's temperature and changes the climate. According to the EPA, every gallon of gasoline your vehicle burns puts 20 pounds of carbon dioxide into the atmosphere.

Buying a fuel-efficient vehicle can save you more than $1,500 per year in fuel costs! Not only that, over the lifetime of the vehicle, it will prevent more than 15 tons of greenhouse gases from polluting the air. You can save a lot of money and help protect the environment by investing in an energy-efficient car.

Hybrid electric vehicles (HEVs) are still new on the market but are beginning to catch the eye of consumers because of their fuel efficiency. They combine the best features of typical (internal combustion) gasoline engines and electric motors.

Calculating Costs

It's very important to understand what you will pay for the car you desire. You may decide to lease, rather than buy a car. You may decide to save up for the down payment for six months in order to make a larger down payment and have a smaller loan. You may change your mind on the type of car you want because one car gets better mileage and seems to have fewer—and less expensive—repair costs.

Owning vs. Leasing

When you own a car (meaning it has been paid in full), the pink slip, or title (proof of ownership) to the car, is yours. If you finance the vehicle through the dealership or through a bank or credit union, the pink slip remains in their possession until the loan is paid in full.

When you **lease** a car, it is like a long-term rental agreement. You make payments for two or three years, but at the end of the lease, the car goes back to the dealer. It is never yours. There are advantages and disadvantages to buying and leasing.

Buying a Car

There are several ways to buy a car:

* You can save up the money and pay cash. For most people, it would take a long time to save this much money.
* You can trade in another car, which will help get the loan amount down.
* You can save up enough for a down payment. On a $20,000 car, the down payment might be one-fourth or one-fifth of the cost ($4,000 or $5,000). You will then get a loan for the remaining $15,000 or $16,000. The length of a car loan used to be two or three years tops, but cars have increased in price. Now, you can get car loans for 36, 48, or even 60 months, depending on the car and your financial situation. The longer the loan, the less the monthly payment, of course. But you will be making payments for a longer period of time and you will pay more because of the interest charges for carrying the loan a longer time. Consider carefully where you are in your life and the amount of stress you want. If it's a time of many changes, when your job or where you'll be living in six months is uncertain, it may not be a good time to saddle yourself with a big three- to five-year financial commitment.

The process of buying a car takes time and practice, but once you know the process, you'll be ready to go!

* Know the invoice price of the car. This is the price the dealer paid. You can find out the invoice price of any make and model of car on the Internet, from *Edmund's,* or from *Consumer Reports.* You can order a full report on a specific make and model of car, including each option, for a fee.
* Decide which options you want and find out the invoice price of each one. Then add up the invoice price of the car plus the options.
* Compare the invoice price with the **sticker price** on the car. This is the manufacturer's suggested retail price. It's usually around 10 percent above the invoice price. Subtract any dealer offers. Also subtract the value of your old car, the trade-in, if you have one. Subtract this amount at the end of the process, *never* at the beginning.
* Now, how much should go to the dealer as profit? Many people feel that around 3 percent is a fair profit. So you will be haggling over the 7 percent.
* What kind of warranty does the car have on the engine, transmission, and other parts?

There are many resources available to help you make a smart car purchase. The more knowledge you have, the better deal you'll be able to strike on the car of your dreams. Remember, be willing to walk away from that dream car if you can't reach a deal that feels right to you.

Search This

Car Prices

Log onto the Internet and go to car web sites, such as the ones sponsored by *Edmund's* or *Kelley Blue Book.* Find out the invoice price of three different cars. Call or visit a car dealership and see how much the sticker price is for each car. How much profit would the dealer make if you paid the sticker price?

Leasing a Car

It's always important to compare the costs of buying and leasing a car. There are added leasing fees that must be calculated when comparing the two to see if you are getting the best possible deal. If you don't know the terminology or leasing process, it's easy to get stuck with a bad deal.

* The first step is to negotiate the price of the car until you agree on its cost, just as you would with a purchase. Say you arrive at a cost of $16,000.
* Next, you must know the amount you will need to pay. If the lease says that the car's value will be at least 65 percent of its current value at the end of the lease, then you will have to pay 35 percent of the $16,000, or $5,600.

* In addition, you will have to make a down payment. Often, it is equal to one month's payment plus a fee that includes a security deposit.
* If you make a down payment of, say, $1,000, you will be financing $5,600–$1,000, or $4,600, for 24 or 36 months. Remember, however, that you are making payments for two or three years on a car you will never own. Still, leasing may allow you to drive a car that you couldn't afford to buy.
* Watch the mileage restriction. You are usually allowed 12,000 miles per year. If you drive more than that, you will have to pay more—often a great deal more.
* At the end of the lease, you return the car and pay for any extra miles or needed repairs. At this point, there is often a large payment required, sometimes several months' worth of payments. Be sure to ask about these payments and factor that into your decision.

Leasing a car has definite pros and cons. Sometimes leasing makes good sense as a tax write-off for a small business. Often, people lease a car because it allows them to drive a fancier, more expensive car than they could afford to buy. This is because lease payments are lower than financing the purchase price of the car. However, it's important to remember that you never own the car. You continue to make car payments forever, unlike a car loan that eventually can be paid in full.

Financing Your Vehicle

A vehicle may be financed through a savings and loan, the bank, a credit union, or the car dealership. Sometimes people decide to finance the loan through the dealership because they get special deals or **rebates** (money back). However, credit unions often have the best rates. Look for programs in your area that are partnerships between a credit union and participating dealerships. They let buyers take advantage of dealer rebates and still finance their car through the credit union—right at the dealership.

Banks, credit unions, and savings and loans have very different interest rates. It pays to shop around. Check the Internet as well. If you know the year, make, and model of car you want, you may be able to get pre-approved for a loan up to a certain dollar amount that is well within your budget with monthly payments you can afford.

Operating Expenses

Buying the vehicle is just the beginning of the costs you must be prepared to pay for the privilege of car ownership. Do some research in your area to find out how much you will likely spend and calculate the monthly payment for the following items:

* License and registration fee (divide by 12).
* Car insurance (get the rate for 6 months and divide by 6).
* Gas and oil.
* Parking (lots, meters, and tickets).
* Car wash.
* Other maintenance.

When you finish, think about the amount of discretionary income you have each month. What percentage does the grand total for the car represent? Some consumer groups feel that 13 percent of your discretionary income is the maximum amount that should be spent on transportation.

Maintenance

Like anything else you own, taking care of your car will make it last longer and require fewer major repairs. Here's the Big 10 of auto maintenance:

1. Check the owner's manual. Follow the maintenance schedule indicated for your car, or ask a mechanic for advice on a used car that's new to you.
2. Get regular lube and oil changes and tune-ups.
3. Wash the exterior and interior regularly.
4. Check all fluid levels and keep them filled.

5. Open the hood and check all belts and hoses for signs of wear (frayed edges and tears).
6. Check tires for wear. Check tire pressure and rotate, balance, and align tires periodically.
7. Check paint. Touch up any scratches or nicks to prevent rusting.
8. Complete recommended preventive maintenance for cold winter (or hot summer) weather.
9. Check headlights, taillights, and brake lights.
10. Check brakes. If they feel low or if the car pulls to the left or right when you apply the brakes, get them checked right away.

Whether you buy a new or used car, you can save money by learning how to do some of the basic maintenance, such as oil changes, yourself.

Search This

Calculate Your Car Payment

Find a source on the Internet that will calculate your car payment. You might try typing "car loan calculator" in a search engine.

Once you've found the web site, type in the number of months you want for

the loan, the interest rate, and the loan amount. Then the program will compute your monthly payment. It's a good way to see what price of car is in your budget and the difference that interest rates can make.

Parking Woes

Angela had it all planned out. She figured it was a lot better to drive her car and park in the paid student parking lot than to ride the bus. She budgeted $3 per day times 12 days per month for a total of $36 for parking. It didn't work out quite that way.

Angela got five parking tickets last month, which she felt was unfair! They were 3-hour meters, and she only missed the expiration by 5 or 10 minutes, each time because the class ran a few minutes over.

Unfortunately, each ticket cost $16. She forgot to pay two of the five tickets within 30 days, so two of the fines doubled. Including the money she put into the parking meter to begin with, how much did Angela actually pay for parking last month? What would you do if you were Angela?

Insurance Coverage and Costs

The cost of insuring your vehicle is another major expense. Young people, especially, often pay high rates. You also pay more or less, depending on the vehicle you're insuring. Before you purchase any car, make sure you know how much it will cost to insure it.

Usually, insurance estimates are given on a six-month basis, so if the rate quoted is $450, that amount may only be for six months. You must divide by six to figure out how much you will have to put aside each month, so when the insurance premium comes due, the money will be there.

If you are in an accident or receive a moving violation of any kind that appears on your record, expect your insurance rates to go up even more.

Get Smart

Fluid Levels

Just like people, cars need their fluids! Without the right levels, cars wear out more quickly and use fuel less efficiently. Check these vital fluid levels for your car regularly:

* Oil.
* Transmission fluid.
* Brake fluid.
* Windshield wiper fluid.
* Antifreeze.
* Water.

There are many ways to get around. For some people, public transportation is an inexpensive, convenient option. For others, traveling by bike or motorcycle works well. Still others walk.

Many people choose to either buy or lease a new or used car. When purchasing a car, there are many things to consider, including financing, operating expenses, maintenance and repairs, and insurance.

New options in transportation are being developed, such as light rail systems and hybrid electric vehicles, which offer exciting new options to drivers.

Deciding on a means of transportation is a decision you'll make many times throughout your life. Each time, the conditions may be very different from the time before. It's important to establish a process for making such an important decision. The good news is, now is the perfect time to start.

Consumer Economics

depreciate—lessen in value. *p. 289*

hybrid electric vehicles (HEVs)— energy-efficient vehicles that run by two sources of power, electric and gasoline. *p. 292*

lease—rent, usually for a long term. *p. 293*

lemon laws—consumer protection laws that require a car manufacturer to replace or repay the consumer for a defective new car that cannot be fixed after several tries. *p. 290*

manual transmission—on a car, gears that are shifted by hand with a gear shift mounted on the steering column or on the floor. *p. 290*

mass transit—public transportation in urban areas. *p. 282*

odometer—instrument on a car that measures the distance traveled in miles. *p. 290*

options—features added to a new car that cost extra and aren't included in the base price. *p. 292*

rebates—special bargains offered by a car dealership that return part of the price of a car. *p. 295*

standard equipment—car features that are included as part of the base price of the car. *p. 292*

sticker price—car manufacturer's recommended retail price, usually about 10 percent above the price the dealer paid the manufacturer. *p. 294*

How Insurance Can Protect You

In this chapter, you will learn about:

- different types of insurance
- how to choose the best insurance for you
- how to keep coverage once it's in place

It's enough to make anyone a little whiny. You save up all your money to buy a house or a car, and then you find out you have to pay more money to insure it! You're perfectly healthy, and yet people advise you to spend your hard-earned money on health insurance. What's the point?

Carla found out the hard way. "I didn't take the value of having insurance seriously until I suddenly got very ill. I was only twenty-two. How could this happen? It was not fair! Most unfair of all was how much I paid for not having health insurance. My hospital bills were staggering. Do you know I am still paying them off four years later? Check on me in six years. Trust me, I'll still be paying."

Insurance Basics

If you lost your backpack, it would be frustrating and inconvenient, but it wouldn't cost much to replace it. However, if your car was totaled, or if you lost your house and all your belongings in a house fire, it would be devastating. There is probably no way you could simply write a check to replace what you lost. That's where insurance comes in.

You purchase insurance to help you pay for the things that could happen to you that you couldn't possibly afford.

Our laws say that if you cause damage to others, even without meaning to, you must pay to compensate them for their losses or injuries. Did a loose stair on your porch result in someone's falling and breaking a leg? You have to pay. Insurance can cover you against these kinds of expenses.

Insurance companies offer different **insurance policies**, or plans, for health, car, homeowner's, disability, and life insurance. The amounts of coverage may vary widely.

How Does Insurance Work?

Let's say you pay $800 a year for your car insurance. You've had the insurance for two years, but you've never had to file a **claim**. (A claim is a request to your insurance company for payment of, or reimbursement for, losses for which you are insured.) You're a good, careful driver, but yesterday there was some unexpected ice on the road. You skidded, hit another car, and drove into a ditch. No one was hurt, but both cars were damaged. The cost for repairs will come to just over $6,000 dollars.

Making it REAL

What if Something Happened?

Imagine each situation below. What type of insurance would you need to protect you from the financial impact of these situations? Consider the consequences of *not* having insurance. What do you think might happen if you didn't have the money to handle these situations?

* You are injured and can't work for eight months.
* Your spouse dies, leaving you with two school-age children to raise alone.

* You accidentally rear-end another car, causing serious damage to both cars.
* You come home from a weekend away to find that a broken water pipe spilled hundreds of gallons of water into your house.
* You need emergency surgery to remove a tumor from your lung.
* You let a friend borrow your car, and he smashes your neighbor's garage door, fence, and prized rose bushes. It's your car, you have to pay.

If you've only spent $1,600 on premiums (2 years x $800), how can the insurance company pay for the damages? It mixes your premiums with everyone else's premiums. Most people don't have accidents often, so the dollars in the pot are greater than the dollars needed to pay out claims.

When you buy insurance, you are sharing the risk with all the other **policy holders**—all the people who buy insurance, pay premiums, and are therefore eligible to file claims. Some of you will need to file claims. Others won't. Everyone, though, is protected *if* something bad happens. That is the value of having insurance and paying premiums, even when it's tempting to use the money for something else.

Insurance Policies		
Type of Insurance	**Purpose**	**Protection**
Health Insurance	Protects in case of illness and other bodily injuries.	Pays for doctor or dental visits, prescriptions, hospital visits, and other illness or injury-related costs.
Car Insurance	Protects persons and vehicles in case of an accident or theft.	Protects against being sued; pays for damage to vehicles and property; may pay for towing and accident-related medical costs.
Homeowner's Insurance	Protects against damage to real property (structures or land) or damage, loss, or theft of personal property (items of value such as furniture, jewelry, or computer equipment).	✳ Pays for damage to a house and belongings due to fire, storms, wind or water damage, theft, or vandalism. ✳ May pay to rebuild a house similar to the one you had or to replace a stolen item. ✳ Separate policies can be purchased for each type of property or combined in one homeowner's insurance policy. ✳ Special insurance policies may be purchased to cover earthquakes or flood damage. ✳ Renter's (or tenant's) insurance covers personal property only.
Disability Insurance	Protects income when you are unable to work and earn a living.	Provides a percentage of income to insured when out of work due to injury or long-term illness.
Life Insurance	Protects the family in the event of the death of a wage-earning family member.	Provides money to the family of someone who has died to help the family pay bills related to the person's death and to help meet ongoing living expenses.

Buying Insurance

Insurance is complicated. When you buy insurance, you are entering into a legally binding contract with the insurance company. You are obligated to make your payments on time, and the company is obligated to pay certain amounts in the event of certain things happening. There are **three** important reasons why you should buy carefully:

1. You want to be sure the protection you believe you are buying will really be there when you need it.
2. You don't want to pay more for it than you must.
3. There is a lot of fine print.

Insurance Agents and Salespeople

Get an insurance agent or sales person you can trust. An agent can explain exactly what you are buying. An agent can provide you with choices, and he or she can work with the company you choose to help you get prompt attention for your claims. It is wise to choose this agent with the same care you would use to choose any other professional. Ask friends, coworkers, your boss, and others. Who do they use? What have their experiences been?

Keeping Costs Down

To some extent, you can control the cost of insurance by:

* Rechecking your needs and the prices of available coverage every year or so.

* Not insuring yourself against events you can afford to pay for on your own.
* Taking the highest deductible you can afford.

A deductible is the amount you pay out of your own pocket before the insurance company pays. All policies assume you will pay some portion of the cost of your losses. Deductibles can range from as little as $100 to as much as $5000.

The higher the deductible you take, the lower your premiums will be. You should take the highest deductible you can afford. Over time, you will save a great deal more money in premiums than you will spend in deductibles.

Individual Protection

Individual protection is designed to protect the assets, car, personal property, or home of an individual or family. It can also protect people in the event that they are unable to work, or a family in the event of a family member's death.

Asset Protection

Insurance protects your **assets**—the things of monetary value that you own. Your assets may include items such as a car, house, and your electric guitar, as well as money you have in savings. If something should happen, you do not want anyone to take your assets in order to pay what can be overwhelming bills. Look around your room and house now. What items of value do you now own? What ones might you have in five years? In ten years?

Car Insurance

Cars are not only expensive to buy, but are expensive to repair as well. If you are in an accident that is your fault, or if the accident is the fault of someone without insurance, it is up to you to pay. How will you do that? If you hit another car and no one is injured, you have the price of fixing one or more vehicles. On top of that, people may be injured or even killed. Property may be damaged if a car drives over a curb and hits a store. You should never drive a vehicle without knowing that there is insurance on the vehicle you're driving. The financial risks are too great.

Get Smart

Irreplaceable Items

What items do you or your family own that absolutely could not be replaced? Even though your grandma's china and your grandfather's saxophone are valuable and important to you, many people put family photographs at the top of the list.

Losing a lifetime of photos is losing an important link to your own history. Here are some ways to ensure the safety of photos that can't be replaced no matter how much insurance you might have:

* Keep old family photos in a lockbox.
* Make copies of photos, and give them to other family members so no one family member has the only photos or family photo album.
* Put your photos on a CD or make a video slide show, so you have a record in more than one format.
* If you live in a location prone to forest fires or flooding, keep photos in a safe place away from home.

Most states now have **financial responsibility laws** that require car owners to carry insurance unless they can prove that they are financially responsible up to a certain dollar amount. If you were extremely wealthy, it's possible you wouldn't need insurance. No matter what happened, you could just write a check to take care of it. Rest assured, however, that the other 99 percent of car owners need insurance.

You are required to keep proof of insurance in your car at all times. Keep it in the glove compartment or in a special clip attachment on your visor.

Car insurance covers:

* ***Your losses***—the costs to repair damages to your car or to replace it if it cannot be repaired. *Collision* coverage pays for damage caused by running into something or someone running into you. *Comprehensive* coverage pays for damages from other sources, such as hail or theft.
* ***Your obligations to others***—the cost to compensate others for injury or death or to repair or replace their property when anyone driving your car caused the damage or injury. This is **liability coverage**.

By the Numbers

When Not to Use Insurance

Say you get in your car one morning to find your case of 25 CDs was stolen during the night. You have insurance on your belongings, both as part of your car insurance and your homeowner's policy. Your car insurance deductible is $250. Your house insurance deductible is $500. How do you decide which insurance policy to use?

For small claims like this, it depends. How much would it cost to replace the CDs? If you use homeowner's insurance, you'll essentially replace all the CDs yourself, since the deductible (the amount you pay up front to file a claim) is $500, probably more than the replacement cost of the stolen items.

So, you figure using your car insurance is the best route to go, but first, ask yourself whether it's worth it. Remember, you must pay your $250 deductible up front, so the insurance will only pay the replacement costs above $250. Will your premiums go up if you file a claim? If so, it probably isn't worth it. Making matters more complicated, you may be required to prove the CDs were in your car.

In the end, you may decide you only really want to replace 10 or 12 of the 25 CDs that were stolen. How much would that cost?

* **Medical expenses**—the costs to care for both the occupants of your car and other people injured by your car as a result of a car accident.

Collision and comprehensive coverage are optional. There are times when you might choose to save money by not buying them. If you are driving an old beater, it may not be worth your insuring its replacement cost.

It is necessary to determine who caused an accident, in order to figure out which insurance company should pay—yours or the other person's. However, suppose the other person doesn't have insurance? To protect against this eventuality, all states require people to carry at least a minimum amount of *uninsured motorist* protection. This is one time when you should consider buying more than the minimum.

Many states also require insurance companies to offer **no-fault auto insurance**. Under no-fault, your insurance company pays the medical bills of people injured in your car, no matter who was at fault.

Coverage Costs and Requirements

Usually, car insurance policies are written on a six-month basis, so if the rate quoted is $450, that is only for six months. You must divide by six to figure out how much you will have to put aside each month so when the insurance premium comes due, the money will be there. If you are in an accident or receive a moving violation of any kind that appears on your record, expect your insurance rates to go up.

A new car will require insurance coverage that an older car will not. It's important to reevaluate your coverage to make sure that you're not paying for coverage you no longer need.

EXAMPLE: If you are driving an older car, the amount of collision and comprehensive coverage needed when it was new no longer applies. Now the dollar value of the car is worth very little, even though it's worth the world to you. The insurance company will not pay you more than its market value, no matter how much you originally insured it for.

Problem Solving

If you find yourself in a position where you are denied coverage, here's what to do:

* Call your agent or the insurance company. Find out why you were denied coverage and request to see a copy of your file.
* Research other insurance companies. Even if you are denied coverage by one company, you may be accepted by another.
* If you know that your driving record is keeping you from getting car insurance, find out about special high-risk pools in your state. Such pools divide up all poor-risk applicants among many insurance companies so these high-risk people can continue to be insured. It will cost substantially more money to be insured in this way. Over time, as your driving record improves, you will qualify for lower-priced insurance. If it doesn't improve, you may find yourself unable to drive.

Car Insurance Factors

Factors Involved in Cost	Explanation
Age, type, and value of the car.	Newer cars and fast, sporty cars cost more to insure than a typical four-door sedan.
Cost to repair or replace the car.	Expensive cars will cost more to repair or replace.
Age of driver(s).	In general, older drivers pay less; teenage boys pay the most, based on insurance company accident statistics. Adding a teenage driver to a policy can increase rates by 75 percent or more.
Your marital status.	Married people often pay less than single adult drivers.
Your driving record.	If you have received tickets in the past few years or have been in one or more accidents, your insurance will cost more than insurance for someone with a clean driving record. You will also pay more if you have not been continuously insured in the last year.
Amount of driving you do and under what conditions.	Insurance companies factor in the amount of driving you do per year. If you have long commutes or drive under dangerous driving conditions, you will pay more for car insurance.
Your geographic location.	Rates differ from state to state and between urban, suburban, and rural areas.
Area of town in which you live and work.	It costs more to insure a car if you live or work in a high-crime area with lots of car thefts.

Insurance companies give discounts for car insurance under certain conditions. When purchasing car insurance, think about which of these apply to you and see how much you can save as a result!

* Completion of a driver education course.
* Good student discount.
* Nonsmoker.
* Nondrinker.
* Safe driving record.
* Low number of miles driven per year.
* Anti-lock brakes, airbags, security alarm.

Drive Safely

The best insurance against car accidents is the way you drive. Here are some tips for safe driving:

* Drive safely and defensively. Train yourself to be aware of what's happening around you so you have time to respond in order to prevent an accident before it happens.
* Pay attention. Keep distractions, such as conversations, music, or cell phone calls, to a minimum.
* Keep your car in good condition. Regularly check the brakes, lights, windshield wipers, fluid levels, and tires.

Homeowner's Insurance

Homeowner's (or house) insurance is designed to protect your **real property**— that is, your house, its contents, the land it is on, and any other structures on the property (a garage, barn, or workshop, for example). For many people, buying a house is the biggest financial investment they will ever make. It would be next to impossible to recover financially from the loss of this asset without the help of insurance. The savings institution that carries the mortgage on your house will require you to have homeowner's insurance to protect *its* investment.

Personal Property Insurance

Personal property insurance covers all your personal belongings in case of theft, fire, or other disasters. **Personal property** is defined as all the items you own that can be moved. Personal property includes:

* Antiques.
* Appliances.
* Bicycles.
* Clothing.
* Computer equipment.
* Furnishings.
* Household items (bedding, dishes, books).
* Jewelry.

Personal property insurance is typically a part of any homeowner's policy. It covers losses at home and also items lost or damaged away from home (a camera lost on a river trip or golf clubs stolen from your car). **Renter's insurance** policies are designed to insure your personal belongings in a house you do not own.

Vehicle, homeowner's, renter's, and personal property policies combine to cover your possessions.

Imagine what it would be like to suffer the loss of all your belongings. Having insurance certainly doesn't make up for the terrible loss, but it can help you financially to begin to start over.

Personal and Family Protection

Life and disability insurance policies protect you and your family in case you cannot earn an income due to death, injury, or illness. They are designed to protect people and lost income, rather than replacing possessions.

Health Insurance

Health insurance is designed to protect you and your family in the event of illness or bodily injury. Medical costs can be overwhelming if you have to pay them all yourself. You may be lucky enough to have good medical insurance through your employer, but if not, you should purchase coverage yourself. (See pages 204–10 for more information about health insurances.)

Life Insurance

Life insurance is designed to protect people left behind when someone dies. It provides survivors with money, which is called a "death benefit." Generally, life insurance is only needed by someone who has **dependents**—family members such as a spouse or children who rely on the person for financial support.

Life insurance can lessen the financial blow to the family in the event of the death of a wage-earning family member.

You buy life insurance for the amount it will pay in the event of the death of the insured individual.

EXAMPLE: Joe takes out a $100,000 policy.

There are **two** main types of life insurance:

1. Cash-value insurance.
2. Term insurance.

When You Can't Afford Insurance

Health care and health insurance are expensive. There may be times when it is simply not affordable. At these times, do you have options? Fortunately, yes. There are government programs that can help, such as Medicaid. County health departments and state programs may also be able to help.

There are many free clinics around the country. One of these, Volunteers in Medicine (VIM), started with one clinic in South Carolina and now has 15 clinics nationwide. The brainchild of retired physician Jack McConnell, VIM clinics offer free or low-cost care to uninsured people,

including doctor visits, prescriptions, and referrals to social service agencies and medical specialists when necessary. There have been cases of people with advanced cancer and other serious illnesses beating their diseases, thanks to the free treatment and surgery they received from physicians and other health-care providers.

In addition to volunteer physicians, VIM clinics rely on community volunteers to help keep clinic doors open evenings and weekends. These long hours and dedicated medical and community volunteers mean VIM's doors are always open to help the uninsured.

Cash-Value Insurance

Cash-value insurance costs more than term insurance, but it has certain advantages. The policy grows in value over time as you pay into it. Should you decide for any reason to quit keeping it, you can cash out for the value you have accumulated. (This amount will be less than you've actually paid, because part of what you are paying for is protection.)

This kind of policy can reach a point in your life when it is fully paid up—often in 20 or 25 years. The protection and cash benefits continue, but you don't continue paying premiums.

The premium costs will not change as you grow older. If you are interested in this

kind of insurance, you should compare the return on the savings part of it to other investment choices, such as bonds.

Term Insurance

Term insurance is much cheaper than cash-value insurance, but it is only in force for the term of the policy—usually one year. It is never paid up. It has no cash value. Many individuals find it an excellent choice when they need coverage for only a few years. A spouse who stays home to care for children may want term insurance on the working spouse's life for the years when the children are small.

Term insurance policy costs go up as you get older. A 20-year-old can buy $100,000 worth of coverage for much less than a 50-year-old can. However, you can buy policies that guarantee not to raise your rates for as long as 20 years.

Disability and Income-Protection Insurance

When an illness or accident prevents you from going to work, you have more than just medical bills to worry about. You lose your income. How will you pay your bills? How will you live? **Disability insurance** both covers medical costs and provides you with income to pay the ordinary costs of living.

Disability insurance is often offered as a benefit by employers. Social Security, too, offers disability coverage to workers who have qualified by paying into the system for a certain amount of time. In addition, insurance companies sell this protection.

Role Model

Disability Insurance

Greg was 33 years old. He had worked for nine years as a computer programmer, and he made a good salary that supported his two young daughters and his wife who stayed home to care for the girls. One day, he was diagnosed with a serious illness, and within six months, he could no longer work.

He had excellent medical insurance that paid the medical bills, but what about the loss of income? Suddenly, Greg's salary was not there, and he and his wife had house payments, food, utilities, a car payment, day care, and other monthly expenses. They did not have much money in savings and did not have family who could help them financially.

Luckily, Greg and his wife had disability insurance to fall back on. Without it, they probably would have had to sell their house.

You can get income protection in several ways:

* **Workers' compensation:** an employer program required by state governments and paid for by the employer. Workers' compensation provides income, medical-care expenses, and retraining for employees injured on the job.
* **Employer-sponsored coverage.** Premiums may be deducted from your paycheck. The employer may also cover part of the premium cost.
* **Individual disability policy,** for which you pay the entire premium.

When purchasing individual coverage, buy a policy that covers you for *no less than* 60 percent of your annual income. Review carefully any conditions that might be excluded from coverage. Also, check the **waiting period**—the amount of time you must wait after the disability or illness before you can collect benefits.

Unemployment Compensation

There is one final avenue of protection against loss of income—**unemployment compensation**. This is a program administered through state governments and paid for with your payroll taxes. If you are released from your job through no fault of your own, you should contact your state unemployment office to learn for what benefits you qualify. You will be asked to complete certain forms. Your previous employer will be contacted. You will be expected to look for work and may be required to show evidence of your search.

Maintaining Coverage

Insurance coverage is only there as long as your payments are up to date. You take a big risk when you pay late or skip a payment.

Imagine this. You're a careful driver and have never been in an accident. In fact, you don't drive all that much or very far. Now you're a little short on cash, so you've let the due date slip by without sending in your money. The company notified you that it would cancel if you didn't pay, but you didn't get around to it. Then, this morning as you turned a corner, a kid on a bike skidded in front of you. You hit her and knocked her down. She went to the hospital. You called your insurance agent and found you're no longer covered. Now what will you do? You could be looking at a fine for driving without coverage and huge expenses.

Don't make this kind of mistake. Make sure you are insured continuously by making timely payments. Also, if you change from one policy to another, make sure there are no days in between policies when you're not insured.

Community Protection

It can't happen here! We humans have the ability to fool ourselves in the most amazing ways. We can't imagine anything really bad happening to us . . . until it happens. The news, however, is filled with examples of whole neighborhoods that were devastated by a tornado, natural gas explosion, or forest fire.

When Disasters Strike

Throughout history, natural disasters of all kinds have occurred and will continue to occur. They include:

* Earthquakes.
* Forest fires.
* Tornadoes.
* Hurricanes.
* Windstorms.
* Floods.

Can you think of any more to add to the list? It is likely that you or someone you know has experienced one of these natural disasters.

Individuals can minimize the damage due to natural disasters to some degree by having some things in place (in addition to adequate insurance) before anything happens. For example:

* Think twice before building a house on the edge of an unstable hill, no matter how beautiful the view. The same is true of building a house right next to a river that regularly overflows its banks (in this case, flood insurance is very expensive).
* If you live in an area where earthquakes occur, earthquake-proof your house. Bolt down your water heater. Secure your cupboard doors with child safety latches to help minimize loss due to breakage.

My Notebook

Insurance Incidents

Think back over the last year. Recall all the times when you might have benefited from insurance, and write them down.

* How often were you sick? Did you go to the doctor? Did you buy medicine?
* Did you have any injuries? Any trips to the emergency room?
* Were you involved in any bicycle or car accidents?
* Did you miss any income due to illness, accident, or injury?
* Was anything of yours stolen?
* Was your neighborhood damaged by any disasters, such as a tornado, earthquake, fire, or flood?

You may be surprised by how many things have happened that were easier to deal with by having insurance.

* Make a list of valuables to take upstairs if a flood occurs.
* Have all your important papers in one place to grab in case of evacuation.
* Keep important papers in a safety deposit box at a bank.
* Have a family evacuation plan in case of fire or other emergency.

* Keep a list of items to pack in the car if you leave your house due to the threat of a hurricane or other natural disaster.
* Make sure batteries in smoke alarms work. Experts recommend changing them twice a year, when we change the clocks for daylight savings time.
* Consider other alarms for your home, such as a carbon monoxide alarm.

Can you think of other ways to minimize the damage caused by natural disasters?

There are also disasters that are anything but natural. Terrorist attacks are an example. So are explosions at chemical processing plants or a dam that bursts. Can you think of other unnatural disasters?

These disasters—natural or unnatural— all have one thing in common: They affect more than one family. Sometimes an entire neighborhood or town is affected.

In addition to the loss of life and houses, public buildings and businesses may be lost with a resulting loss of jobs. In many cases, the damage may also have an impact on the area's **infrastructure**, which may include the roads, public utilities (including water and power), public transportation, emergency services, and public safety (including police, fire, and ambulance service).

In such cases, individuals cannot take care of the problem through their individual insurance policies alone. It is too enormous. Help must come from government at all levels and from relief organizations such as the Red Cross.

Rebuilding

In the case of disasters that touch not just one house but an entire community, government steps in to help people. Agencies providing disaster relief go to work to provide temporary living quarters and food to people. Low-interest loans are made available for rebuilding. Procedures to quickly process insurance claims are initiated. Again, no one can sufficiently remove the pain and suffering of people who have experienced such devastation. But with the help of agencies, volunteers, and the government, people can slowly begin to put their lives back together again over time.

Chapter 16 Wrap-up
HOW INSURANCE CAN PROTECT YOU

Insurance protects you from the costs of major events you can't control and can't possibly pay for. Illness, death, injury, fire, car accidents—these are the kinds of events you buy insurance to cover. Insurance is complex, and you should find a professional—an agent or the sales person at a respected company—to help you.

At some time you may need car insurance, renter's or homeowner's insurance, life insurance, and disability insurance. Unemployment compensation is available through your state government. It is wise to have as much coverage as you can afford.

WORDS TO KNOW

asset—possession that has monetary value. (In the plural, *assets* are all the property owned by a person or business that could be used to pay debts.) *p. 303*

claim—request to your insurance company for payment of, or reimbursement for, losses for which you are insured. *p. 300*

dependents—people, usually family members, who rely on you for financial support. *p. 308*

disability insurance—coverage that helps with living and medical expenses if you cannot work due to injury or illness. *p. 310*

financial responsibility laws—laws requiring proof that you are financially responsible up to a certain dollar amount. *p. 304*

infrastructure—structure of a community or nation that includes the roads, public utilities (including water and power), public transportation, emergency services, and public safety (including police, fire, and ambulance service). *p. 313*

insurance policy—contract offered by an insurance company that details what kinds of events are covered, how the amount of payment will be calculated, and how much the insured will pay for the coverage. *p. 300*

liability coverage—type of insurance that pays the costs of your obligations to others for whose death, injury, or loss you are responsible. *p. 304*

life insurance—form of insurance that provides survivors with money, called a death benefit, if you die. *p. 308*

no-fault auto insurance—type of car insurance that pays medical expenses to policy holder and others injured in his or her car regardless of who caused the accident. *p. 305*

personal property—all the items you own that can be moved. *p. 307*

policy holder—person who buys insurance, pays premiums, and is therefore eligible to file claims if necessary. *p. 301*

real property—house, the land it is on, and any other structures on the property. *p. 307*

renter's insurance—property and liability insurance for people who live in a rented home. *p. 307*

unemployment compensation—government-run program operated by the states and paid for with payroll taxes. It provides cash benefits to people who have lost their jobs through no fault of their own. *p. 311*

waiting period—specified amount of time you must wait before collecting benefits. *p. 311*

How to Get Help

In this chapter, you will learn about:

- consumer protection agencies
- government agencies
- legal services

"I'm going to scream if I get one more bill from that stupid place!" fumed Alana. "I paid my bill and said I didn't want any more products."

"We paid a $600 security deposit on the apartment. We followed every instruction and still the landlord refuses to give us back our deposit!" explained Radu and Matt, almost in unison.

"My so-called friend moved out of the apartment and took things that weren't hers, including my CD player. I've talked to her, sent her letters, and left messages on her answering machine. Is there anything I can do to make her give my stuff back?" asked Tina.

"I bought a computer from a mail-order company," explained Kevin. "When it came, it had this loud hum in it. I took it to be repaired, still under warranty. The repair shop had bad news. The computer I paid for had been removed from the case and a cheap one put in its place with serial numbers that don't match. I've tried to reach the company, but nobody will talk to me. What can I do?"

In each of these situations, there seems to be a legitimate complaint. Unfortunately, attempts to resolve the issues thus far haven't worked. For you as a consumer, it's important to know where to go for help.

Seeking Consumer Help

Planning ahead, budgeting carefully, researching products, comparing prices, and documenting your transactions are the best ways to protect yourself from consumer problems. But even when you do everything right, sometimes you will run into problems. What can you do?

* Investigate consumer protection agencies that exist to help consumers.
* Make your voice heard by voting on consumer-related issues.

Consumer Protection Agencies

Consumer protection agencies exist at the federal, state, and local levels. They watch over specific areas, enforce rules and regulations, and penalize those who break the law. Private agencies also help consumers.

When you feel you have been treated unfairly by a business, it's often a good idea to start with the Better Business Bureau.

Better Business Bureau

The Better Business Bureau (BBB) is a non-profit organization with offices in almost every state nationwide. The BBB has no legal authority to settle a dispute, but it helps promote honest business practices in several important ways. It:

* Helps resolve disputes by contacting the business when a dispute has been reported.
* Keeps a file of complaints against local businesses and shares this information with consumers upon request.
* Publishes information booklets.
* Makes information available through its web site.
* Brings consumer complaints to the attention of businesses.
* Helps educate the public about fraudulent business practices and current "scams" reported to them, and suggests how to avoid becoming a victim.
* Investigates unfair advertising and selling practices.
* Refers fraudulent businesses or consumer complaints to the appropriate government agency.

The BBB's Business Reliability Reports provide a valuable service for consumers. You can search by a specific business name and see the general history of complaints and the resolution of those complaints over a three-year period.

EXAMPLE: Alicia wanted to see where to take her car for major service. She had narrowed it down to two garages in her town. She typed in their names and locations on the web site. One garage had only two complaints, both of which were resolved to the consumer's satisfaction. The other had a very high number of unresolved complaints. Now Alicia's choice was easy.

The BBB web site also allows consumers to search the history and legitimacy of charitable organizations. You can use it to learn how much of the money you are giving is spent doing the work you're supporting.

Federal Trade Commission

The Federal Trade Commission (FTC) is a federal agency established in 1914. The FTC:

* Promotes free, fair business competition.
* Investigates unfair and deceptive trade practices.
* Enforces consumer protection legislation in areas such as labeling, packaging, and advertising.
* Protects businesses from unfair competition.

The FTC may open an investigation of a business or industry as a result of complaints from consumers, inquiries from Congress, or reports on consumer-related topics. The FTC has the authority to issue a **cease and desist order** against any business it believes is engaging in unlawful practices. This legal order means that the business must stop doing whatever is in question unless a court overturns the decision.

The FTC web site has a Consumer Complaint Form. Completed forms from consumers can help launch an investigation of fraud. Complaints regarding the Internet, telemarketing, identity theft, and other fraud-related issues are entered into a secure, online database available to hundreds of civil and criminal law enforcement agencies worldwide.

Consumer Protection Legislation

In the last century, many laws were passed to protect consumers and guide the practices of business and industry. Such laws didn't just "happen." They occurred because people made their collective voices heard.

Consumer-related bills continue to be debated and put before Congress. Contact your congressional representatives if you have concerns. Make your voice heard!

Seeking Legal Help

Sometimes a phone call, letter, or visit with a store manager doesn't help, and the Better Business Bureau can't solve your problem. When all else fails, you can seek legal help.

When you seek legal help, it means you see someone who knows the law. This person may be an **attorney**—lawyer— who is legally qualified to represent you in legal proceedings.

You may choose to go to a legal service group such as Legal Aid for assistance with a **civil matter**—a personal or constitutional matter, anything that is not a criminal matter. Child custody, bankruptcy, and a landlord-tenant dispute are all civil matters.

For a **criminal matter**—any matter where a crime has been committed—you need the help of a public defender or private attorney. Parole violations, drug arrests, and burglary are examples of criminal matters.

When Do You Need Legal Help?

There are many situations in which you might need or want to seek the advice or help of a lawyer:

* **You've been arrested.** Say you were arrested for breaking into someone's house. Whether or not you are innocent or guilty, you need a lawyer who will defend you. If you cannot afford a lawyer, the court will appoint a public defender to represent you in court.

* **You're being sued.** In this case, you probably need a lawyer to help you respond to the lawsuit filed against you. If you choose to sue someone, you will also need a lawyer to help you.

* **You are starting a small business.** To set up the legal documents to officially begin your business, you need to see a lawyer who specializes in this area of the law.

* **You want help protecting your rights.** Sometimes, you might need advice relating to your rights as a tenant. You might have a question about a contract—a legally binding agreement you are about to sign. You may believe you have been discriminated against because of your race, religion, age, physical disability, or sexual orientation.

Many contracts are signed without the need of legal assistance. These contracts include:

* Car loans.
* Credit card applications.
* Health club contracts.
* Extended service contracts.
* House insurance contracts.

Lease Agreement

The day you move into your first apartment, you may sign a rental agreement or a lease. It may be the first contract you sign. A lease is a binding contract between you, the **tenant**, and your landlord (property owner). Most leases are for a period of one year, but can be shorter or longer.

A lease protects both you and your landlord. It outlines the rights and responsibilities of you and your landlord. You may want to have a lawyer read over the first lease agreement you sign to make sure you understand what you are signing. Read it carefully. Does it outline things like:

* When the rent is due?
* When late charges, if any, are imposed?
* What happens if you miss a payment?
* If pets are allowed?
* Deposits required, such as cleaning or a security deposit?

* Rules regarding allowing people to move in with you whose names aren't on the lease?
* Noise restrictions?
* What you may do to your apartment (paint, hang things on the walls, when you may schedule repairs yourself)?

After you and your landlord sign the lease, keep a copy of it in a safe place. If any changes in the lease are made, they must be initialed by both you and your landlord.

A Tenant Loses

Kellyn B. was so excited to rent an apartment in New York City with a working fireplace. She loved lighting fires in it throughout the winter. It made the apartment cozy.

One day, a fire broke out in the wall behind her fireplace, causing considerable damage to the building and her apartment. She was very concerned about the damage done to her apartment, and she was very disappointed not to have a working fireplace anymore. The fireplace had been the whole reason she'd chosen the apartment.

Kellyn told the landlord of her concerns and expected him to repair the damages, including the fireplace. But after a couple of months, the repairs still weren't made. Kellyn decided to pay the landlord less money each month than she had agreed to in her lease. She reasoned that the apartment without a working fireplace was worth less than it had been when the fireplace worked.

But her landlord did not agree. He sued her for the amount of rent he believed she still owed him, and he won. The judge decided that a fireplace wasn't an essential feature of the apartment.

Landlord's vs. Tenants' Rights

Here are some questions regarding your rights as a tenant. These rights vary from state to state. It is wise to know tenants' rights in your state.

Tenant Rights	
Questions	**Answers**
Can my landlord raise the rent?	Landlords usually are required to give renters a month's notice before raising the rent.
Can my landlord shut off the water or electricity if I don't pay my rent?	Usually, no. Check tenants' rights in your state.
How long does my landlord have to return my security deposit?	Usually a month.
What can I do if I don't get my security deposit back in a reasonable length of time (usually within a month)?	If there is no reason for the landlord to keep your security deposit, you can take him or her to Small Claims Court.
Can my landlord evict me (tell me I have to move) from my apartment with no notice?	No, but check your lease and laws governing eviction in your state.
What happens if I want to move before the lease is up?	You are required to give the landlord 30 days notice before moving. You should pay the last month's rent, rather than just letting the landlord keep the security deposit you paid when you moved in. The landlord could take you to Small Claims Court over payment of the months left on your lease.
Can you refuse to pay the rent if your landlord doesn't fix something major that you have requested be fixed?	Such problems may include a lack of heat or hot water, bad wiring, leaks in the walls or ceiling, broken windows, or unsafe appliances provided by the landlord. The answer maybe yes, but make sure you have a lot of documentation. First, try to negotiate with the landlord. Don't refuse to pay rent for nonessential things.

If You Want to File for Bankruptcy

Sometimes people get in a financial bind they cannot seem to get out of. Whatever the reason, the person in trouble can no longer deal with the amount of debt. When there are no other solutions, **bankruptcy** is a last resort. Bankruptcy is a legal process that frees a person from responsibility for his or her debts.

To file bankruptcy, you need a lawyer. There are two types of bankruptcy: Chapter 7 and Chapter 13. If you have an income, Chapter 13 allows you to pay off some bills over three to five years. Chapter 7 removes all debts, with a couple of exceptions (taxes and alimony).

But don't think bankruptcy is ever an easy way out! It takes time and money to file for bankruptcy. It is difficult emotionally, no matter what the reasons. Also, your credit record is damaged for ten years. It takes time and effort to build a new credit history.

If You're Making a Major Decision or Life Change.

In the course of your life, you will probably make many major decisions. Some decisions are made by many people every day without the help or advice of a lawyer, while other situations require legal help. For example:

* ***You are getting married.*** If you want a **prenuptial agreement**—a legal document that protects the assets of one or both parties in the event of a separation or divorce—you will need a lawyer.

* ***You are having a baby***. You may want to make a will (if you don't have one already) to make sure your child is provided for if you die.
* ***You're adopting a child.*** You will want a lawyer to draw up papers that make sure you have a legal right to your child.
* ***You are getting divorced.*** Many couples represent themselves in a divorce and don't need to hire a lawyer to represent them. "Do-it-yourself" divorce kits exist, but check the laws in your state. These types of no-fault divorces work best when people have no joint property to divide, no children, and no disagreements on how to end the marriage. When this isn't the case, a lawyer is necessary to help finalize child custody arrangements, visitation rights, child support, and the division of property. Even in simple divorces, having a lawyer look over the agreement can protect you from financial harm later.
* ***You want to make a will***. This is a legal document describing what you want to happen with your personal property, including what you leave to your children, if you should die.
* ***You want to control life-support decisions for yourself.*** An **advance health directive** is a legal document that contains instructions on what medical and other decisions you want made on your behalf when you cannot speak for yourself. Check with a lawyer in your state to make sure you use a document that will be honored in your state.

Your Will

Imagine that you want to make a will. Think about what you would like done with your possessions. Look around. What special or unique items do you own? These could be jewelry, a pet, a musical instrument, your car, money in your savings account, or specific articles of furniture or clothing.

Is there someone you want to give specific items to, either because they need them or because you know they would like them and feel the object would remind them of you? The person might be a sibling, friend, parent, or other family member. You may also want to give something to your favorite charity.

Selecting Legal Services

When you want to buy a TV, you shop around. It's the same when seeking legal services. There are good and bad lawyers with varying years of experience and types of expertise. How can you find the best legal help for you?

First, carefully define what you want or need. Is it:

* *Information?* (You want to know if do-it-yourself divorces are legal in your state.)
* *Advice?* (What should you do next in dealing with a company that is ruining your credit record because a dispute over work you did hasn't been settled?)
* *Help in dealing with a criminal matter?* (You have been attacked and want to press charges.)

You don't want to pay for a lawyer's time if you don't need it. Sometimes, you can get a quick question answered over the phone.

When you have a question specific to you, chances are you'll need to talk to a lawyer. Many lawyers will agree to a free initial consultation.

Like teachers and doctors, lawyers have specific areas of expertise. If the problem involves the field of medicine, you will want to find a medical malpractice lawyer. For a question regarding a book or music contract, you will want to consult a lawyer who specializes in entertainment law. If you are arrested, you will need a good criminal lawyer.

To find a lawyer in your area, contact the American Bar Association in your local phone directory. The ABA is a clearinghouse of information on lawyers. Each state has its own individual bar association—the Texas State Bar Association, for example. It can provide you with a list of lawyers with the expertise you need. The ABA cannot answer specific legal questions or give advice.

When Consulting a Lawyer

For a Criminal Matter	For a Civil Matter
1. Bring arrest warrant and court documents. Bring any material that helps prove your innocence or any other relevant information (phone bills, employment records, correspondence that pertains to the problem).	1. Bring any relevant photographs, documents, or information regarding a lawsuit against you, a lawsuit you want to file, or any other problem you have.
2. Ask: Do I need a lawyer to represent me in court?	2. Ask: Does the lawsuit have merit? Do you believe I could win?
3. Find out the cost (if paying for the lawyer yourself).	3. Be prepared to pay some costs for a defense or to file legal documents against someone else.
4. Be prepared to give a full and truthful account of the situation.	4. Be prepared to state what you want from a lawsuit you want to file and what you are willing to give in a lawsuit against you if the claim is valid.

Your Legal Options

Before you head straight to a lawyer's office, consider these options.

Legal Aid Society

Legal Aid is a nonprofit organization designed to deal with civil matters that include housing, Social Security, family problems, neighbor disputes, food stamps, consumer problems, utility service, and much more. It provides legal help for low-income people who cannot afford attorney fees. Criminal matters are referred to a public defender.

Public Defender

The public defender's office is a state and federal agency to represent **indigent** people—people who have no funds to pay for legal representation. A public defender is assigned to represent any individual in court who cannot afford his or her own attorney.

Mediation and Arbitration

Mediation is a good way to settle disputes or disagreements that aren't able to be resolved by the people involved. In the process of **mediation**, a neutral third party helps to resolve a dispute. After listening to both sides, the mediator suggests a way to resolve the dispute. However, the parties involved are not required to accept the mediator's recommendations.

An **arbitration** process is much the same as mediation except that the arbitrator's decision is binding, or final. The main advantage to mediation and arbitration is that family, neighborhood, and other disputes can be settled informally outside of court. The process is simpler, the resolution faster, and the cost much lower than taking the case to court.

By the Numbers

The Cost of Legal Help

Kate and her friend Sam had similar legal problems. Kate went straight to the family lawyer. She paid her lawyer $200 an hour for five hours' work plus another $125 in filing fees. It took more than a year, but she won the case! The award was for $3,800, but she had to pay the lawyer and other costs. How much money did she take home?

Sam decided to take his case to Small Claims Court. He settled his case for $2,900. The process took six months.

Who got to take home more money? Who do you think made the better choice, and why?

Small Claims Court

An individual representing him- or herself goes to Small Claims Court to resolve financial or property issues up to a certain amount of money. No lawyer is needed. Instead, you act as your own lawyer. The claims (the amount of money you can recoup) range from about $1,000 to $5,000 maximum, depending on the state. The benefits of Small Claims Court include:

* Faster resolution to a problem.
* No lawyer fees.

Filing a Lien

If someone owes you money, you can file papers in court. If the court agrees that the money is owed you, a **lien** can be filed against the person owing the money. A lien is a legal document that means that any property the person owns or money in the bank can be taken to pay the debt owed you.

Legal Action

There are two kinds of legal action you might take. You can file a **class action lawsuit**. Although laws vary from state to state, class action lawsuits are designed for groups of people who have experienced the same problem.

EXAMPLE: Consumers who have had car accidents where injuries and deaths occurred due to the same auto problem have filed class action lawsuits against the auto company.

You can also file a lawsuit on behalf of yourself or someone in your family where just one person is represented. This, of course, can be costly and time-consuming.

In some cases, a lawyer may take your case without requiring you to pay any money up front. When a lawyer takes a case on a **contingency** basis, he or she is paid when the lawsuit is settled. Typically, the lawyer fee is one-third of the settlement if you win. If you lose, the lawyer does not get any money and neither do you. However, when a lawyer takes a case on contingency, the client is often asked to pay some out-of-pocket money to cover filing fees and other expenses.

Remember, the court system is crowded. Civil and criminal lawsuits can take two to three years to get to court. It is also costly to take cases to court. For these reasons, it is often worthwhile for all parties to solve cases out of court whenever possible.

Seeking Government Help

The U.S. government has programs and services designed to address problems involving access to and the cost of needed services. It is helpful to know about these agencies and programs.

Housing

The federal government has several housing and housing-related programs. The help varies from assistance with questions and concerns to programs that help people meet a specific goal, such as buying a house.

Government Housing Programs		
Program	**Issues Addressed**	**Program Details or Services**
Housing and Urban Development (HUD)	✳ Lack of safe, affordable housing for low-income people, the elderly, and people with disabilities. ✳ Tenants' rights.	✳ Section 8 provides rent subsidies to renters based on the ability to pay. ✳ Subsidized housing. ✳ Homeless programs. ✳ Supportive housing for the elderly and people with disabilities.
Veterans Administration (VA)	✳ Affordable housing at low interest rates.	✳ VA home loans to people who are serving or who have served in the military, and their dependents.
Legal Aid	✳ Discrimination in housing. ✳ Sexual harassment.	✳ Housing discrimination is illegal. This means that no one may refuse to rent to you because of your race. Check with Legal Aid regarding other forms of discrimination based on religion, sexual orientation, disability, national origin, or age. ✳ Sexual harassment is illegal. Contact Legal Aid if you are being sexually harassed by your landlord.
State and Local Agencies	✳ Financial assistance with rent in order to avoid eviction.	✳ Many cities have programs to help people who are in danger of being evicted. Contact your local social services agency, Salvation Army, or church.

Health Care

The government has state and federal programs to address people's health-care needs. The U.S. Department of Health and Human Services provides information on adoption, accessibility, child care, civil rights, family assistance, Head Start, Medicaid, teen pregnancy, and substance abuse programs.

Food

The government operates a food stamp program through the Social Security Administration to individuals and households who qualify. A Special Supplemental Food Program for Women, Infants, and Children provides food to pregnant and nursing women, infants, and children under the age of five, as well as access to health services and nutrition education.

Food distribution programs through the Department of Agriculture distribute food to needy individuals and households and to organizations that serve meals to low-income people. The department also operates school breakfast and lunch programs and distributes free meals and snacks to needy children during the summer months when school is not in session.

Teen Issues

In many states there are state and local agencies that focus on access to health care for teens. Even as a teenager, you have a right to health care, medical insurance, and any prescriptions your doctor may prescribe, regardless of whether your family can assist you.

Medicaid is a federally funded health insurance program for low-income people. Medicaid covers most medical costs and prescriptions. If your family receives public assistance, you probably have Medicaid coverage. Some states have insurance programs for children who don't qualify for Medicaid and who are unable to get health insurance through their parents.

There are low-cost or free clinics that provide medical and dental care in many communities. Contact your local social services agency for more information.

Know the laws regarding consent in your state. **Consent** means your voluntary, informed agreement to, say, medical care. Find out at what age a person may give his or her own consent for treatment. When must a parent be notified? Find out whether consent is necessary in these cases and under what conditions:

* Emergency.
* Alcohol or drug treatment.
* Reproductive health.
* Surgery.

If you are 18 years of age and have the ability to understand, you can make your own medical decisions. Even as a minor, if you have the ability to understand, you may also have consent under certain conditions.

As a teenager it's important to know your legal rights regarding confidentiality in medical issues such as:

* HIV testing.
* Drug or alcohol treatment.
* General health.

In legal terms, **confidential communication** is something you have said to a lawyer, doctor, or spouse that they cannot be forced to reveal in court. For adults, no one can violate the confidentiality of their medical treatment without their consent. However, this is not always true for minors. Ask whether information about you that you give to a health care professional can be given to someone, including your parents, without your written permission.

Education

The government has many programs available to aid in obtaining access to educational programs. The Head Start program is for young children. There are student aid programs to help college students pay for college. GI Bills help veterans, reservists, and their dependents pay for the cost of a higher education and other special training programs.

Family and Personal Problems

There are programs at all levels of government to help people and families with a range of problems that include:

* Alcohol and drug abuse.
* Job training/retraining.
* Abuse.
* Homelessness.
* HIV/AIDS.
* Teen pregnancy.
* Mental health issues.

Finding Social Services

Help exists in almost any area you can think of, including housing, food programs, drug and alcohol treatment, mental health counseling, and job retraining programs. Unfortunately, it can sometimes be frustrating to figure out where to go for information on these services.

Where to Look

You can find out about many federal, state, and local programs at your local public library. The library may have brochures you can take with you, or you can use the Internet or other resources to get the information you need. Many telephone directories have a special section in the front containing federal, state, and local agencies in your area.

There may be an information clearing-house in your city. It's kind of like "one-stop shopping" for information about agencies and programs. If there is one in your town, take advantage of it! It will save you many phone calls and visits to separate locations.

Your area likely has local groups that focus on:

* Battered women.
* Abused children.
* Children of alcoholic parents.
* Drug or alcohol addiction.
* Teen pregnancy.
* AIDS.
* Job training/retraining.
* Providing food for people in need.
* Support for people with mental health problems.
* Support to help people who have experienced the loss of a loved one.
* Health-care clinic for indigent people.
* Shelter for homeless people and families.

How to Ask

It may be helpful to call before you go in. Write down questions you want to ask and take notes as you are talking. Here are some questions to ask:

* Who qualifies for the program?
* What do I need to bring as proof?
* Where do I go?
* What are the hours?
* Does anyone in my family need to come with me?
* How long does it take to be certified?
* What can I expect once I am accepted for the program?
* Is there anything else I should know before I come in?

When you begin calling, one agency may refer you to another, so be prepared for a hunt for the perfect person or agency at times. Try not to be discouraged by automatic telephone systems. They are a fact of life in the 21st century. (One hint: When you want to talk to someone, try not to push any buttons. See if there is an option for people with rotary dial phones. If so, just stay on the line until you are connected with an operator—it's the easiest way to reach a human being.)

Rights and Responsibilities

Make sure you qualify under the guidelines of the agency you are seeking help from. Federal agencies have detailed procedures for ensuring you meet the guidelines for eligibility. It is fraud to accept assistance if you do not legally qualify for it. However, in many cases, there are community groups who are eager to help anyone who walks in the door.

You can also volunteer your time to help at one or more of these agencies. Almost all community groups depend on volunteers just like you. It is a good way to give back to your community.

Chapter 17 Wrap-up
HOW TO GET HELP

If you have a consumer-related problem and have been unable to resolve it, don't give up. There are many organizations that can help you. The Better Business Bureau is a good place to start.

Sometimes, you may have to resort to taking legal action. There are many organizations and types of legal assistance available, so it's good to know your options. The government also has programs available to help in housing, health, education, and other areas.

Knowing where to go for different types of legal and government help may come in handy many times in your life. Even if you don't need to access these resources, you may be able to help a friend, family member, or coworker who does.

advance health directive—legal document that gives instructions on medical decisions you want made on your behalf when you cannot speak for yourself. *p. 322*

arbitration—mediation process where the arbitrator's decision regarding the resolution of a dispute is binding, or final. *p. 325*

attorney—person who is legally qualified to represent you in legal proceedings; lawyer. *p. 319*

bankruptcy—legal process that makes a person no longer responsible for his or her debts. *p. 322*

cease and desist order—legal order requiring a business to stop doing whatever is in question unless a court overturns the decision. *p. 318*

civil matter—personal or constitutional issue; any disagreement that is not a criminal matter. *p. 319*

class action lawsuit—lawsuit filed by a group of people who have experienced the same problem. *p. 326*

confidential communication—protected conversation that a doctor, lawyer, or spouse cannot be forced to reveal in court. *p. 329*

consent—voluntary, informed agreement to do something, for example, undergo medical treatment. *p. 328*

contingency—lawsuit where the lawyer agrees to being paid from the settlement she wins for you; you don't pay up front. *p. 326*

criminal matter—any situation in which a crime has been committed. *p. 319*

indigent—without funds. *p. 325*

lien—legal document that allows property or money to be taken to pay a debt owed. *p. 326*

mediation—process whereby a neutral third party helps resolve a dispute. *p. 325*

prenuptial agreement—legal document that protects the assets of one or both parties in the event of a separation or divorce. *p. 322*

tenant—person who pays rent to use or occupy a building, land, or property owned by someone else. *p. 319*

will—legal document describing what you want to happen to your personal property in the event of your death. *p. 322*

CHAPTER 18

How to Invest for Your Future

In this chapter, you will learn about:

- planning for your financial future
- the power of compound interest
- investing money

Sophie always loved animals, and from when she was 10 years old, she was sure she wanted to be a veterinarian. She knew that her parents would help her as much as they could but that she would need to pay for a large portion of her education expenses herself.

Sophie took every opportunity she could find to earn money and vowed to save one-third of everything she earned for the next eight years. Sophie's mom explained to her that there were better places than banks for saving toward a long-term goal. She steered Sophie to a mutual fund that invested conservatively. Although Sophie wanted her money to grow as much as it could, she didn't want to take big risks. She couldn't afford to lose any of it, if she was to reach her goal. Sophie's approach used the basic principles of investing—understanding about risks and returns.

Long-Term Planning

Careful planning, budgeting, and smart shopping are just the beginning when it comes to securing your financial health. As you get more experienced with handling money in the short term, you also need to start thinking about your financial life in the long term. Saving and investing your money are the key to future financial well-being. When you save and **invest**, you put your money in stocks, bonds, or other instruments where it will grow for the future.

Financial planning sounds like a pretty serious and, let's face it, *challenging* topic. It conjures up visions of a large boardroom with lots of charts and graphs on the walls. Men and women sit at an enormous, long table looking at papers filled with numbers and dollar signs. But this is a misleading image, because financial planning isn't just important for businesses. It's essential for everyone.

Whether we're teenagers with a part-time job or multimillionaires in charge of a vast fortune, money is something that all of us must deal with in some way. Whether you have a lot or a little, you have to decide what you're going to do with it. So, why not be smart about your money?

Long-term planning involves investments that are focused on goals and needs that will arise many years in the future.

Time Is Money

When it comes to saving and investing, time is on your side. No matter what your income level, starting to save when you're young makes an enormous difference. Not only do you develop good saving habits, but your money has more time to grow.

If you put your money in a safe deposit box, buried it like treasure in a hole beneath a tree, or hid it under your mattress, then it would not grow. But you know better. Your money is earning interest. And the interest is earning interest.

We call that **compound interest**—interest earned on both your principal (the amount you invested) and on the interest it earns.

When asked if he could name the seven wonders of the world, Baron de Rothschild said, "I don't know what the first seven are, but the eighth wonder of the world is compound interest."

Albert Einstein called compound interest, "The most powerful invention of mankind."

Follow these **two** tips to reap the greatest benefit from compound interest:

1. Start to save and invest sooner rather than later.
2. Leave your money in as long as you can.

One easy-to-remember example of this is the following fact: *Money invested at seven percent interest will double in 10 years.* Notice there are two important parts to this equation: the percentage and the number of years. You need to know both to describe growth with compound interest.

Basic Principles of Investment

When you have money to invest, you are faced with a variety of choices about what to do with your money.

You might buy a one-year bank certificate of deposit (a CD) paying $4\frac{1}{2}$ percent. This is a very safe way to invest. You know at the start the interest it will pay and how long it will go on paying it. You can be certain the money will be there (because of Federal insurance) at the end of that time.

On the other hand, you may want to get a higher rate of return on your money. You may have heard that people were getting a 15 percent return from investing in a certain stock, and you'd like to do that. Now, you can't be certain that because a stock paid 15 percent in the past it will continue to do so. Also, there is no certainty that the stock will bring the price you paid for it when you decide later to sell it. So, this stock investment is much riskier than the bank CD.

These examples demonstrate **one** basic principle of investing:

1. The greater the risk, the greater the return.

How do you choose which kind of investment to make? Your goals provide an important guide.

Long-Term Goals

When you save money for a vacation or to be able to pay the occasional major repair on your car, you have a short-term goal. You want to take that vacation later this year. You'll probably have to have new tires next year. For those purposes, you'll probably just put your money in a savings account at your bank, or buy a CD for the short term.

But when you save for something more than a couple of years off, then you have a long-term goal. Investing, rather than merely saving, is what you do to reach a long-term goal.

Long-term goals many people invest for include:

* College education.
* Buying a home.
* Retirement.

"I didn't realize the Wilson's house was on the market."

Your College Education

A college education gives people experiences that improve their ability to appreciate life. It can also provide a network of friends who will support you in many ways through the years. A college degree also greatly improves your chances of finding work you enjoy and that pays a good salary. The more education you get, the more you qualify for jobs that pay the highest salaries.

Many colleges are very expensive. To attend one of these becomes a long-term goal because you need to save and invest over a long period of time to accumulate enough money to pay for it. Parents often start college saving plans when their children or grandchildren are quite young. If you have 18 years or so to save, you can afford to "ride out" some of the ups and downs of the economy, and you can accept a certain amount of risk.

Buying a Home

A home is the most expensive purchase most people will make in their lives. However, to buy one, you do not need to save the full price. You need only save the down payment amount plus the additional percentage points and fees associated with the purchase. Depending on your income and the price of the house you're willing to start with, many careful people can save a down payment in under five years. It takes discipline.

Retirement

Most people expect to live long enough to retire. Some people even make it a goal to retire early in order to pursue interests outside their work. But once you stop working, where will the money you need to live on come from?

* Social Security.
* Company retirement plan.
* Personal savings.

For most people, the answer is some combination of all three. Social Security is not enough for most people to live the way they have become accustomed to living. Some companies have good retirement plans for their workers, but you earn your retirement with them over many years of employment. Increasingly, people do not stay working for one company for long periods of time. So, it is wise to plan on having to fund much of your retirement yourself. As you have many, many years before you have to think about retirement, you should look at it as a *very* long-term goal.

Remember that time is money. If you save only $50 a week for 30 years, you'll have more than $307,000 at an 8 percent return. At 10 percent, you'd have over $450,000. Historically, the stock market has returned between 8 and 10 percent over the long term.

Investment Tools

There are many ways to invest money. Some people buy land. Some people feel safest when they put their money in precious metals, buying gold and silver. Some invest in objects they expect to be able to sell later at a higher price—like fine art or rare stamps. These are unusual investments and require a great deal of specialized knowledge to earn any return. The basic tools for most investors include:

* Stocks.
* Bonds.
* Mutual funds.

These tools, composed of bond or stock certificates, are known as **securities**.

Developing a Strategy

Your strategy for reaching long-term goals may be made up of different parts. It might look like this:

1. Commit to investing a certain amount of money regularly, perhaps $100 a month to start.
2. Use a savings account at the bank until you have the minimum amount needed to invest in a higher-yielding tool.
3. Make a minimum investment in a balanced mutual fund.
4. Continue to make regular contributions to that fund, perhaps through automatic withdrawals from your checking account.
5. Evaluate your goals and your investments periodically—once a year, for instance.
6. Make changes as needed.

Get Smart

Saving Strategies

One way to save money is to set aside a certain percentage of *every bit of money* that comes your way, whether it's from a part-time job or money from a family allowance. If you commit to saving 10 to 20 percent of all money you earn, without exception, you'll be amazed at how quickly it will grow. Put it in a savings account that pays a good rate of interest.

Some people save money by saving all their loose change. Whenever you have coins, just put them in a jar until it's full and then take it to the bank. This is a fairly painless way to save, because generally you won't even miss the small amount of change you set aside each day, but it will mount up over time. People have saved up for vacations to faraway places in this way!

Stocks

Many Americans invest in **stocks**. A stock is a share of a company. When you buy a share, you actually become one of the owners. Here's how it works.

Large companies need a great deal of money to operate and grow, and so they seek investors. The investors give them money in exchange for stock certificates that prove they own a certain number of shares. The investors get a share of the profits and the right to make certain decisions about the company. The stock certificates themselves have value, and investors sell their certificates to each other. Every day, huge numbers of stock are bought and sold in the major stock markets of the world.

To watch how the stock certificates change in price, you can read the financial pages of any major newspaper or follow any of the financial channels on TV. Try it. Pick a company and keep track of its price for a month. Pretend that you had bought it on the first day you looked it up, at the price shown that day. What happened to it? Did the price stay steady? If you sold it on the 10th day, would you have made a little money? How about at the end of the month?

People are interested in both the dividend a company pays (that's the share of profits distributed to investors) and the changing value of the stock.

Your Life

Stock Exchanges

Most stocks are bought and sold on one of these major stock exchanges:

* New York Stock Exchange (NYSE).
* NASDAQ (National Association of Securities Dealers Automated Quote system).
* American Stock Exchange (Amex).
* Regional exchanges.

Stock indexes and averages measure and report how the prices of various groups of stock change. Their reports help us know how the economy is doing. The most frequently quoted indexes and averages are:

* ***Dow Jones Industrial Average:*** provides data on 30 actively traded blue chip stocks, such as industrial corporations, American Express, Walt Disney, and other service firms.
* ***Standard and Poor's Composite Index:*** rates 500 mostly NYSE-listed companies, along with some Amex and NASDAQ stocks.
* ***NASDAQ Composite Index:*** includes about 4,700 companies. The NASDAQ originally focused on small companies, but now includes many large, high-technology companies such as Microsoft.
* ***Amex Market Value Index:*** rates the performance of stocks listed on the American Stock Exchange.

Many different kinds of things can affect the day-to-day value of a stock, but over the long term, the guide to its value is the performance of the company. So, when you buy a stock, you should know as much as you can about the company. Investors ask these kinds of questions about a company before they invest in it:

* Does it make a product people want and will go on wanting?
* Is it financially strong? Or does it have more debt than it can handle?
* Does it make the kind of profit we expect in this market?
* Are the people at the top of the company honest, reliable, and good at what they do?

To learn the answers to such questions, investors read newspapers and business magazines. They talk to people who know or listen to them on the media. They also use their own good common sense. Some people form investment clubs and share the work of tracking stocks and researching companies. Use the search words "investment clubs" on the Web to find out more about these.

Bonds

When you buy a **bond**, you are making a loan. (When you buy a stock, you are buying a part of a company.) Corporations, including governments, issue bonds to raise money. A bond is designed to pay a specified rate of interest at the end of a certain period of time. So, for example, you could buy a 10-year $100 bond guaranteed to pay six percent. It would pay six percent

a year every year for the 10-year period. If you sold it to someone else, it would pay that person for the remaining years of the term.

Like stocks, investors are interested in both the interest that the bond will pay and its price.

Government Bonds

Government bonds are issued by federal, state, and local governments as a means of raising money for government projects. Some are safer than others, depending on the financial health of the town or state. U.S. Savings bonds are among the safest securities instruments you can invest in because their value—the price they sell for—cannot change.

Corporate Bonds

Corporate bonds are bonds issued by corporations. Their prices fluctuate. When interest rates fall, bond prices generally go up. Think about it. If you are holding a bond in a strong company that pays seven percent and the most anyone can get in a bank CD is $5\frac{1}{2}$ percent, wouldn't people want it? Your bond may be worth more than when you bought it.

As with stocks, you need to know the financial health of a company whose bonds interest you. You wouldn't loan money to someone without knowing you had a very good chance of getting it back. There are **two** major corporations that help investors in bonds:

1. Standard & Poor's.
2. Moody's.

These corporations rate bonds from AAA (the highest quality) to D (the bond will not pay any interest). Bonds with the highest ratings sell at the highest prices. You wouldn't be able to get anyone to buy a D-rated bond. It wouldn't be "iffy," it would be a bust!

Mutual Funds

A **mutual fund** invests in a number of different tools. It sells you shares in itself. There are many different kinds of funds:

* Stock funds.
* Bond funds.
* Funds that invest only in foreign stocks.
* Funds managed to produce income.
* Funds that are managed to produce growth.

Mutual Funds		
Type	**Fund Composition**	**Characteristics**
Stock Fund	Group of stocks with similar characteristics: type of product, company size, expectations for growth, high dividends.	Designed to meet investors' goals— growth (long-term) or income now— and level of risk.
Bond Fund	Group of bonds of similar corporations, including government corporations.	Like stock funds, but in general are less risky and grow more slowly.
Money-Market Fund	Group of financial institutions' plans for paying interest on cash deposits.	Are very safe, provide immediate access to your money, but pay a low return.
Mixed or Balanced Fund	Various mixes of stocks, bonds, and money market funds.	Like stock funds, but the greater variety gives the manager more flexibility to meet fund goals.

There are several others as well. You can pick a fund for almost any investment purpose you can think of.

The primary reason to purchase shares of a mutual fund is **diversification**. You don't have all your money in one place. Purchasing fund shares is generally less risky than purchasing individual stocks or bonds. It makes you less likely to lose money when one particular company is not doing well. Most retirement plans invest in mutual funds.

Working With a Financial Advisor

In the beginning, you will need to make your investments and evaluate your plan by yourself. Over time, you may accumulate enough wealth (think of it, wealth!) to want the services of an investment counselor. When that time comes, he or she will ask you:

* What are your goals? What are you saving for?
* How much money do you have to invest?
* How long can you leave it invested before you want or need to take some of it out?
* Are you a risk-taker? Or are you fairly conservative? What is your comfort level for risk?

As you can see, these are the same questions you must be able to answer when you invest—at any level.

Investments
and Financial Planning

"I retire on Friday and I haven't saved a dime. Here's your chance to become a legend!"

Retirement Plans

Because it is so important to have enough money to be able to retire comfortably, the government has provided tax breaks to corporations and individuals that set aside money for retirement. Some retirement savings plans include:

* Individual retirement accounts (IRAs).
* KEOGH plans.
* Employer-sponsored plans.

Individual Retirement Accounts (IRAs)

Individual retirement accounts (IRAs) are personal retirement accounts. Some employers offer IRAs as part of their benefits package. However, anyone can open an IRA, even if you already participate in your company's plan. Funds from IRAs may be withdrawn without penalty as early as age 59 but not later than age 70.

If you withdraw funds from this kind of account before age 59, you will be charged a penalty, and the money you withdraw will be taxed as income for that year. There are a few exceptions to this rule.

EXAMPLE: You may withdraw money to help buy a first home, but the money must be repaid, usually within a year, to avoid penalties.

There are **two** basic types of IRAs:

* **Tax-deferred.** In these plans, the money you save grows tax-deferred. Tax-deferred means that the money saved will not be taxed until it is withdrawn many years in the future. Also, when an employee leaves a company, he or she may *rollover* the amount of his or her employer-sponsored plan into an IRA to continue saving for retirement. Tax-deferred IRAs include Traditional, SIMPLE, and SEP IRAs.
* **Non tax-deferred.** A Roth IRA is not tax deferred. Some people prefer to pay the taxes now, while they have a job. The benefit is that you pay no taxes when you withdraw the money after retirement, no matter how much interest has accrued.

KEOGH Plans

KEOGH plans are tax-deferred pension accounts designed for employees of unincorporated businesses or for people who are self-employed, either full or part time. KEOGH assets may be placed in stocks, bonds, money-market funds, certificates of deposit, mutual funds, or limited partnerships. Like IRAs, KEOGH funds grow without being taxed until they are withdrawn as early as age 59, but not later than age 70.

Employer-sponsored Plans

Employer-sponsored savings plans are usually available from larger corporations. They are designed to help you save money toward your retirement. Currently, they include:

* **"401(k)" plans:** You can deduct a percentage of your salary to invest for retirement. Often, your employer will also contribute some portion of money to your 401(k) account. Non-profit organizations sometimes offer a similar plan, the 403(b). You can't withdraw money until age 59.
* **Stock ownership:** You can buy discounted stock in the company you work for.
* **Company pension plans:** Your employer puts money away in a variety of pension plans for your retirement.
* **Profit-sharing plans:** You have the opportunity to be paid dividends based on your company's earnings.

Online Investment Simulation

One way to try your hand at buying and selling stock is to go on the Internet and experiment with some online investment simulations. Playing trading games online will give you a good feeling for how investing works without running the risk of losing any money!

One well known game is called the Stock Market Game. It's run by the education division of the Securities Industry Association. More than 700,000 kids played the game nationally in 1999 and interest in it continues to grow.

Since investing rules vary from state to state, you should go to the web site to find the online address of your state's Stock Market Game.

Being a wise consumer goes a long way toward establishing your financial health. But planning for the future is also important.

The earlier you begin to save money, the faster it will grow, thanks to compound interest. Get in the habit of saving a percentage of your income now. Invest your savings wisely, and you will give yourself a financially secure future.

Consumer Economics

WORDS TO KNOW

bonds—interest-bearing instruments issued by government agencies or corporations. You are paid back within a specified period of time at a fixed rate of interest. *p. 339*

compound interest—interest paid on both the principal (the original amount invested) and the interest added to it. *p. 334*

diversification—reduction of investment risk by investing in several different stocks, bonds, or other securities so you don't have all your money invested in one place. *p. 341*

Individual Retirement Accounts (IRAs)—personal retirement accounts. *p. 342*

invest—put money in stocks, bonds, or other instruments that will allow it to grow. *p. 334*

mutual fund—large grouping of stocks, bonds, options, futures, currencies, or money-market securities managed by investment companies. *p. 340*

securities—stock and bond certificates. *p. 337*

stock—ownership shares in a company. *p. 338*

References

CHAPTER 1

Baron, Renee. *What Type Am I? Discover Who You Really Are.* Penguin USA, 1998.

College Planning. http://university.smartmoney.com/Departments/CollegePlanning/

Earning Money: Investigating Careers. http://www.themint.org/earning/index.php

Gardner, Howard. *Intelligence Reframed: Multiple Intelligences for the 21st Century.* New York: Basic Books, 2000.

Heiman, J.D. *MTV's Now What?! A Guide to Jobs, Money, and the Real World.* New York: Basic Books, 1989.

Myers, Isabel Briggs with Peter Myers. *Gifts Differing: Understanding Personality Types.* Palo Alto, CA: Davis-Black Publishers, 1995.

Setting Your Financial Goals. Project Moneysmart. http://www.chicagofed.org/consumerinformation/projectmoneysmart/budgetworksheetns.cfm

CHAPTER 2

College Financial Aid. http://www.finaid.org

Education Loans. http://www.ed.gov

Interview Center: Virtual Interview. http://interview.monster.com

Kaplan, Benjamin R. *How To Go To College Almost For Free.* Gleneden Beach, CA: Waggle Dancer Books, 2000.

Resumés and Cover Letters. http://jobstar.org/tools/resume/index.cfm

Richardson, Bradley G. *Jobsmarts for Twentysomethings.* New York: Vintage Books, 1995.

Scholarships. http://www.fastweb.com

CHAPTER 3

Budgeting Basics. Project Moneysmart. http://www.chicagofed.org/consumerinformation/projectmoneysmart/budgetworksheetns.cfm#budgeting

CNN.com's Money 101. Making a Budget. http://money.cnn.com/pf/101/lessons/2

Dacyczyn, Amy. *The Complete Tightwad Gazette: Promoting Thrift as a Viable Alternative Lifestyle.* Random House, 1999.

Financial Clutter: What to Keep and What to Get Rid of. http://www.suzeorman.com/resources/managingdebt.asp?section=clutter

Heady, Christy, and Heady, Robert. *The Complete Idiot's Guide to Managing Your Money.* New York: Alpha Books (Macmillan), 2002.

Keeping a Money Diary. http://www.themint.org/tracking/keepingamoneydiary.php

Kobliner, Beth. *Get a Financial Life: Personal Finance in Your Twenties and Thirties.* NY: Simon and Schuster, 1996.

Pond, Jonathan. *1001 Ways to Cut Your Expenses.* New York: Dell Books, 1992.

Project Moneysmart: Chicago Federal Reserve Bank. http://www.chicagofed.org/consumerinformation/projectmoneysmart/index.cfm

Spending Money. http://www.themint.org/spending/index.php

Taxi: IRS Interactive Tax Site for Students. http://www.irs.gov/taxi

Tyson, Eric. *Personal Finance for Dummies.* New York: Hungry Minds, 2000.

Where Your Paycheck Goes. http://www.themint.org/tracking/whereyourpaycheckgoes.php

Why You Need to Save. http://www.themint.org/saving/index.php

CHAPTER 4

CNN.com's Money 101. Basics of Banking and Saving. http://money.cnn.com/pf/101/lessons/3

CNN.com's Money 101. Taxes. http://money.cnn.com/pf/101/lessons/18

Credit and Debit Cards. http://www.nolo.com/lawcenter/index.cfm/catID/734BECB6-ADDE-4041-AEC595AF30EA15CE/subcatid/A255AF52-3FB9-4A67-A55A147C244F92F6

How Banks Work. http://www.themint.org/saving/howbankswork.php

Keeping Track with a Check Register. http://www.themint.org/tracking/usingacheckregister.php

Mintzer, Rich. *Getting Out of Debt: Repair Bad Credit and Restore Your Finances!.* Avon, MA: Fastread Series, Adams Media Corp., 2001.

Morris, Kenneth, Morris, Virginia, and Siegel, Alan M. *The Wall Street Journal Guide to Understanding Money and Investing.* New York: Fireside Press, 1999.

Pond, Jonathan. *1001 Ways to Cut Your Expenses.* New York: Dell Books, 1992.

Project Moneysmart: Financial Institutions. http://www.chicagofed.org/consumerinformation/projectmoneysmart/index.cfm

Scalzi, John, ed. *the Rough Guide to Money Online: How to Bank, Invest, and Make Money Work on the Internet.* Rough Guides, 2000.

Young Fisher, Sarah, and Shelly, Susan. *The Complete Idiot's Guide to Personal Finance in Your 20s and 30s.* New York: Alpha Books (Macmillan), 1999.

CHAPTER 5

Aghili, Shaun. *The No-Nonsense Credit Manual :How to Repair Your Credit Profile, Manage Personal Debts and Get the Right Home Loan or Car Lease.* New York: Ils Publications, 1998.

BankRate. http://www.bankrate.com

Bierman, Todd. *The Fix-Your-Credit Workbook: A Step by Step Guide to a Lifetime of Great Credit.* New York: St. Martin's Press, 1998.

CNN.com's Money 101. Controlling Debt. http://money.cnn.com/pf/101/lessons/9

Managing Your Credit Cards. http://university.smartmoney.com/Departments/DebtManagement/CreditCards/

McNaughton, Deborah. *The Insider's Guide to managing Your Credit: How to Establish, Maintain, Repair, and Protect Your Credit.* New York: Berkley Books, 1999.

Owing Money and Credit Cards. http://www.themint.org/owing/index.php

Sember, Brette McWhorter. *Repair Your Own Credit and Deal With Debt.* Naperville, IL: Sphinx Publishing, 2001.

Strong, Howard. *What Every Credit Card User Needs to Know: How to Protect Yourself and Your Money.* New York: Owl Books (Henry Holt and Co.), 1999.

Using Credit Wisely. Project Moneysmart. http://www.chicagofed.org/consumerinformation/projectmoneysmart/index.cfm

CHAPTER 6

Buchholz, Todd G. *From Here to Economy: A Short Cut to Economic Literacy.* New York: Plume, 1996.

Fed101: Understanding the Federal Reserve System. http://www.kc.frb.org/fed101html/

Friedman, David D. *Hidden Order: The Economics of Everyday Life.* New York: HarperCollins, 1997.

Landsburg, Steven E. *The Armchair Economist: Economics and Everyday Life.* San Francisco: Free Press, 1995.

Mankiw, N. Gregory. *Principles of Microeconomics, 2nd edition.* Cincinnati, OH: South-Western College Publishers, 2000.

Peanuts and Crackerjacks. http://www.bos.frb.org/peanuts/leadpgs/intro.htm

Sowell, Thomas. *Basic Economics: A Citizen's Guide to the Economy.* New York: Basic Books, 2000.

Walden, Michael L. *Economics and Consumer Decisions.* Dubuque, IA: Kendall/Hunt Publishing, 2001.

CHAPTER 7

Brobeck, Stephen, ed. *Encyclopedia of the Consumer Movement.* Santa Barbara, CA: ABC-CLIO, Inc., 1997.

Consumer Protection. http://www.ftc.gov/ftc/consumer.htm

Green, Mark, with Youman, Nancy. *The Consumer Bible: 1001 Ways to Shop Smart.* New York: Workman Publishing, 1998.

Mayer, Robert. *The Consumer Movement: Guardians of the Marketplace.* New York: Macmillan Library Reference, 1990.

CHAPTER 8

Barfield, Rhonda. *Eat Healthy for $50 a Week.* New York: Kensington Publishing, 1996.

Benkendorf, Jayne. *The Food Storage Bible.* Edmond, OK: Ludwig Press, 1999.

Food and Nutrition Information Center. http://www.nal.usda.gov/fnic/

Frugal Living: Food—All About Food. http://frugal-living.about.com/cs/food/

Gateway to Government Food Safety. http://www.foodsafety.gov/

Lieberman, Alice, with Raff, Jason. *Tricks of the Trade: A Consumer Survival Guide.* New York: Dell Books, 1998.

Margen, Sheldon, MD, and the Editors of the University of California at Berkeley Wellness Letter. *The Wellness Encyclopedia of Food and Nutrition.* New York: Rebus, 1992.

Nutrition.gov. http://www.nutrition.gov/home/index.php3

Tisdale, Sallie. *The Best Thing I Ever Tasted: The Secret of Food.* New York: Riverhead Books, 2000.

CHAPTER 9

Audette, Vicki. *Dress Better for Less.* Minnetonka, MN: Meadowbrook Press, 1981.

Begoun, Paula. *Don't Go to the Cosmetics Counter Without Me, 5th Edition.* Seattle, WA: Beginning Press, 2000.

Feldon, Leah. *Dress Like a Million (On Considerably Less).* New York: Villard Books, 1993, Universe.com, 2001.

Green, Mark, with Youman, Nancy. *The Consumer Bible: 1001 Ways to Shop Smart.* New York: Workman Publishing, 1998.

Lieberman, Alice, with Raff, Jason. *Tricks of the Trade: A Consumer Survival Guide.* New York: Dell Books, 1998.

Lurie, Alison. *The Language of Clothes.* New York: Owl Books (Henry Holt and Co.), 2000.

CHAPTER 10

Friel, John C., PhD, and Friel, Linda D., MA. *The Seven Best Things (Smart) Teens Do.* Deerfield Beach, FL: Health Communications, 2000.

Greenberg, Peter. *The Travel Detective: How to Get the Best Service and the Best Deals From Airlines, Hotels, Cruise Ships, and Car Rental Agencies.* New York: Random House, 2001.

Meyer, Stephanie H., and Meyer, John. *Teen Ink, Our Voices, Our Visions.* Deerfield Beach, FL: Health Communications, 2000.

Raab, Evelyn. *Clueless In The Kitchen: A Cookbook For Teens.* Buffalo, NY: Firefly Books (U.S.) Inc., 1998.

Shellenberger, Susie, and Johnson, Greg. *Cars, Curfews, Parties and Parents.* Bloomington, MN: Bethany House Publishers, 1995.

CHAPTER 11

Agency for Health Care Research and Quality. http://www.ahcpr.gov/consumer/

Benson, Herbert, MD, and Stuart, Eileen, RN. *The Wellness Book: The Comprehensive Guide to Maintaining Health and Treating Stress-related Illness.* New York: Fireside (Simon and Schuster), 1993.

Brody, Jane. *The New York Times Book of Health: How to Feel Fitter, Eat Better, and Live Longer.* New York: Random House, 1998.

Dillard, James, and Ziporyn, Terra. *Alternative Medicine for Dummies.* New York: Hungry Minds, 1998.

Fitness. http://www.nutrition.gov/html/links.php3?topic=health%20management&subtopic=fitness

Health Finder. http://www.healthfinder.gov/

University of California at Berkeley Wellness Letter, ed. *The New Wellness Encyclopedia.* New York: Mariner Books (Houghton Mifflin), 1995.

CHAPTER 12

"Be E-Wise: How to Shop Safely Online." Washington, DC: National Consumers League, 2000.

E-commerce Complaints. http://www.econsumer.gov/english/index.html

Gookin, Dan. *Buying a Computer for Dummies, 2nd edition.* New York: Hungry Minds, 1999.

"Internet Auctions: A Guide for Buyers and Sellers." Washington, DC: U.S. Federal Trade Commission, February 2000.

Lowery, Joseph W. *Buying Online for Dummies.* New York: Hungry Minds, 1998.

Rappeport, Amy and Gates, Susan. *The BizRate.Com Guide: The Best of Online Shopping.* Marina Del Rey, CA: BizRate (Publishers' Group West), 2000.

Scribbins, Kate. *Should I Buy? Shopping Online 2001: An International Comparative Study of Electronic Commerce.* London: Consumers International, 2001.

Smith, Robert Ellis. *Ben Franklin's Web Site: Privacy and Curiosity from Plymouth Rock to the Internet.* Providence, RI: Privacy Journal, 2000.

CHAPTER 13

Burnham, Richard. *Housing Ourselves: Creating Affordable, Sustainable Shelter.* New York: McGraw-Hill, 1998.

CNN.com's Money 101. Buying a Home. http://money.cnn.com/pf/101/lessons/8

Do It Yourself Moving. http://www.homestore.com/Moving/DIY/default.asp

Janik, Carolyn. *Homeology: How to Be Sure the House You Buy Is the Home You Really Want.* Washington DC: Kiplinger Books, 1998.

Mortgages. Project Moneysmart.
http://www. chicagofed.org/consumerinformation/
projectmoneysmart/index.cfm

Packing and Storage. http://www.homestore.com/
Moving/Storage/Default.asp

Sacks, Ed. *The Savvy Renter's Kit.* Chicago: Dearborn
Publishing, 1998.

Thomsett, Michael C. *How to Buy a House, Condo,
or Co-Op.* Yonkers, New York: Consumer Reports
Books, 1996.

Young Fisher, Sarah, and Shelly, Susan. *The Complete
Idiot's Guide to Personal Finance in Your 20s and 30s.*
New York: Alpha Books (Macmillan), 1999.

CHAPTER 14

Ashwell, Rachel. *The Shabby Chic Home.* New York:
Regan Books, 2000.

Consumer Reports editors. *Consumer Reports Buying
Guide 2002.* Yonkers, NY: Consumer Reports
Books, 2001.

Dumke, Lourdes and Sternard, Denise. *How to
Decorate and Furnish Your Apartment on a Budget.*
Roseville, CA: Prima Publishing, 2001.

McKevitt, Anne and Warrington, Shelley. *Style on a
Shoestring: Simple Ideas for Fantastic Rooms.* San
Francisco: Bay Books, 1998.

CHAPTER 15

Bennett, Jim. *The Complete Motorcycle Book: A
Consumer's Guide.* New York: Facts on File, 1999.

Car Buying Tips. http://www.carbuyingtips.com

CNN.com's Money 101. Buying a Car.
http://money.cnn.com/pf/101/lessons/17

Consumer Reports Books Editors. *Consumer Reports
Used Car Buying Guide 2001.* Yonkers, New York:
Consumer Reports Books, 2001.

Edmund's Staff. *Edmund's Used Cars and Trucks Prices
and Ratings: 1991–2000 American and Import.* Alhambra,
CA: Edmund Publications, 2001 (annual publication).

Kelley Blue Book Staff. *Kelley Blue Book Used Car Guide,
July–December 2001: Consumer Ed, 1986–2000, Used Car
and Truck Retail Values.* Irvine, CA: Kelley Blue Book
Publishers' Group, 2001 (annual publication).

Lyle, Pique. *How to Buy or Lease a Car Without Getting
Ripped Off.* Avon, MA: Adams Media, 1999.

Motavalli, Jim. *Forward Drive: The Race to Build the Car
of the Future.* San Francisco: Sierra Club Books, 2000.

Pavelka, Ed (ed.). *Bicycling Magazine's New Cyclist
Handbook.* Emmaus, PA: Rodale Press, 2000.

Sutton, Remar. *Don't Get Taken Every Time: The
Ultimate Guide to Buying or Leasing a Car in the
Showroom or on the Internet—5th Edition.* New York:
Penguin, 2001.

To Buy or To Lease. http://www.smartmoney.com/
autos/leasing/index.cfm?story=buylease

CHAPTER 16

CNN.com's Money 101. Auto Insurance.
http://money.cnn.com/pf/101/lessons/22

CNN.com's Money 101. Health Insurance.
http://money.cnn.com/pf/101/lessons/16

CNN.com's Money 101. Home Insurance.
http://money.cnn.com/pf/101/lessons/19

CNN.com's Money 101. Life Insurance.
http://money.cnn.com/pf/101/lessons/20

Morris, Kenneth, Morris, Virginia, and Siegel, Alan M.
*The Wall Street Journal Guide to Understanding Money
and Investing.* New York: Fireside Press, 1999.

Pond, Jonathan. *1001 Ways to Cut Your Expenses.* New
York: Dell Books, 1992.

CHAPTER 17

Bankruptcy FAQ. http://www.nolo.com/ lawcenter/
ency/article.cfm/objectid/1FF752C2-0C80-4539-
8B159557A55CC17D/catID/575C3BE9-F0C1-448E-
B5F43D22FE36E9F2

Green, Mark J. *The Consumer Bible: 1001 Ways to Shop
Smart.* New York: Workman Publishing Co., 1998.

Leiberman, Marc R., and Strohm, Richard L. (ed.).
*Your Rights as a Consumer: Legal Tips for Savvy
Purchases of Goods, Services and Credit.* Broomall, PA:
Chelsea House, Layman's Law Guides, 1997.

Norrgard, Lee E., and Norrgard, Julia M. *Consumer
Fraud: A Reference Handbook.* Santa Barbara, CA:
ABC-CLIO, 1998.

Parsi, Nicolettes, Ph.D., J.D., and Robinson, Marc.
Understanding Consumer Rights. New York: DK
Essential Finance Series, 2001.

Plain-English Law Centers. http://www.nolo.com

Phillips, Ellen. *Shocked, Appalled, and Dismayed!
How to Write Letters of Complaint That Get Results.*
New York: Vintage Books, 1999.

Smith, Wesley J., and Ostberg, Kay (ed.). *The Smart Consumer: A Legal Guide to Your Rights in the Marketplace.* Washington, DC: HALT: Americans for Legal Reform, 1999.

Ventura, John. *The Credit Repair Kit.* Chicago: Dearborn Trade, 1998.

CHAPTER 18

Allen, Robert G. *Multiple Streams of Income: How to Generate a Lifetime of Unlimited Wealth.* New York: John Wiley & Sons, 2000.

Bramford, Janet. *Street Wise: A Guide for Teen Investors.* Princeton, NJ: Bloomberg Press, 2000.

Chatzky, Jean Sherman. *Talking Money: Everything You Need to Know About Your Finances and Your Future.* New York: Warner Books, 2002.

CNN.com's Money 101. Basics of Investing. (See also lessons 5–7, 10, 13–15, and 23) http://money.cnn.com/pf/101/lessons/4

Dominguez, Joe, and Robin, Vicki. *Your Money or Your Life: Transforming Your Relationship With Money and Achieving Financial Independence.* New York: Penguin Books, 1992.

Downes, John, and Goodman, Jordan Elliot. *Barron's Finance and Investment Handbook—Fourth Edition.* Hauppauge, NY: Barron's Educational, 1995.

Investing 101. http://university.smartmoney.com/Departments/Investing101/

Lerner, Joel J. *Financial Planning for the Utterly Confused—Fifth Edition.* New York: McGraw Hill, 1998.

Miller, Ted. *Kiplinger's Practical Guide to Your Money.* Washington, DC: Kiplinger Books, 1998.

Places to Invest Your Money. http://www.themint.org/investing/index.php

Retirement/401(k). http://university.smartmoney.com/Departments/Retirement401k/

Toohey, Bill, and Toohey, Mary. *The Average Family's Guide to Financial Freedom: How You can Save a Small Fortune on a Modest Income.* New York: John Wiley & Sons, 2000.

Credits

Index

Boldfaced numerals tell you where the word or phrase is defined.

D

F

I

M

Q

R

S

Y

W